Saddle Up, Colorado!

The Statewide Equestrian Trail and Travel Guide

Text and photography by
Sherry and **Scott Snead**

WESTCLIFFE PUBLISHERS
westcliffepublishers.com

ISBN-10: 1-56579-530-X
ISBN-13: 978-1-56579-530-3

TEXT & PHOTOGRAPHY COPYRIGHT: Sherry H. and J. Scott Snead, 2007. All rights reserved.
MAPS COPYRIGHT: F + P Graphic Design, Inc., 2007. All rights reserved.

EDITORS: Jennifer Jahner and Jenna Samelson Browning
DESIGN: Rebecca Finkel, F + P Graphic Design, Inc., Fort Collins, CO
PRODUCTION: Craig Keyzer and Barrett Webb

PUBLISHED BY: Westcliffe Publishers, Inc.
P.O. Box 1261
Englewood, Colorado 80150
westcliffepublishers.com

PRINTED IN CHINA BY: Hing Yip Printing Co., Ltd.

LIBRARY OF CONGRESS CATALOGING-IN-PUBLICATION DATA:

Snead, Sherry H. and J. Scott.
Saddle up, Colorado! : the statewide equestrian trail and travel guide / text and photography by Sherry H. Snead and J. Scott Snead.
p. cm.
Includes index.
ISBN-13: 978-1-56579-530-3
ISBN-10: 1-56579-530-X
1. Trail riding—Colorado—Guidebooks. 2. Trails—Colorado—Guidebooks. 3. Colorado—Guidebooks I. Snead, J. Scott. II. Title.
SF309.256.C6S64   2006
798.2'309788—dc22

2006021649

For more information about other fine books and calendars from Westcliffe Publishers, please contact your local bookstore, call us at (800) 523-3692, or visit us on the Web at **westcliffepublishers.com**.

COVER PHOTO:
Riding in Maroon Bells-Snowmass Wilderness

PREVIOUS PAGE:
A scenic view from the Ben Tyler Trail

PLEASE NOTE:
Risk is always a factor in backcountry and high-mountain travel, and travel with horses presents an additional set of risks. Many of the activities described in this book can be dangerous, especially when weather is adverse or unpredictable, and when unforeseen events or conditions create a hazardous situation. The authors have done their best to provide the reader with accurate information about backcountry travel, as well as to point out some of its potential hazards. It is the responsibility of the users of this guide to learn the necessary skills for safe horseback riding and to exercise caution in potentially hazardous areas. The authors, publisher, and sponsors disclaim any liability for injury or other damage caused by backcountry traveling or performing any other activity described in this book.

Riding and handling equines carry inherent risks, and the capabilities of individual riders and horses vary significantly. It is strongly recommended that this book be used as a reference only and not as a substitute for independent verification of current conditions. The responsibility for the health and safety of the rider and his or her horse rests with the rider.

The authors and publisher of this book have made every effort to ensure the accuracy and currency of its information. Nevertheless, books can require revisions. Please feel free to let us know if you find information in this book that needs to be updated, and we will be glad to correct it for the next printing. Your comments and suggestions are always welcome.

Acknowledgments

My heartfelt appreciation goes to my husband, Scott, for his support during the writing of this book. Scott's knowledge of the out-of-doors, innate sense of direction, outstanding horsemanship skills, wilderness ethics, and hours of proofreading allowed me to pursue my dream of writing an equestrian guidebook.

Our book wouldn't have come to fruition without Scott's father, Larry Snead, and his introducing us to Westcliffe Publishers owner John Fielder. Thank you, Larry. And thank you, John Fielder. What a pleasure it has been working with you, learning from you, and getting to know the man behind the lens.

To the dedicated and talented staff at Westcliffe Publishers: Thank you for your patience, you have been fabulous to work with.

Along the way, we met a number of wonderful horse-loving people who opened their hearts, homes, and barns to accommodate us and our mounts in their bed-and-breakfasts, ranches, and horse hotels. We truly appreciate the kindness and hospitality you extended to us.

Throughout the entire process, our family, friends, riding buddies, and horse clubs were incredibly encouraging. Thanks for being our cheerleaders all the way.

We had great input and support from many land agencies, including the Division of Wildlife and all of the city, county, and state parks. The U.S. Forest Service, whose employees were invaluable, assisted with ride selection, trail information and conditions, directions, campsite locations, and more. A special thank-you to Ralph Swain and his Wilderness Rangers for their effort and time reviewing trails and making recommendations.

We could have never accomplished our book without the commitment of our special friend, Mary Seibert, and her family, Boyd and Brandon. They house-, horse-, and dog-sat, and took such good care of all of us.

Researching and writing this book required a lot of time. With the help and dedication of some veteran equestrian friends, we were able to meet our goals.

Our friends Jim and Julie Chaney from the Backcountry Horsemen of America (BCHA) organization, who are as experienced and knowledgeable as they come, have added so very much to the content, photography, and fun of this book. Many thanks to both of you. Julie contributed rides 4, 14, 18, 20-22, 26, 27, 30-36, 43-45, 96, 97, and assisted with many others.

Betsy Beineke, a local practitioner of Eastern medicine and passionate horsewoman, contributed research for rides 41, 42, 48-50, 55, and 95. Thank you for all of your help.

A very special thank-you goes to Dr. Leon Anderson, DVM, his wife, Trisha, and the staff at Elizabeth Animal Hospital for the absolute finest veterinary care available. We can't thank you enough for taking such excellent care of all 10 of our four-legged children, who mean the world to us.

Happy trails,
SHERRY SNEAD

Foreword

You are about to embark on a wonderful journey with *Saddle Up, Colorado! The Statewide Equestrian Trail & Travel Guide*, a one-of-a-kind guide filled with important information and maps describing Colorado's equestrian trails. Its publication could not have come at a more significant time.

In 2005, the American Horse Council published *The Economic Impact of the Horse Industry on the United States,* a comprehensive study that gauged the horse industry's economic impact. The results were both a source of pride and a harbinger of things to come for all who love horses and their place in our lives.

The study concluded that the industry has an economic impact in Colorado of $1.6 billion, pays more than $21 million in annual taxes, generates 21,300 jobs, and involves 102,000 Coloradans. Our horses are engaged in many disciplines, including racing, showing, recreation, ranching, and farming. Recreational riding is dramatically increasing. Of Colorado's 256,000 horses, 106,600 are involved in recreational activities, and 7,800 of the 21,300 jobs in Colorado's horse industry are in the recreational sector. That is the good news.

The good news is tempered by population growth and the continuing erosion of economic and management resources, placing increasing pressure on the agencies that control access to Colorado's trails, curtailing and even banning such access to equestrians. The Colorado Horse Council, Colorado's Back Country Horsemen of America, and other groups are working with the National Park Service, Colorado State Parks, the Division of Wildlife, the Forest Service, the BLM, and other agencies to relieve that pressure.

As you ride Colorado's trails and make them your own, be good stewards of the land and mindful of the information contained in this book. It will help you to have many wonderful rides and help ensure that those who come after you have the opportunity to do the same. Enjoy.

—CHRISTOPHER D. WHITNEY
President, Colorado Horse Council

Introduction

I have always had an overwhelming desire to have horses in my life. Born and raised in Lexington, KY, the "Horse Capital of the World," my love affair with horses began at the age of five. On my mother's front lawn one humid summer afternoon, a photographer with an adorable pony walked into my life. He asked if my mother would like to have a photograph of her children, dressed as cowgirls, sitting atop the pretty pony. I think it was from that day on that I had "it," a deep passion for horses. If you have purchased this book, I suspect you have "it," too. I feel so very fortunate that my life has been touched by the grace and magic of horses. I can think of no better way to explore Colorado than from the back of a favorite four-legged friend.

When we moved to Colorado in 2001, my husband Scott and I were amazed at how difficult it was to determine where to go riding. We felt certain there would be many books about Colorado's horse trails. Much to our dismay, we were not able to find a single trail book for equestrians in any library!

A couple of years later, Scott's father introduced us to renowned photographer and Westcliffe Publishers owner John Fielder. An astute outdoorsman and businessman, John also recognized the huge void and need for an equestrian guidebook on Colorado. We developed a concept, and soon Scott and I were researching, writing, and photographing what would become *Saddle Up, Colorado! The Statewide Equestrian Trail & Travel Guide.*

Many of the 100-plus routes in this book lie within Colorado's fabulous national forest and wilderness areas, taking you on trails to many of Colorado's majestic peaks. Pack along a fishing rod and picnic while you enjoy gold-medal streams. Discover the trails in some of the best park systems in the country and take extended weekend trips into millions of acres of land managed by the U.S. Forest Service and the Bureau of Land Management. Explore a multitude of horse camping opportunities or just check into one of the many horse hotels or "B, B, & Bs" (Bed, Barn & Breakfasts) listed. Saddle up and enjoy Colorado from the back of your own four-legged friend!

—SHERRY H. SNEAD
Elizabeth, CO

ABOVE: A group of riders on the Hay Park Trail

RIGHT: Julie Chaney, who researched many trails for this book, in a stand of aspen

BELOW: The Ben Tyler Trail offers riders fantastic views

Contents

State Map 8
How to Use This Guide. 10
Trail Savvy. 12
   Safety Guidelines. 12
   Trail Etiquette 15
   General Regulations 16
   Leave No Trace Principles. 17
Checklists. 20
   Trip Planning 20
   Tack. 20
   Veterinary Supplies 21
   Vehicle 21
   Camping Gear 21
   Personal Gear 21

Chapters
   1: Denver and Colorado Springs Region 22
   2: Central Region 102
   3: North-Central Region 148
   4: Northwest Region 186
   5: West-Central Region. 212
   6: Southwest Region 234
   7: South-Central Region. 258
   8: The Eastern Plains. 278

Appendices
   A: Public Agency Contact Information 300
   B: Trail Accommodations 303
   C: Sponsor. 305
   D: Back Country Horsemen of America 306
Index. 307
About the Authors/Photographers 312

Saddle Up, Colorado

The Statewide Equestrian Trail and Travel Guide

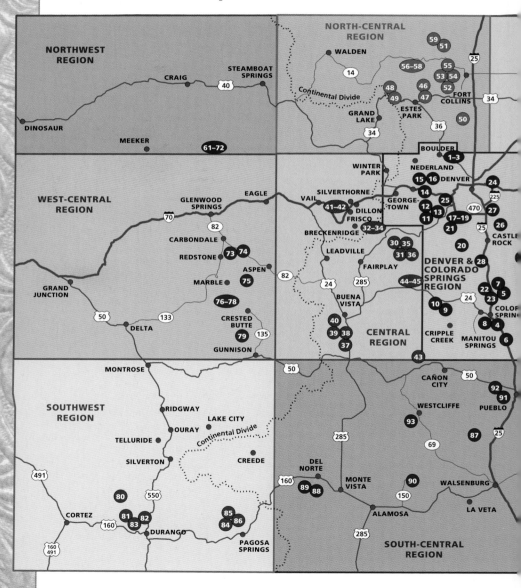

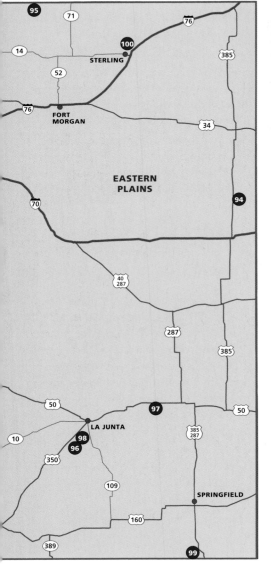

LEGEND

- ◎ City or Town
- (41) State Highway
- (54) U.S. Highway
- (40) Interstate Highway

Symbols used on interior maps

- Paved Road
- Dirt or Gravel Road
- Ride Route
- Other Ride Routes
- Intersecting or Alternate Trail
- ▲ Camping
- P Parking
- TH● Trailhead
- ◎ Corral, City, Town, or Feature along the ride
- Gate
- ● Water Tank or Spring
- Lake or Pond
- River or Creek

How to Use This Guide

Saddle Up, Colorado! divides the state into 8 color-coded regions (Chapters 1 through 8), each with introductory text describing the region. Overnight accommodations for people and horses are then listed. The chapter introduction ends with a listing of the rides in that region. Each ride is listed with its official trail name and number. The individual rides then follow, each with a banner of important information for riders, boxed directions to get to the trailhead, a description of the ride, and a map (some rides share a map). Map icons are explained on p. 9. Each ride has an opening banner with this information:

- **Overall Ride Rating:** Each ride is given a horseshoe rating (ՍՍՍՍՍ) based upon factors such as access, difficulty, terrain, distance, water sources, scenery, and other things. The trails in this book are open to the public as of this writing, but it is the rider's responsibility to check that the trail is still open to equestrians, accessible, and in good condition before setting off.

- **Rating:** Each ride is rated as easy, moderate, or difficult, assuming that the horse and rider are of average ability, experience, training, and conditioning. Add one level up in difficulty for an inexperienced horse or an inexperienced rider. It is never advisable for an inexperienced rider to mount an inexperienced horse, no matter what the degree of trail difficulty.

  Easy trails are typically flat or gently sloping paths of sand, dirt, or crusher fines. The terrain is generally fine for barefoot, or unshod, horses. Loose rocks, bridges, water crossings, and other obstacles or potential hazards are minimal. If there's traffic, it is light, possibly from bicyclists, hikers with dogs, hunters, and fishermen.

  Moderate trails have flat to sloping grades; terrain that requires shoes or protective boots; muddy or wet areas, water crossings, bridges, gates, fencing, trees, downed timber or branches to negotiate; and possibly heavier traffic.

  Difficult trails can have a combination of mountainous, steep, or rocky terrain that requires shoes and extra conditioning of the horse; are longer rides with significant elevation gains and losses; are less maintained, may be remote, and may require some trailblazing. There may be densely forested areas; downed timber and branches; boulders; rock or timber steps; boggy areas; steep side slopes; significant water crossings and bridges; heavy traffic; or other obstacles and hazards.

- **Distance:** Length of trail in miles (one way, unless noted). Connecting trails and loop trails are also identified. If multiple trails are described, a total mileage is often noted for the whole trail or park system.

- **Elevation:** The starting elevation and the highest elevation on the ride. Does not reflect numerous ascents and descents on a particular ride.

- **Best Season:** The best time of year for riding the trail.

- **Main Uses:** Mentions types of recreation and camping, including the following:

    Dispersed Camping: Truck/Trailer camping with stock at non-designated/ undeveloped sites where one can pull off the road to park and set up camp and restrain stock by means of picketing, hobbling, electric fence, portable corrals, or high-lining. No amenities or facilities provided.

    Trailhead Camping: Truck/Trailer camping with stock at a trailhead. Trailhead amenities such as water and restrooms vary per site.

    Backcountry Camping: Camping is in the backcountry via saddle and pack stock, leaving vehicles/trailers parked nearby.

    Developed/Campground Camping: Camping with stock at a designated equestrian campground (usually a spur or loop of a campground set aside for equestrians). Amenities such as restrooms, water, trash services, dump stations, horse pens, and parking for truck/trailer rigs vary per campground.

- **Trailhead Amenities:** Lists bathrooms, water, number of rigs allowed and/or size of trailhead parking, picnic tables, hitching posts, corrals, and camping. Keep in mind that the number of rigs is always dependent on the size of your rig, how others have parked, and if cars have blocked any spots. Park so you won't be blocked in and can leave after your ride.

- **Dogs:** Describes regulations pertaining to dogs on the trail.

- **Shoes:** Indicates whether shoes or protective hoof boots are recommended.

- **Maps:** Offers map resources such as DeLorme *Colorado Atlas & Gazetteer* (for general information and finding the trailhead), National Geographic *Trails Illustrated* maps (provide good trailhead and trail detail), and maps from city, county, and state agencies.

- **Contact:** The governing agency for the area (contact information is on p. 300).

- **Fees:** Current fees, if any, charged at the location (subject to change).

- **Special Regulations:** These are general guidelines only. Always review the Trail Savvy section (p. 12), posted regulations, and area websites for information prior to riding a trail.

- **Special Notes:** Hazards and items of special interest.

After each ride's opening banner, there is either Directions to Trailhead or the ride's descriptive text, and a map of the ride (some rides share a map).

- **Directions to Trailhead:** Driving directions from the nearest town, as well as road conditions, are presented and boxed.

- **Ride description:** the ride's text gives a description of the trail, including trail surfaces, terrain, water crossings, bridges, scenery, history, geology, flora, and fauna, applicability for training, and unique features.

Trail Savvy

Colorado's extensive list of incredible trails is one of its most valuable recreational resources. As our state's population continues to increase, so does the pressure on our trail networks to support more and varied types of recreation. Therefore, it becomes increasingly important that we all participate in protecting this precious resource. As equestrians, we can help educate other trail users about safely and enjoyably sharing the trails with horses. It is also helpful for more experienced riders to share their knowledge with newer riders. Remember that how we behave on trails or at trailheads is a reflection on all equestrians. Please be safe, courteous to other trail users, clean up after your horse, practice "Leave No Trace" ethics and help protect the equestrians' right to ride on public lands now and in the future.

The following general guidelines will help you to be "trail savvy," as well as to practice excellent horsemanship.

Safety Guidelines

- Always contact the local land management agency for trail closures, conditions, hazards, regulations, and additional information before setting out on a ride.

- Carefully check your truck, trailer, horse, and tack before leaving home (see checklists on p. 20 for more information). Doublecheck your horse and tack again before beginning your ride.

- Recognize and respect different levels of riding ability. Understand your and your horse's limitations, and don't ride beyond that comfort level.

- Make sure that you and your horse are prepared and conditioned for the level of riding that you plan to do. Know the route, type of terrain, distance, and difficulty of the ride you are doing. Also make sure that your horse's feet are trimmed and shod or booted, as required for the terrain.

- Carry a map and compass (GPS unit optional). Also take a cell phone, extra clothing, food, water, first aid kit for humans/horses, and any other necessities with you in case of an emergency (see p. 20 for a complete checklist).

- If you are riding in remote areas, you should carry several means of self-rescue: a whistle, a flashlight, and a mirror. The cry for help is three signals repeated every 30 seconds.

- Protective headgear can prevent serious injuries. See the American Medical Equestrian Association's website at *www.ameaonline.org* for serious facts and information that can help you decide if wearing a helmet is right for you.

- If you are riding during hunting season or in hunting areas, remember that you and your horse should be wearing blaze orange.

- It is safer to ride with a buddy or in a group than riding alone. It is best to ride with four or more people/horses. In case of emergency, one person/horse is available to stay with an injured party and two riders/horses can go for help. Horses are herd animals and easier managed when with other horses.

- Always let someone know your itinerary and plan to check in when you have completed your ride.

- Maintain a safe speed and a safe distance of one horse length between other riders. If a horse and rider are having a bad moment, other riders should allow additional space in front of and behind them, as well as time for them to work through their issues. If your horse is a kicker, tie or braid a red ribbon at the base of the tail to alert others to maintain a proper distance.

- Most riders travel at 2.8–3 miles per hour at an average walking pace. Know your average pace and how long your ride should take, and allow enough time to finish your ride before dark. If you are planning to ride at night, use reflectors (like bicyclists do), wear light-colored clothing to increase your visibility, and carry a flashlight.

- At streets, bridges, water crossings, or in any other uncomfortable or unfamiliar situation, dismount and hand-lead your horse until safely on the other side—but only if you and your horse will be more comfortable with you on the ground than in the saddle, and you are sure the horse will not get frightened and trample you. Be observant of your surroundings. That unexpected bicyclist whizzing by, a scary-looking three-wheeled stroller, or other potential outside influences can become trail hazards.

- When tying your horse, be sure to tie high and short enough to prevent your horse from getting tangled or untied.

- Rattlesnakes are known as reclusive animals and tend to avoid horses and humans. They will strike at a horse or rider if threatened or startled. When it is warm, rattlesnakes tend to lie in shady areas. During the spring and fall, you are more likely to see a rattlesnake lying on or crossing a trail. The best way to avoid a strike while riding your horse is to watch for and avoid them. If you do not see the rattlesnake but you hear the rattle, immediately stop and freeze your horse. Stand still, attempt to locate the snake, let the snake settle down, and allow it to move away (or quietly move you and your horse directly away). A rattlesnake's effective strike range is about half its body length.

- Bees are an accident waiting to happen. If you are allergic, be sure that you always carry your medication with you. If you notice bees in your immediate area, steer clear! Turn and ride in the opposite direction. If they attack, dismount your horse, leading it away as quickly as possible.

- The weather in Colorado is often unpredictable and can have a serious impact on riding activities, especially at higher elevations. So before you ride, be sure to check the local weather forecast. Be as prepared as you possibly can. Always carry raingear, a heavier jacket, warm and dry clothes (if possible), extra food, water, matches in a waterproof container, and firestarter. Some of the weather-related hazards to be familiar with are:

  Lightning: We generally see lightning and thunderstorms in Colorado during summer afternoons. If you find yourself on a high mountain ridge as a storm starts rolling in, it is best to descend to a lower elevation as quickly as possible. The experts say a low spot in the land, such as a ditch, is the preferable place to be, as lightning takes the shortest path from the sky to the earth. The safest action is to head back to your truck and trailer at the first sign of a storm. If you find yourself in a serious lightning storm cannot make it back to your trailer, get off, away from your horse and trees to the lowest possible spot in the land.

  Hypothermia: This general lowering of the body's core temperature usually occurs when a person is exposed to extreme wet or cold for a long period of time; wind and exhaustion often compound the victim's condition. Warm, dry clothes, hot liquids, and rest are best for treating hypothermia. At the first sign of hypothermia, the best treatment is taking cover, getting out of wet clothes, adding dry layers and drinking warm liquids. Don't wait until you are soaked or cold—by that time it may be too late.

  Dehydration: The low moisture content in Colorado's atmosphere, combined with high altitudes, can quickly cause dehydration. Drink more than you would at home during your normal routine, more than you are thirsty for, and carry more water than you think you will need. Don't wait until you are thirsty or sick—by that time, it's too late.

  Altitude sickness: The lack of oxygen at high altitudes can cause altitude sickness. General symptoms include dizziness, shortness of breath,

loss of appetite, and nausea. The effects of high altitude are different for everyone, so pay close attention and if you feel any of these symptoms, seek lower ground.

Trail Etiquette

- Stay on designated trails. Creating your own trail causes erosion, damages habitat and creates new trails which cannot be maintained. Do not cut switchbacks. Avoid muddy trails choosing alternate dry trails whenever possible to minimize trail damage. Should you run into a wet or muddy area on an otherwise dry trail, ride through the wet or muddy puddles instead of around them whenever possible to avoid trail widening.

- Share the trail. Stay on the right; pass on the left on non-motorized trails and opposite on motorized trails or roads. Greet and communicate openly with other trail users.

- When passing another trail user, slow to a walk, communicate your intent to pass on the left, travel at a safe distance and speed around the other user, and thank them politely.

- Downhill traffic yields to uphill traffic. Bicyclists and hikers yield to horses whenever possible. Although horses generally have the right of way, sometimes it may be safer and more practical for the horse to pull off the trail, rather than another user. So use good judgment, be courteous to other trail users, and be sensitive to the environment.

- Never trot or canter off without permission, leaving your riding partner in the dust.

- Always leave gates as you find them.

- At water crossings, try to cross at a low, rocky place, being cognizant of fragile vegetation. It is best if you can cross one at a time, allowing each horse ample time to drink without crowding. When your horse is ready, move on a bit to make room for the next horse, but wait for the next horse to drink and catch up. Don't let your horse eat or play in the water.

- If you are attending a group ride, ask ahead of time what the ride rules are. Do not start until all riders are mounted and ready to go. Arrive on time and be ready to ride when the group is ready. If you are confirmed to be present for a ride but can't make it, call the trail boss. Don't take an unsafe or untrained horse on a group ride. Don't pass the trail boss or lead rider, or fall behind the drag rider.

- Please clean up after your horses (and others, if necessary). Carry a muck bucket, apple picker/manure fork, and shovel. If there is no place to properly dispose of manure, put it in your trailer and dispose of it at home in your normal fashion. Do not just throw the manure off to the side of the parking area. Many non-equestrian trail users complain about manure, so less manure means fewer complaints and ultimately more places to ride. At trailheads and within 100 feet of parking areas, developed or paved areas, and campsites, manure should be thoroughly cleaned up. Manure piles outside this zone should be removed and scattered in the grass. Any pawed ground should be filled in.

- Give something back to the land you enjoy riding on by volunteering for trail-advocacy groups or trail-building and maintenance projects. Among others, the Back Country Horsemen of America (see p. 306) is a worthy equestrian organization dedicated to preserving the use of saddle and pack stock; this group works on many trail-improvement and maintenance projects utilizing horses and works to protect public land resources through education.

General Regulations

- Check all trails and trailheads for posted signage regarding regulations.
- Check trail regulations before your trip to to determine whether or not dogs are allowed on the trail.
- It is good practice to register at Forest Service trailheads before heading out on a ride. This is very helpful in managing resources as well as identifying equestrians as a user group.
- Keep vehicles and trailers on maintained roads and parking areas unless otherwise specified. Lock vehicles and trailers with valuables out of sight.
- No motor vehicles, bikes, carts, or motorized equipment are permitted in wilderness areas.
- In the wilderness, camping with pack and saddle stock is prohibited within 100 feet of lakes, streams, trails and other water sources unless otherwise specified.
- In the wilderness, hobbling, picketing or tethering of stock is prohibited within 100 feet of lakes, streams, trails and other water sources unless otherwise specified.
- Certified weed-seed-free forage products are required on all federally managed public lands in Colorado. Failure to do so is subject to fines. It is recommended that animals be fed certified weed-seed-free feed at least three days before entering backcountry areas. Feeding pelleted or processed feeds in addition to hay or grazing forage is a convenient, light-weight, and economical way to feed horses while traveling. For certified weed-seed-free hay providers and additional information, contact the Colorado Department of Agriculture in Lakewood at 303-239-4149 or *www.ag.state.co.us/dpi/*.
- Most Forest Service wilderness areas have group size limitations. The size limit may vary from one wilderness to another, but it is frequently 10–25 people and/or stock.
- Do not allow your dog to disturb wildlife or livestock. Make sure to clean up after your dog and keep him in strict voice and sight control at all times. Many public lands require dogs to be on leash.

Leave No Trace Principles

The Leave No Trace Center for Outdoor Ethics unites four federal land management agencies—the U.S. Forest Service, the National Park Service, the Bureau of Land Management, and the U.S. Fish and Wildlife Service—with manufacturers, outdoor retailers, user groups, educators, and individuals who share a commitment to maintain and protect our wildlands and natural areas for future enjoyment. The following Leave No Trace principles lie at the foundation of the organization's education, awareness, and training initiatives.

Leave No Trace also provides a highly recommended, detailed, 32-page booklet specific to saddle and pack stock use. To get more information on Leave No Trace Horse Use, please visit *http://archive.lnt.org/LNTPublications/LNTHorseS&E.php* or call 1-800-332-4100.

Plan Ahead and Prepare

- Know the regulations and special concerns for the area you'll visit.
- Prepare for extreme weather, hazards, and emergencies.
- Schedule your trip to avoid times of high use.
- Visit in small groups. Split larger parties into groups of 4–6.
- Repackage food to minimize waste.
- Use a map and compass to eliminate the use of marking paint, rock cairns, or flagging.

The trailhead parking at Weminuche Trail can easily accommodate many large rigs.

Travel and Camp on Durable Surfaces

- Durable surfaces include established trails and campsites, rock, gravel, dry grasses, or snow.
- Protect riparian areas by camping at least 200 feet from lakes and streams.
- Good campsites are found, not made. Altering a site is not necessary.
- In popular areas:
  - Concentrate use on existing trails and campsites.
  - Ride single file in the middle of the trail, even when wet or muddy.
  - Keep campsites small. Focus activity in areas where vegetation is absent.
- In pristine areas:
  - Disperse use to prevent the creation of campsites and trails.
  - Avoid places where impacts are just beginning.

Dispose of Waste Properly

- Pack it in, pack it out. Inspect your campsite and rest areas for trash or spilled foods. Pack out all trash, leftover food, and litter.
- Deposit solid human waste in catholes dug 6 to 8 inches deep at least 200 feet from water, camp, and trails. Cover and disguise the cathole when finished.
- Pack out toilet paper and hygiene products.
- To wash yourself or your dishes, carry water 200 feet away from streams or lakes and use small amounts of biodegradable soap. Scatter strained dishwater.

Well-prepared riders begin a pack trip on the Brookside McCurdy Trail.

Leave What You Find
- Preserve the past: Examine, but do not touch, cultural or historic structures and artifacts.
- Leave rocks, plants, and other natural objects as you find them.
- Avoid introducing or transporting non-native species.
- Do not build structures, furniture, or dig trenches.

Minimize Campfire Impacts
- Campfires can cause lasting impacts to the backcountry. Use a lightweight stove for cooking and enjoy a candle lantern for light.
- Where fires are permitted, use established fire rings, fire pans, or mound fires.
- Keep fires small. Only use sticks from the ground that can be broken by hand.
- Burn all wood and coals to ash, put out campfires completely, then scatter cool ashes.

Respect Wildlife
- Observe wildlife from a distance. Do not follow or approach them.
- Never feed animals. Feeding wildlife can damage their health, alter natural behaviors, and expose them to predators and other dangers.
- Protect wildlife and your food by storing rations and trash securely.
- Control pets at all times, or leave them at home.
- Avoid wildlife during sensitive times such as mating, nesting, raising young, or in the winter.

Be Considerate of Other Visitors
- Respect other visitors and protect the quality of their experience.
- Be courteous. Yield to other users on the trail.
- Step to the downhill side of the trail when encountering pack stock.
- Take breaks and camp away from trails and other visitors.
- Let nature's sounds prevail. Avoid loud voices and noises.

Checklists

Trip Planning

- Pre-determine the area you will be visiting, how to get there, where you will camp, what trails you will ride, and what you need to take.
- Tell a loved one where you are going and when you are expected home.
- Acquire maps and learn about the area's rules and regulations.
- Make sure that you and your livestock are in the appropriate physical condition for the area's terrain and the difficulty, length, and elevation of the trails.
- Check the weather conditions.
- Take your own water, even if the area you're visiting supposedly offers water, and take weed-seed-free hay or pellets; for certified weed-seed-free hay providers and additional information, contact the Colorado Department of Agriculture at 303-239-4149 or *www.ag.state.co.us/dpi/weedfreeforage*.
- Always carry food and water for humans, a flashlight, and blankets or sleeping bags.
- Do a safety check on your truck and trailer, including your tires, hitch, oil, lights, spare tire, and brakes, as well as your trailer doors, window closures, and floor.
- Be sure to bring your insurance and registration paperwork for your truck and trailer, plus your hauling certificate/brand inspection and health certificate for your livestock; know if the places you are traveling to have additional health requirements such as a Coggins test.

Tack

- Bailing twine and/or shoelaces (handy for a lot of things)
- Blankets
- Blaze orange during hunting seasons
- Brand inspection, hauling card, health records, and weed-seed-free hay certificate
- Bridle, bit, and reins
- Buckets (for feed, water, manure; collapsible for trail)
- Extra rope
- Extra tack (for emergency)
- Fly spray and fly mask
- Grooming aids, brushes, and sprays
- Halter and lead rope
- Hay bags
- Hobbles, highline, picket, electric fence, or portable panels
- Hoof boot, extra shoe, hammer, nails, and shoe puller
- Hoof pick
- Manure fork/shovel and bucket
- Multipurpose knife
- Pack saddle and panniers
- Repair kit with leather, shoelaces, Chicago screws, leather punch
- Saddle and pad
- Saddle bags
- Shipping and sport boots
- Vet kit (small for saddle bags, large for trailer)
- Water and refillable containers (for people and horses; allow for 20 gallons per horse per day)
- Weed-seed-free hay, grain, pellets, or cubes
- Zip/wire ties

Veterinary Supplies

- Acepromizine tranquilizer
- Antibiotic scrub, solution, salve, or ointment
- Banamine paste and/or injection
- Betadine
- Bran
- Hot/cold pack
- Large rolled gauze and cotton (for leg wrapping)
- Leg wraps
- Liniment
- Lubricant
- Oral antibiotic tablets (trimethoprim sulfa)
- Phenylbutazone (Bute) paste and/or tablets
- Rubbing alcohol
- Saline
- Scissors
- Stable blanket
- Sterile gauze pads (various sizes)
- Stethoscope
- Syringes and needles
- Thermometer
- Topical wound-care ointment, salve, spray, or powder
- Tweezers
- Vet wrap
- Waterproof tape

Vehicle

- Flares
- Jack
- Lug wrench
- Motor oil
- Portable air compressor/ battery charger
- Self-sealing tire repair kit
- Spare tire
- Trailer/truck tool kit
- Vehicle registration and insurance card

Camping Gear

- Batteries
- Bedding and blankets or sleeping bags
- Camp stove/grill
- Charcoal
- Cleaning supplies
- Foil/plastic wrap
- Food
- Funnel
- Generator and gas (plus lock and cable)
- Lantern
- Matches/lighter
- Napkins
- Newspaper
- Paper plates and towels
- Plastic cups/utensils
- Plastic food-storage containers
- Plastic zip-closure bags (small and large)
- Pots and pans
- Propane
- Saw
- Scissors
- Shovel
- Toilet deodorizer for RV
- Towels and washcloths
- Trash bags
- Water

Personal Gear

- Ball cap or hat and helmet
- Bandanna or handkerchief
- Battery-operated radio
- Binoculars
- Blaze orange to wear in hunting seasons
- Camera
- Cell phone and car charger
- GPS device (optional)
- First-aid kit
- Fishing equipment
- Flashlight/batteries
- Insect repellent
- Jackets (heavyweight, lightweight, and rain)
- Jeans
- Lip balm
- Maps and compass
- Matches in waterproof container/lighter
- Medications and toiletries
- Pet supplies
- Rain gear
- Riding boots (also suitable for walking)
- Riding gloves and chaps
- Shirts (both long- and short-sleeved)
- Snacks
- Sunglasses and sunscreen
- Water canteen
- Whistle and mirror (for emergency signaling)

Chapter 1

Denver and Colorado Springs Region

Thirsty horses stop for a drink at Monument Preserve.

Colorado residents are fortunate to have a multitude of excellent trails within minutes of the Denver and Colorado Springs metropolitan areas (see DeLorme *Colorado Atlas & Gazetteer* maps 39–41, 50–51, and 62–63). Avid trail-riding enthusiasts have little chance of boredom with such a fine selection of trails right in their backyard.

The metro and surrounding areas offer something for every interest and skill level. Choose from short, easy trails or longer, more challenging rides. Select a trail from one of several state parks or ride one of the city or county parks. Take a scenic trip through a pristine open space or explore a regional trail. Whatever your interest, the metro areas have it all, right here where the great Rockies meet the plains.

The challenge lies in knowing where to find the trails and organizing all the "horsy" details. The following pages provide you with the information you need to make trail riding around Denver and Colorado Springs fun, safe, and effortless. So strap on your boots, load up your equine friend, and get ready for some great riding!

Accommodations

🏠 🐴 🚐 H2 Ranch Bed & Breakfast and Horse Motel

6665 Walker Road   719-495-2338
Colorado Springs, CO 80908   www.bbonline.com/co/h2stables

Innkeepers Ed and Arlene Housley are the owners of this lovely bed-and-breakfast. The horse facilities are large and well kept, with private paddocks, a guest pasture, indoor stalls, and an indoor and outdoor arena. The bed-and-breakfast consists of two queen bedrooms that share a bath, accommodating a total of four people. Breakfast is included and arrangements may be made for evening meals. The Housleys welcome campers and living quarters in their camper section. Electric hookup is available, but there is no hookup for city water. With beautiful views of Pikes Peak and the surrounding mountains, this is a good base camp if you wish to ride the many trails in the area.

🐴 🚐 Jefferson County Fairgrounds

15200 W. 6th Avenue   303-271-6600 • www.co.jefferson.co.us/fair
Golden, CO 80401   Office Hours: Mon.-Fri., 8:00 am to 5:00 pm

Jefferson County Fairgrounds is a horse-friendly facility located near Golden, Colorado, and convenient to many of the Jefferson County rides detailed in this book. The fairgrounds are situated on 100-plus acres and offer 102 covered 10x10 box stalls, and a host of amenities including water hydrants, manure bins, wash racks, indoor and outdoor arenas, stall barns, exhibit halls, conference rooms, RV sites, a bathroom and shower house, a dump station, a picnic pavilion, and convenient trailer parking. Box stalls rent for $15.00 per night per horse. Stalls must be stripped back to the dirt upon leaving to avoid a $5.00 cleaning charge. RV sites are available for $15.00 per night per RV as follows: 6 back-in (60') sites with 50 amp service; 26 pull-through (40') sites with 30 amp service; and 8 parallel (55') sites with 30 amp service. For reservations call the main number or email Debra Adams at *dadams@jeffco.us*. Local hotel accommodations can be found online at *www.hotelsbycity.com/colorado/golden-hotels.html* and *www.hotelsbycity.com/colorado/lakewood-hotels.html*.

DIRECTIONS

If you are coming west on I-70, take Exit 262, which is the Colfax Street exit. The exit is a downhill ramp. At the light turn left (east) onto W. Colfax. Turn right at the second stoplight, which is Colorado Mills/Denver West Blvd. & Indiana. At the 5th stoplight to 6th Ave. Frontage Road, turn right. This will take you to the Fairgrounds entrance on the left.

If you are coming east on I-70, take Exit 261 which is 6th Ave. East. Stay in your righthand lane as it immediately becomes the exit ramp to Indiana Street. Take the Indiana Street exit. Turn right onto Indiana Street and then turn right, (west), onto 6th Ave. Frontage Road (first light). This will take you to the Fairgrounds entrance on the left.

Norris-Penrose Event Center (formerly Penrose Equestrian Center)

1045 W. Rio Grande St.   719-635-1101
Colorado Springs, CO 80906 www.penroseequestrian.com

Situated on 150 acres of beautiful terrain adjoining the Pike National Forest, the Norris-Penrose Event Center is just 2 miles from downtown Colorado Springs, with convenient access to shopping, lodging, and restaurants. Recreation includes playgrounds, off-leash dog area, nature center, community garden, sports fields, and picnic pavilions. The nearby Pike National Forest and Bear Creek Regional Park offer a multitude of riding opportunities. The center includes a climate-controlled indoor arena, boarding barns, wash racks, five outdoor arenas, concessions, plentiful parking, restrooms and showers, and 52 camper sites with water and electric hookups ($25 per night, with dump station available). Overnight stabling is possible in one of 340 show stalls (depending on availability; the center fills quickly during scheduled events). Horse owners must supply their own buckets, feed, and shavings, available on-site for $6 per bag. Overnight stabling is $17 per horse per night for the first night and $12 for each additional night (you do the care and cleaning). Please call ahead for availability and reservations.

 SS² Bed, Barn & Breakfast

39773 CR 21   303-646-3637
Elizabeth, CO 80107 E-mail: ssnead@myawai.com

SS² Bed, Barn & Breakfast is a lovely 5,200-square-foot home and equestrian facility situated on 40 acres halfway between Colorado Springs and Denver. Located 20 miles east of I-25 on the edge of the Black Forest and only 15 minutes from the Colorado Horse Park, it is within an hour's drive of most trails within the Denver metro area. Horses are accommodated either at the barn in box stalls with runs (cleaned daily) or in a paddock, pasture, or round pen. The two indoor suites of the beautifully decorated western-style ranch are reserved for guests of the two-legged variety. The large suites have their own private amenities including a sitting area with a fireplace, a great room with a widescreen TV and stereo, a full bath, and a patio. Breakfast is included and arrangements can be made

for other meals. SS² Bed, Barn & Breakfast is run by authors Sherry and Scott Snead. Feed is provided or you can provide your own for a reduced fee. Current health certificates and vaccinations required.

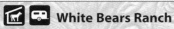 **White Bears Ranch**

5277 Teller CR 1
Cripple Creek, CO 80813   719-689-0455

White Bears Ranch is located 20 minutes from Dome Rock State Wildlife Area and Mueller State Park on 40 acres, with an additional 300 acres of land to ride. Horse accommodations include pasture turn out and nine box stalls (three with covered runs) in a charming older barn. A guest lounge is available at the barn. White Bears welcomes tent and RV camping without hookups, though potable water is available at the barn. The fee is $10 per horse per night for self-care (you feed and clean). Beautiful views of Pikes Peak and Crystal Peak can be enjoyed from the ranch. Look for additional accommodations and services in the future as the new owners are currently remodeling.

Rides

Boulder

1 Doudy Draw and Community
   Ditch Trails 26
2 Greenbelt Plateau and Marshall
   Mesa Trails 29
3 Mesa Trail 30

Colorado Springs

4 Bear Creek Regional Park and
   Palmer/Red Rock Loop Trail... 32
5 Black Forest Regional Park ... 35
6 Fountain Creek Regional Trail 38
7 Fox Run Regional Park.......... 40
8 Garden of the Gods 42

Divide

9 Dome Rock State Wildlife Area 46
10 Mueller State Park 49

Evergreen/Morrison

11 Alderfer/Three Sisters Park ... 51
12 Elk Meadow Park 53
13 Lair O' the Bear Park............ 55

Golden

14 Apex Park and Lookout
   Mountain Park.................... 57
15 Golden Gate Canyon
   State Park 59
16 White Ranch Park................ 62

Littleton

17 Chatfield State Park 64
18 Highline Canal Trail 67
19 Deer Creek Canyon Park....... 69
20 Indian Creek Trail (No. 800).... 72
21 Sharptail Ridge Trail System .. 75

Monument

22 Monument Preserve 77
23 New Santa Fe Regional Trail .. 80

Other Denver Area Rides

24 Barr Lake State Park
   (Brighton) 83
25 Bear Creek Lake Park
   (Lakewood)........................ 85
26 Cherry Creek Regional Trail
   (Parker) 88
27 Cherry Creek State Park
   (Aurora)............................ 93
28 Greenland Trail (Larkspur)..... 97
29 Homestead Ranch Park
   (Elbert) 100

1 Doudy Draw and Community Ditch Trails

Overall Ride Rating	○○○○○
Trail Rating	Easy
Distance	Doudy Draw, 3.3 miles one way; Community Ditch, 3.6 miles one way. Can extend your ride and and loop with Marshall Mesa and Greenbelt Plateau.
Elevation	5,650–6,100 feet
Best Season	Year-round
Main Uses	Equestrian, hiking, mountain biking. Wheelchair accessible; no camping
Trailhead Amenities	Room for six to eight trailers if you arrive very early or on weekdays. Restrooms, trash receptacles, and picnic tables across the street at the Mesa trailhead (not suitable for horse trailer parking). There is an additional restroom 0.3 mile south of the Doudy Draw trailhead near the intersection with the Community Ditch Trail at the picnic area. Bring your own water for horses and people.
Dogs	On leash south of the Community Ditch Trail and west of the Flatirons Vista trailhead; otherwise under voice and sight control with a city of Boulder Voice and Sight tag displayed.
Shoes	Barefoot okay
Maps	DeLorme *Colorado Atlas & Gazetteer,* p. 40; National Geographic *Trails Illustrated 100, Boulder/Golden;* City of Boulder Open Space & Mountain Parks map (www.bouldercolorado.gov)
Contact	City of Boulder Open Space & Mountain Parks
Fees	None
Regulations	Vehicles parked on Eldorado Springs Dr. could be ticketed. Call ahead (303-441-3440) to arrange parking for group rides. See the Trail Savvy section (p. 12), website and posted regulations for additional information.
Special Notes	Arrive very early for parking. If the lot is full, park at the Greenbelt Plateau parking lot, 0.1 mile east of the intersection of CO 128 and CO 93 on the north side of the road.

Directions to Trailhead

From Boulder, head south on CO 93 (Broadway). Go right (west) at CO 170 (also Eldorado Springs Dr.) and continue for about 1.75 miles to the trailhead and gravel lot on the left (south) side. To start at the opposite end of the trail at the Flatirons Visa trailhead, continue south on CO 93, two miles past CO 170. The trailhead is on the west side of the road and can accommodate three to four trailer rigs depending on size. Trail access is to the west of the lot.

From the Doudy Draw trailhead, access the trail through the gate on the south side of the parking area and ride south along the paved path as it passes between two mesas. The trail picks up the stream and arrives at the picnic area and restroom at 0.3 mile. Historical remnants remain in a small building on the northeast edge of the picnic area that served as the milk house for the original Doudy family. The stream was rerouted to flow through the building and over canisters of milk to keep them cold until they could be taken to market. Here, the trail connects to the 3.6-mile Community Ditch Trail, which can be taken east to extend your ride.

The Doudy Draw Trail is more open than shaded, providing incredible views of the valley and surrounding landscape, including Eldorado Mountain, Crescent Mountain, and Coal Creek Peak. The terrain is suitable for barefoot horses, as it is mostly flat to gently sloping and largely free of rock. Native grasses such as wheatgrass, blue grama, brome, and needle grass dominate, but yucca, skunkbrush, and a variety of wildflowers also grow along the route. The midgrass prairie occasionally gives way to some tall-grass prairie and even ponderosa pine at the southernmost end of the trail. From here, ride due east toward the Flatirons Vista trailhead where the trail ends. This area is home to a wide variety of wildlife, including great horned owls, deer, coyotes, many songbirds, black bears, mountain lions, birds of prey, mule deer, and numerous other species.

Community Ditch Trail This trail can be added to your ride on the way out or on the way back. The route intersects the Doudy Draw Trail 0.2 mile from the picnic area. Barefoot horses should be fine picking their way around the few rocks. The trail crosses a sizeable, horse-safe bridge and follows the Community Ditch, one of the first irrigation projects in the area in the early 1900s. The trail is 1.7 miles from the Doudy Draw Trail to CO 93 and 1.9 miles from CO 93 northeast to its end at the Marshall Mesa trailhead.

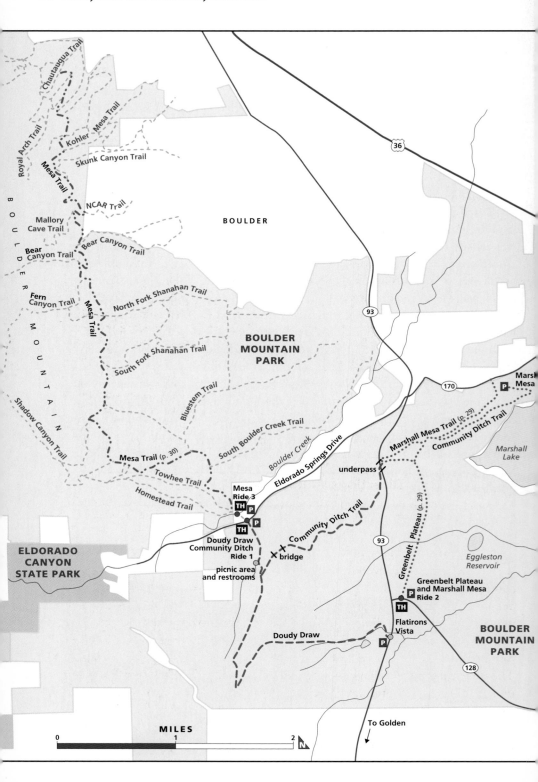

BOULDER

Chautauqua Trail

Royal Arch Trail

Kohler Mesa Trail

Skunk Canyon Trail

Mesa Trail

NCAR Trail

Mallory Cave Trail

Bear Canyon Trail

Bear Canyon Trail

Fern Canyon Trail

Mesa Trail

North Fork Shanahan Trail

South Fork Shanahan Trail

BOULDER MOUNTAIN PARK

Bluestem Trail

Shadow Canyon Trail

South Boulder Creek Trail

Boulder Creek

Eldorado Springs Drive

Marshall Mesa Trail (p. 29)

Community Ditch Trail

Marshall Mesa

Marshall Lake

Mesa Trail (p. 30)

Towhee Trail

Homestead Trail

Mesa Ride 3

TH P

Doudy Draw Community Ditch Ride 1

TH P

picnic area and restrooms

bridge

Community Ditch Trail

underpass

Greenbelt Plateau (p. 29)

ELDORADO CANYON STATE PARK

Doudy Draw

Greenbelt Plateau and Marshall Mesa Ride 2

Flatirons Vista

TH P

Eggleston Reservoir

BOULDER MOUNTAIN PARK

To Golden

MILES

0   1   2

N

93

36

93

170

128

2 Greenbelt Plateau and Marshall Mesa Trails

(For Trail Map see p. 28)

Overall Ride Rating	○○○○○
Trail Rating	Easy
Distance	5.7-mile loop
Elevation	5,640–6,100 feet
Best Season	Year-round
Main Uses	Equestrian, hiking, mountain biking
Trailhead Amenities	Room for 6-8 trailers (minus any car parking); arrive early for better parking. Kiosk and trash receptacles but no other amenities available. Bring your own water.
Dogs	On leash or under voice and sight control with a city of Boulder Voice and Sight Tag displayed.
Shoes	Barefoot okay
Maps	DeLorme *Colorado Atlas & Gazetteer,* p. 40; National Geographic *Trails Illustrated 100, Boulder/Golden;* City of Boulder Open Space & Mountain Parks map (www.bouldercolorado.gov)
Contact	City of Boulder Open Space & Mountain Parks
Fees	None
Regulations	Call ahead (303-441-3440) to make parking arrangements for group rides. See the Trail Savvy section (p. 12), website and posted regulations for additional information.
Special Notes	The trail is mostly unshaded, so bring a hat and sunscreen

Directions to Trailhead

From Boulder, go south on CO 93 (Broadway) past CO 170 for approximately 1.75 miles. Turn left (east) at CO 128. The parking lot is on the left (north) side of the road.

Access the trail through the gate on the north side of the parking area, traveling north on a level, wide path good for barefoot horses. The Boulder Mountains dominate the landscape on the west; to the east is Marshall Lake. Scattered ponderosa pine provides occasional relief from the sun. This area is wonderful for winter riding. The Greenbelt Plateau connects to the northeast with the Community Ditch Trail. Follow this trail for approximately 1.7 miles east around the northern side of Marshall Lake to meet the Marshall Mesa Trail. The three trails connect for a nice 5.7-mile loop. The Marshall Mesa Trail has interpretive signs explaining the coal-mining and geologic history of the area. At the Marshall Mesa trailhead, turn west and follow the trail back, either to the Community Ditch or all the way to CO 93. You can then pick up the Greenbelt Plateau Trail again and head south back to your rig.

3 Mesa Trail (For Trail Map see p. 28)

Overall Ride Rating	◡◡◡◡◡
Trail Rating	Easy
Distance	6.9 miles one way, plus many connecting trails and loops
Elevation	5,655 feet–6,000 feet
Best Season	Year-round
Main Uses	Equestrian, hiking. Wheelchair accessible.
Trailhead Amenities	Park at the Doudy Draw parking area, which has room for six to eight trailers. You must arrive very early or on weekdays to get good parking. The Mesa trailhead is directly across the highway on the north side. Due, to the limited amount of turn-around space and high density of vehicular traffic, the trailhead is limited to smaller two-horse trailers and/or weekday or extremely early arrivals. Restrooms, trash receptacles, and picnic tables are available. Bring your own water for horses and people.
Dogs	On leash on the Towhee Trail; otherwise under voice and sight control with a city of Boulder Voice and Sight Tag displayed.
Shoes	Recommended
Maps	DeLorme *Colorado Atlas & Gazetteer*, p. 40; National Geographic *Trails Illustrated 100, Boulder/Golden;* City of Boulder Open Space & Mountain Parks map (www.bouldercolorado.gov)
Contact	City of Boulder Open Space & Mountain Parks
Fees	None
Regulations	Vehicles parked on Eldorado Springs Dr. may be ticketed. Call ahead (303-441-3440) to arrange parking for group rides. See the Trail Savvy section (p. 12), website and posted regulations for additional information.

Directions to Trailhead

From Boulder, go south on CO 93 (Broadway) and turn right (west) at CO 170. The Mesa trailhead is at mile 1.7 on the right (north) side, but park at the Doudy Draw trailhead across the street. Once you have tacked up, cautiously walk your horses across CO 170 to access the Mesa Trail.

The trail heads north out of the parking area across a large but horse-safe bridge that spans South Boulder Creek. Depending on your comfort level, you may want to dismount and lead your horse across. The granite/gravel/natural-dirt path is 6–8 feet wide at the beginning and crosses gently rolling high-plains prairie to the first trail intersection, where the Mesa Trail connects with the Towhee and the Shadow Canyon trails. A little piece of Boulder's history can be found here in the remnants of an 1874 stone addition made to the homesite of Boulder's first settler. The Mesa Trail offers expansive views of the Front Range, foothills, and the valley to the east.

The vast network of interlaced trails make for seemingly endless options. You can ride the Mesa Trail all the way north through grassy prairies, ponderosa pine stands, and montane forest to Chautauqua Park. Or take any one of a number of connecting trails east or west to various points of interest, from major peaks like Green Mountain and Bear Peak to the historic McGilvrey Cabin on the Towhee Trail or the Old Schoolmarm Cabin on the Mesa Trail. The area is rich with wildlife, including peregrine falcons and red-tailed hawks. Your horse should be shod or booted for this adventure, as there are rocky areas to negotiate as you transition from prairie-type terrain to boulders, shrubs, and forest.

4 Bear Creek Regional Park and Palmer/ Red Rock Loop Trail

Overall Ride Rating	☺☺☺☺☺
Trail Rating	Bear Creek Regional Park, easy; Palmer/Red Rock Loop Trail, difficult
Distance	10 miles of trails in Bear Creek Regional Park; Palmer/Red Rock Loop Trail is 5.5 miles.
Elevation	5,900–7,800 feet
Best Season	Year-round within Bear Creek Regional Park; spring to fall on the Palmer/Red Rock Loop Trail.
Main Uses	Equestrian, hiking, mountain biking
Trailhead Amenities	Unlimited trailer parking, restrooms, campground, stalls, water hydrants, emergency phone, on-site administrative offices, and indoor and outdoor arenas (fee charged for camping, stalls and the indoor arena) at the Norris-Penrose Event Center (formerly Penrose Equestrian Center). For overnight fees and camping facilities, see Accommodations (p. 24).
Dogs	On leash within El Paso County Regional Parks; off leash within Pike National Forest but under voice control.
Shoes	Barefoot okay on the Bear Creek Regional Park trails; shoes are recommended on all other trails.
Maps	DeLorme *Colorado Atlas & Gazetteer,* p. 62–63; National Geographic *Trails Illustrated Map 137, Pikes Peak/Cañon City;* Recreation Guide Map Co. *Colorado Springs and the Pikes Peak Area Map and Guide No. CO-2;* El Paso County Parks and Recreation map, Bear Creek Regional Park (http://adm2. elpasoco.com/parks/prktrail.asp)
Contact	City of Colorado Springs; El Paso County Parks and Recreation; Pike National Forest, Pikes Peak Ranger District
Fees	For camping, stalls and indoor riding arena fees, see Norris-Penrose Event Center (p. 24).
Regulations	Horses prohibited on Bear Creek Regional Park Nature Center trails and within the half-mile dog loop. See the Trail Savvy section (p. 12), website and posted regulations for additional information.
Special Notes	The main east-west trail crosses 21st St. midway through Bear Creek Regional Park on the north side. There is a crosswalk signal with a push button high enough to be reached from horseback. All riders should be ready to cross before the button is pushed, as the walk signal is short. If you are unsure of your horse's ability to handle this type of obstacle, dismount and walk your horse across. After this crossing is the dog walk area. Although dogs are to be on a leash outside of this area, dog handlers often stretch the boundary and allow their dogs in the nearby creek to play. Expect to see dogs off leash anywhere within the park.

Directions to Trailhead

From I-25 in Colorado Springs, exit onto US 24 west. At 8th St. (the first major intersection west of I-25), turn left (south). Take 8th St. to W. Rio Grande Ave., the second stoplight, and turn right (west). Swing wide due to a close curb and utility poles, but watch for oncoming traffic. Follow W. Rio Grande Ave. up the hill to the Norris-Penrose Event Center on the left. Follow the entry drive to the left and down to the long barns that house the show stalls. Park in the large gravel lot nearby.

Pick up the Bear Creek Regional Park trail system by following the equestrian center access road adjacent to the parking lot east about 200 feet, where you meet the wide crusher-fine trail going to the right across Bear Creek. For an easy ride, choose any combination of the 4-foot-wide crusher-fine trails that loop around the regional park, staying east of Bear Creek Rd. and the Section 16 trail system. All trails are well signed.

For a greater challenge and wonderful views, head west to the Palmer/Red Rock Loop by following the trail paralleling the creek and crossing the bridge after the community garden. Ride past the playground, cross 21st St. (see Special

Notes), cross another bridge just past the dog walk area, and continue up the hill. The trail will drop down near Orion Dr. to skirt private property. Take the left-hand trail at the Y and continue west, passing through by hills covered with scrub oak. The Bear Creek Nature Center and restrooms are at the end of the trail to the right. Soon the trail narrows to a single track and drops steeply to cross Bear Creek one more time before crossing Bear Creek Rd. Drop slightly to the left and continue following the trail right and up to cross Upper Gold Camp Rd. This is the car parking lot and trailhead for the Section 16 trail system.

The trail resumes its ascent as you reach the foothills of Pikes Peak. A nice short loop to the right takes you along some beautiful red rock walls and returns to the main Red Rock Loop Trail. Now the trail really starts to climb, with the scrub oak giving way to tall ponderosa pine as the route enters Pike National Forest. Be cautious where the trail crosses Hunters Run, a tributary of Bear Creek. The crossing is a slab of granite and can be slick under shod hooves. The trail assumes a much more gentle descent through Bear Creek Cañon Park and ends at High Dr. Turn left and follow the road northeast along Bear Creek. At the road intersection, take Bear Creek Rd., the middle fork, back to the earlier bridge crossing. Return to Norris-Penrose Event Center by backtracking through Bear Creek Regional Park.

5 Black Forest Regional Park

Overall Ride Rating	♡♡♡♡♡
Trail Rating	Easy
Distance	4 miles with multiple loops
Elevation	7,180–7,400 feet
Best Season	Year-round
Main Uses	Equestrian, hiking. Bicycles allowed on the first 0.3 mile of trail. Wheelchair accessible
Trailhead Amenities	No amenities at the trailhead (first parking area on Milam Rd.), which can accommodate about four trailers. The main portion of the park, roughly 1 mile north of the trailhead and parking, has restrooms, drinking water, picnic pavilions, sports fields, tennis courts, and playground. Bring water for your horses.
Dogs	On leash
Shoes	Barefoot okay
Maps	DeLorme *Colorado Atlas & Gazetteer,* p. 51; El Paso County Parks and Recreation map, Black Forest Regional Park (http://adm2.elpasoco.com/parks/prktrail.asp)
Contact	El Paso County Parks and Recreation
Fees	None
Regulations	See the Trail Savvy section (p. 12), website and posted regulations for additional information.
Special Notes	Renovations due to a neighboring housing development will add a new trailhead, additional trail mileage, and 200 acres to this park. Detailed information was not available at the time of this writing. Check with El Paso County Parks and Recreation (see Appendix, p. 300) for an updated map and information.

Directions to Trailhead

From Parker Rd. and Mainstreet in Parker, take CO 83 (Parker Rd.) south to Shoup Rd. Go left (east) on Shoup Rd. for 2.5 miles, turning left (north) onto Milam Rd. Trailer parking and the trailhead are at the first turn to the right. (The main parking areas 1 mile north are difficult for horse trailers.)

This wonderful urban park just north and east of Colorado Springs is set within a 200-square-mile area of dense ponderosa pine forest known as the Black Forest. The trail system travels northeast out of the parking area and makes numerous small circuits through this shady little wonderland. Wide, natural-dirt paths weave between the trees in eight little loops, or you can make larger loops by combining two or more trails. This forest is home to the infamous Abert's squirrel, otherwise known as the tassel-eared squirrel, as well as porcupines, Stellars jays, mule deer, and many other types of wildlife.

Black Forest Regional Park offers a leisurely half-day ride with spectacular views of Pikes Peak and the Front Range. This is also a good opportunity to expose a young horse or new rider to easy trails in a lovely forested setting.

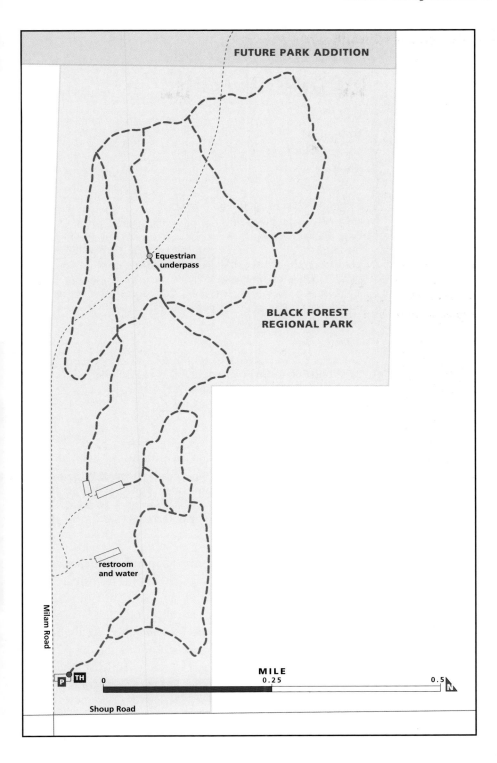

FUTURE PARK ADDITION

Equestrian
underpass

BLACK FOREST
REGIONAL PARK

restroom
and water

Milam Road

MILE
0   0.25   0.5

N

Shoup Road

6 Fountain Creek Regional Trail

Overall Ride Rating	☺☺☺☺☺
Trail Rating	Easy
Distance	10 miles one way
Elevation	5,600 feet
Best Season	Year-round
Main Uses	Equestrian, hiking, mountain biking
Trailhead Amenities	No amenities at the Willow Springs parking area, which can hold 4-6 rigs. Arrive early or on a weekday to get parking. Although large, this is not a pull-through lot; it is possible to get blocked in by cars, so position your trailer carefully. The smaller Duckwood trailhead is 1 mile south with restrooms, water, and parking for 2-3 trailers. Restrooms can also be found in Fountain Creek Regional Park. Bring your own water.
Dogs	On leash
Shoes	Barefoot okay
Maps	DeLorme *Colorado Atlas & Gazetteer,* p. 63; El Paso County Parks and Recreation map, Fountain Creek Regional Trail (http://adm2.elpasoco.com/parks/prktrail.asp)
Contact	El Paso County Parks and Recreation
Fees	None
Regulations	See the Trail Savvy section (p. 12), website and posted regulations for additional information.
Special Notes	As of this writing, the first of two parking areas at Willow Springs is closed due to contamination in the ponds. Pass this first closed lot to get to the second open parking area. Contact El Paso County Parks and Recreation for updates.

Fountain Creek, a floodplain with associated spring-fed ponds and marshes, is the main attraction of the Fountain Creek Regional Trail. This primarily wide, gravel-and-sand trail travels along the wetland sanctuaries of Fountain Creek, where wildlife-viewing gazebos have been installed. Be a little cautious, as these are unfamiliar sights to most horses. Waterfowl can also take flight unexpectedly. Wildlife abounds within the park and surrounding habitats.

Beginning at the Willow Springs trailhead access, ride north past Willow Springs Ponds (closed) and Ceresa Park for 4.3 miles to the intersection with Academy Rd. It is another 1.2 miles north to the intersection with US 85/87. Just a bit beyond is the junction with the City of Colorado Springs Sand Creek Trail, which heads northeast from the Fountain Creek Trail. The trail ends where the Monument Creek Trail picks up.

Directions to Trailhead

WILLOW SPRINGS: From Denver, go south on I-25 to the Fountain exit (Exit 132) and turn left (east) on CO 16. At 0.5 mile, take a right (south) on US 85/87 and another right immediately after on Willow Springs Rd. Continue 0.4 mile to the second parking lot described above. DUCKWOOD: This smaller lot is located 1 mile south of Willow Springs on US 85/87.

Return to your trailer to ride the trail past the nature center and the regional park, 1 mile south of the parking area. Another 0.75 mile south puts you at the Duckwood trailhead, and a mile past that at the junction with the Hanson trailhead and the end of the trail.

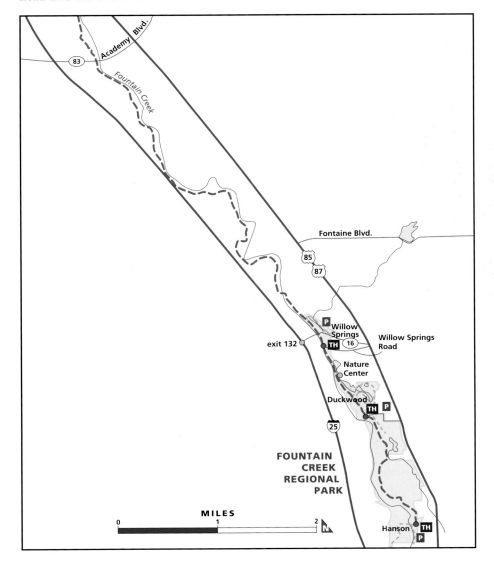

7 Fox Run Regional Park

Overall Ride Rating	UUUUU
Trail Rating	Easy
Distance	3.5 miles total with several loops
Elevation	7,350 feet
Best Season	Year-round
Main Uses	Equestrian, hiking, mountain biking.
Trailhead Amenities	Restrooms, seasonal drinking water, picnic tables, playgrounds, sports fields, and interpretive signs at trailheads and throughout the park. Bring water for your horse. Parking lots allow for several large rigs depending on how many cars are parked.
Dogs	On leash
Shoes	Barefoot okay
Maps	DeLorme *Colorado Atlas & Gazetteer,* p. 51; El Paso County Parks and Recreation map, Fox Run Regional Park (http://adm2.elpasoco.com/parks/prktrail.asp)
Contact	El Paso County Parks and Recreation
Fees	None
Regulations	Horses not allowed on trails around the ponds. See the Trail Savvy section (p. 12), website and posted regulations for additional information.
Special Notes	Weekday and off-season riding is recommended—the park is busy and parking lots full on warm weekends. Sports fields on the south end make this portion especially crowded.

Directions to Trailhead

From I-25 north of Colorado Springs, take Exit 156A. Slow down as you exit; it is a sharp turn from the highway. Proceed east on North Gate Rd. 3.2 miles to Rollercoaster Rd. Turn left and go 1.5 miles to the park entrance. A second entrance is located to the west on Stella Dr.

ALTERNATE ROUTE: From CO 83, head west on North Gate Rd. for 0.5 mile, then north on Rollercoaster Rd. for 1.5 miles to either the Stella Dr. or Rollercoaster Rd. entrances.

There are several gravel lots suitable for trailers. The Pine Meadows Picnic Area on the south side of the park (left from the Stella Dr. entrance) has a loop-around parking area. The Fallen Timbers trailhead, at the center of the park, has a lesser-used loop-around parking lot with adequate trailer parking, but it is closed in the winter months. The most popular loop-around parking area for equestrians is at a trailhead outside of the main part of the park on the northeast side, farther north of the main entrance on the west side of Rollercoaster Rd.

This lovely park of gentle, rolling hills receives heavy use. The wide trails are hoof-friendly and the park is an excellent place for green horses or junior riders. It is easy to ride for several hours by utilizing the park's roads and making figure-eight tracks. Trail map signage at every major intersection make it impossible to get lost. On the west side, a concrete underpass offers good practice in navigating an unusual trail obstacle with minimal distractions. On the other side, the trail goes past a reservoir and dead-ends, requiring riders to turn back.

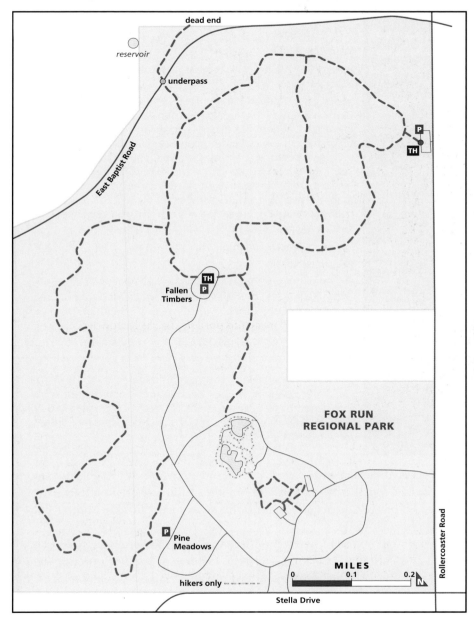

8 Garden of the Gods

Overall Ride Rating	○○○○○
Trail Rating	Easy to moderate
Distance	Approximately 15 total miles of trails; outer loop of the whole park just under 8 miles
Elevation	6,250–6,600 feet
Best Season	Year-round
Main Uses	Equestrian, hiking, rock climbing, mountain biking (within southeast area only)
Trailhead Amenities	Loop-around, paved parking for four to six rigs at the Spring Canyon South Picnic Area on Garden Dr. at the far south end of the park. Longer rigs may have problems pulling out due to the small turning radius and concrete curbing. Picnic tables, grills, and a dumpster are available here. The Garden of the Gods Trading Post on Beckers Lane has restrooms, telephones, a hitching post, food, and a gift shop. Restrooms, water, and trail maps are available at the visitor center on 30th St. Camping and overnight stabling is available at the Norris-Penrose Equestrian Center south of US 24 (see Accommodations, p. 24).
Dogs	On leash. Owners must pick up after dogs.
Shoes	Recommended
Maps	DeLorme *Colorado Atlas & Gazetteer*, p. 62; National Geographic *Trails Illustrated Map 137, Pikes Peak/Cañon City*; Garden of the Gods Visitor Center map
Contact	Garden of the Gods Visitor and Nature Center; Colorado Springs Parks, Recreation, and Cultural Services
Fees	None
Regulations	Horses not allowed in the central gardens area or on the Central Garden Trail, Hamp Trail, or Rock Ledge Ranch Historic Site. Please do not tie horses to trees. No alcohol is permitted. See the Trail Savvy section (p. 12), website and posted regulations for additional information.

This incredible city-owned park is truly one of a kind. It was given to the city of Colorado Springs in 1909 by the children of railroad magnate Charles Elliot Perkins in fulfillment of his wish that it be kept forever open and free to the public.

Recognized by the Department of the Interior as "a nationally significant natural area," the site is a National Natural Landmark. It offers towering sandstone formations, a wonderful view of Pikes Peak, hiking paths, the Rock Ledge Ranch Historic Site (with a living history museum), which was placed on the National Register for Historic Places in 1979, and many other amenities.

Directions to Trailhead

From I-25 in Colorado Springs, take exit 141/westbound US 24. Follow this west for approximately 2.5 to 3 miles toward Old Colorado City. You can turn right on either 31st St. at the stoplight or Ridge Rd. (no stoplight). Turn left and follow Colorado Ave. through town to Beckers Lane. Turn right and follow this through the residential neighborhood to the Garden of the Gods Trading Post and into the park by turning right onto Garden Lane (one-way street). The South Spring Canyon parking lot will be on your left. Parking in this lot is a challenge. There are two entrances. Signs recommend turning in at the first entrance as the second one is marked on the pavement as an exit. Either way will force you to go against a directional arrow in order to park in the designated angled parking.

ALTERNATE ROUTE: From I-25 in Colorado Springs take exit 146, Garden of the Gods Road. Head west for 2.5 miles. At the stoplight, turn left onto 30th St. and proceed 1.5 miles to the park entrance on the right (Gateway Rd.). At the stop sign, go right on one-way Juniper Way Loop. Turn right on Garden Rd. staying right when it becomes a one-way street. Turn left on Garden Lane, pass the Garden of the Gods Trading Post, and head to the parking lot on the left. Do not go past Balanced Rock; it is a very busy area and very tight for trailers.

Because so many of the roads in the park are one-way, it is best to return to I-25 by exiting the parking lot and turning left (one-way) on Garden Lane to Garden Drive. At this point you have two options. You can either turn left (one-way), continue the loop to the left back to the Trading Post and turn right at Beckers Lane. Or you can turn right on Garden Drive and then right again on Juniper Way Loop (one-way) and follow this out to Gateway Road, where you will turn right back out to 30th St. at the Visitor Center.

This is quite possibly one of the most visually stunning parks in the entire state. Be sure to bring a camera to capture the outstanding views. Red sandstone rocks seem to stand on end as a result of one of the most recent geological events in the Rocky Mountain area, which means that these formations are younger than the Rocky Mountains. There are multiple trails in this 1,320-acre park. Most of the terrain is relatively easy with only a few short steep or rocky sections. There are a small number of seasonal water crossings and a few places where there are patches of solid rock. Some trails occasionally cross the road, so be aware—traffic is usually heavy, especially on the weekends. Due to these concerns, this area is not recommended for training green horses or inexperienced riders. There are many branches of trails that either carry the same name or are not signed at all, which may cause you a bit of confusion. If you feel you are going the wrong direction, don't hesitate to turn around and find a more suitable route.

This suggested approximately 8-mile loop is only one of many options that riders can take to enjoy the distinctive formations. Pikes Peak views, as well as detailed city scenes, are offered from the higher points of this route. Leave the parking lot to the south on the Balanced Rock Trail following the road past the Trading Post and around the ridge toward Garden Drive. Stay right at the Y to cross the road and head onto Cabin Canyon Trail. Turn left to follow the more western portion of this loop toward the Spring Canyon parking lot. Turn left again onto the Siamese Twins Trail. Here you are allowed to ride right through the formations, giving you a very close view. Here is also the largest slab of rock to cross, which often worries riders, however, the abrasive sandstone allows a good grip. Note that there are often other park visitors wandering around the formation who can easily spook some horses with their unexpected appearance.

After leaving the Siamese Twins, continue down the hill toward the road to pick up the Palmer Trail. Turn north and climb the hillside along the western portion of the park for views of the Central Garden formations. From this vantage point, you can try to identify Sentinel Rock, Pulpit Rock and the Three Graces, as well as many others. This is a more narrow section of the trail, but

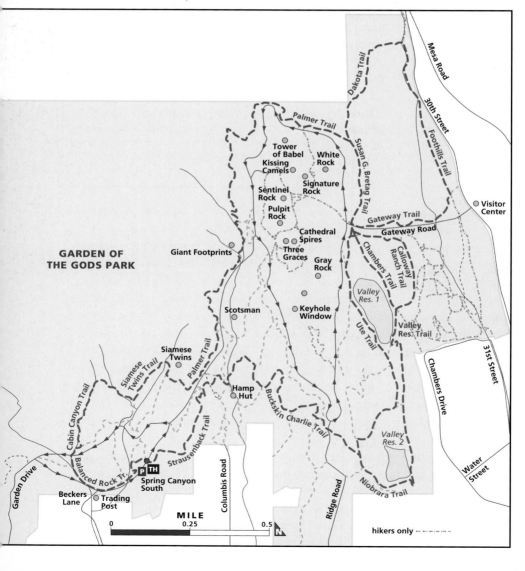

it is very navigable. Continue the loop around the Tower of Babel at the far north end of the park. As you come to White Rock, the Dakota Trail will turn left and appears to leave the park (though it doesn't). This is where bighorn sheep are sometimes spotted. Watch for the interpretive signs detailing their habitat and placement in the park. At this point you can either add a mile to your trip by taking the Dakota Trail over to the Foothills Trail, which is paved and has typical urban trail traffic, and then back west along the Gateway Trail, where you will cross one wooden foot bridge. Or you can turn right onto the Susan G. Bretag Trail. For this riders will need to cross Gateway Rd., which can be difficult, even

with the crosswalk, but be patient and do not allow your horse to rush across the road. Once safely across, you can choose either the Ute Trail to the right, which stays in the lower meadow and crosses one wooden foot bridge or you can ride the Chambers Trail to the left and on to the Valley Reservoir Trail. Or you can opt to stay on the east side of the ridge on the narrow Galloway Ranch Trail which offers beautiful views into the historic Rock Ledge Ranch. Mountain bikes are allowed to ride in this area of the park. The Niobrara Trail follows the ridge crest on the far southeast, adding some challenge and scenery. After coming through the meadow or off the ridge switchback, the trail crosses Ridge Rd. and becomes the Buckskin Charlie Trail. This area can be particularly confusing with a myriad of trails running in all directions. Continue to head in a generally southwest direction possibly coming upon the Old Colorado City Trail or Arnold Trail, which are both pretty, one-way trails that end at neighborhood streets. If you find the Scotsman Trail and emerge at the Scotsman Picnic Area with its hitching rails, head back south until you stumble onto the Strausenback Trail. There is an unexpected, steep downhill on the Strausenback Trail, but it brings you directly back to the trailers.

9 Dome Rock State Wildlife Area

Overall Ride Rating	℧℧℧℧℧
Trail Rating	Moderate
Distance	9.5-mile Dome Rock Loop, plus a large network of interconnected loops and out-and-back trails
Elevation	8,880–9,800 feet
Best Season	Year-round
Main Uses	Equestrian, hiking, hunting.
Trailhead Amenities	Room for six to eight large rigs in the spacious, graveled parking area. There is a seasonal creek on the northeast side of the lot for watering your horses. Trailhead also has a water spigot and portable toilet.
Dogs	Not permitted
Shoes	Barefoot okay
Maps	DeLorme *Colorado Atlas & Gazetteer*, p. 62; National Geographic *Trails Illustrated Map 137, Pikes Peak/Cañon City*
Contact	Colorado Division of Wildlife
Fees	All adults visiting state wildlife areas must have a current habitat stamp, which can be purchased for $5 at local sporting goods stores and other retailers that sell hunting and fishing licenses.
Regulations	Public access is prohibited December 1 through July 15 to protect critical winter habitat for elk and bighorn sheep on the Spring Creek Trail, Dome View Trail, and Dome Rock Trail from Jack Rabbit Lodge. See the Trail Savvy section (p. 12), website and posted regulations for additional information.
Special Notes	The entrance gate is very small and takes a sharp turn. The hill down into the parking area is steep and makes a sharp left turn. Many large rigs negotiate the road with no problem: just take your time, swing wide getting into the gate, and go slow. The riding is well worth the extra care you'll take to park. No mountain bikes are allowed on this trail.

Directions to Trailhead

From Colorado Springs, take US 24 18.5 miles through Woodland Park to Divide. Turn left (south) on CO 67 toward Cripple Creek and Mueller State Park. Drive approximately 5.5 miles (past the Mueller State Park entrance) to the fork in the road. Take the right fork, signed as CR 61 (Fourmile Rd.). Follow this road for 2 miles until you see a sign on the right for Dome Rock State Wildlife Area. Make a sharp turn right through a narrow gate, head down a steep hill, and go around to the left for the clearly marked trailhead parking lot.

This 6,980-acre region of outstanding horse country makes for one of my favorites. The options are nothing short of fabulous. You can choose a short out-and-back ride or an all-day loop ride. If you would like to do more exploring, stay overnight in one of the nearby boarding facilities (see Accommodations, p. 23) or camp north of US 24 in one of the many dispersed sites off of Forest Service roads. Adjacent Mueller State Park (see Ride 10, p. 49) is also outstanding.

The Dome Rock Trail (No. 46) heads west from the parking area, following Fourmile Creek downhill to the 8,200-foot base of Dome Rock. Along the way are looming canyon walls, sandy washes, beaver ponds, beautiful rock outcroppings, mountain views, remnants of an old mine, and gorgeous, grassy meadows. Be prepared, too, for numerous water crossings. Stop to enjoy a picnic lunch when you reach the Jack Rabbit Lodge, an old hunting lodge that burned in the 1940s. All that remains are the rustic rock chimney, portions of the original foundation, old bedsprings, and a few glass shards.

At this point, you have ridden about a third of the 9.5-mile Dome Rock Loop and can see the prominent 9,039-foot Dome Rock in the distance. Continuing west brings you to Dome Rock, or you can head north on the Cabin Creek Trail (No. 45) into Mueller State Park. To complete the Dome Rock Loop, follow Trail No. 46 until it intersects the Spring Creek Trail (No. 43). The section from Jack Rabbit Lodge to this point is only open from July 16 to November 30 each year due to the bighorn sheep lambing season. The trail continues east, connecting with the Willow Creek Trail (No. 40). Again, you have several water crossings as well as significant overlooks from high points.

The trail system is a combination of wide double tracks, old stagecoach roads, sandy washes, and single tracks. Trails on the north-facing hillsides are veiled by dense Engelmann spruce forest, while those on the south-facing slope offer more expansive views through sparsely vegetated limber and bristlecone pine. Keep an eye out for one of the few remaining resident herds of bighorn sheep in the state. The Dome Rock Loop is a great introduction to the area, but don't miss exploring the other wonderful trails that crisscross this state wildlife area.

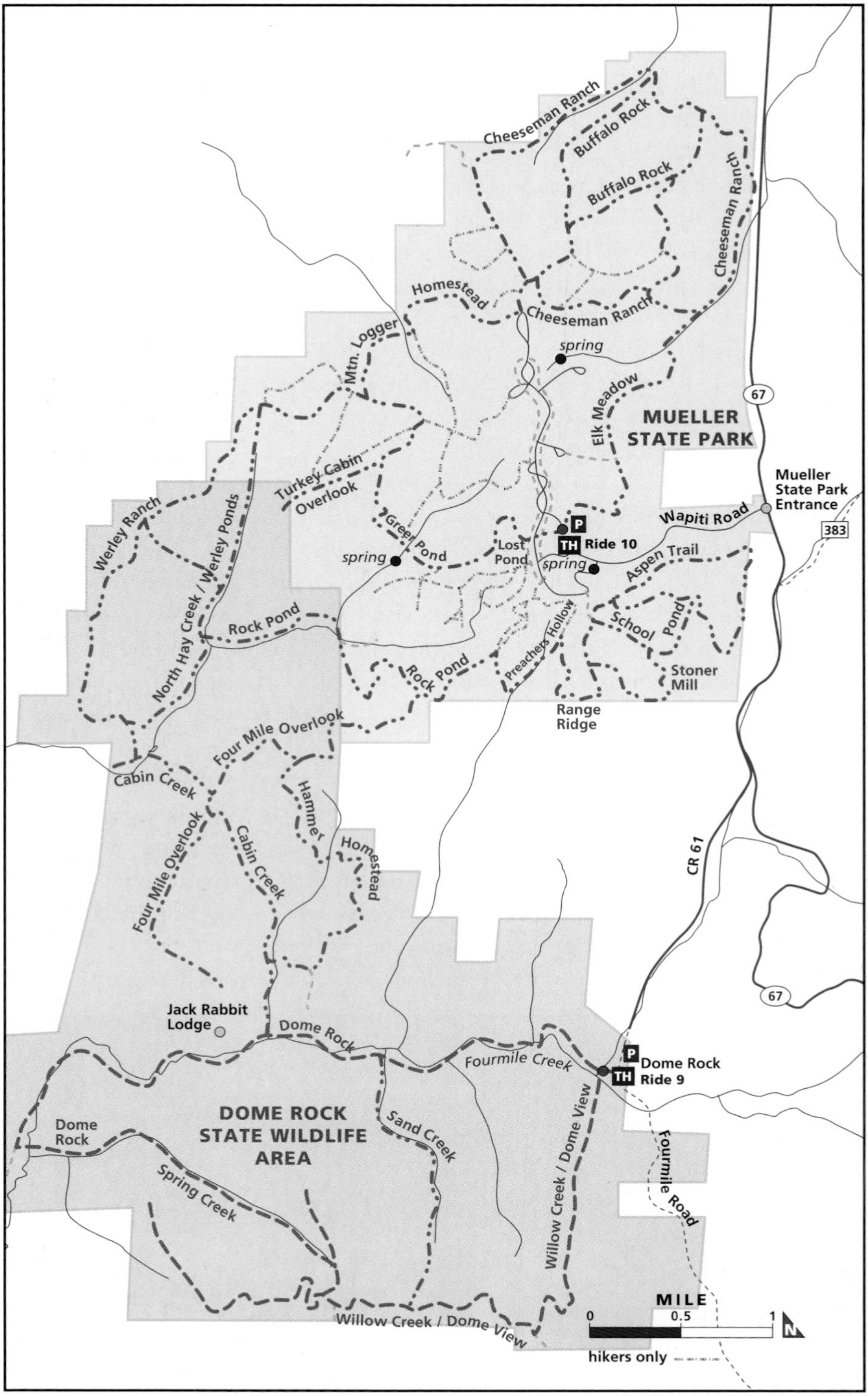

Cheeseman Ranch
Buffalo Rock
Buffalo Rock
Cheeseman Ranch
Homestead
Cheeseman Ranch
spring
Mtn. Logger
Elk Meadow
67
MUELLER
STATE PARK
Turkey Cabin
Overlook
Mueller
State Park
Entrance
Wapiti Road
383
Green Pond
P
spring
Lost
Pond
TH Ride 10
Aspen Trail
Werley Ranch
North Hay Creek / Werley Ponds
spring
Preachers Hollow
School
Pond
Rock Pond
Rock Pond
Stoner
Mill
Range
Ridge
Four Mile Overlook
CR 61
Cabin Creek
Hammer
Four Mile Overlook
Cabin Creek
Homestead
67
Jack Rabbit
Lodge
Dome Rock
Fourmile Creek
P
TH
Dome Rock
Ride 9
Dome
Rock
DOME ROCK
STATE WILDLIFE
AREA
Sand Creek
Willow Creek / Dome View
Fourmile Road
Spring Creek
MILE
0   0.5   1
Willow Creek / Dome View
N
hikers only

10 Mueller State Park
(For Trail Map see p. 48)

Overall Ride Rating	UUUUU
Trail Rating	Easy
Distance	27-mile trail system of interconnecting loops
Elevation	8,800–9,680 feet
Best Season	Year-round
Main Uses	Equestrian, hiking, mountain biking, fishing, hunting, picnicking
Trailhead Amenities	Equestrians must park at the large parking area at the livery lot, which has 12 designated trailer spots. Restrooms are found in the park and as you leave the trailhead on Livery Trail (No. 20) and Lost Pond Trail (No. 11). No overnight stabling or camping for horses within the park. See accommodations on p. 25.
Dogs	On leash in developed portions of park; prohibited on trails or in the backcountry
Shoes	Barefoot okay
Maps	DeLorme *Colorado Atlas & Gazetteer*, p. 62; National Geographic *Trails Illustrated Map 137, Pikes Peak/Cañon City;* Colorado State Parks map, Mueller State Park (http://parks.state.co.us)
Contact	Mueller State Park
Fees	$5 daily park permit or $55 annual state parks pass
Regulations	See the Trail Savvy section (p. 12), website and posted regulations for additional information.
Special Notes	Rental horses are available through Golden Eagle Outfitters and can be reached at the livery 719-686-7373 (May-September) or 719-687-2316 (off season office). Hunting is permitted beginning in October. Be sure that you and your horse wear blaze orange and check at the park entrance to confirm the hunting area boundaries at the time of your visit.

Directions to Trailhead

From Colorado Springs, take US 24 18.5 miles through Woodland Park to Divide. Turn left (south) on CO 67 toward Cripple Creek. Drive approximately 5 miles to the park entrance on your right, where you will pay and pick up a large-scale trail map. Follow Wapiti (Elk) Rd. through the park and take the second right for the livery parking area, just after the Bootleg Picnic Area on your left.

Mueller State Park is one of Colorado's most popular parks due to its accessibility, excellent facilities, and scenery. Trails are numerous, from short 1-mile circuits to long loops encircling the entire park. Ride for an hour, ride for a day, or overnight your horse at one of the nearby stabling facilities and visit for longer (see Accommodations, p. 25). The park scenery includes incredible views of Pikes Peak, the Collegiate Peaks, and the Sangre de Cristo Mountains. Open, grassy meadows are painted with wildflowers in the summer and aspen in the fall. The trails are meticulously maintained and connect with the nearby Dome Rock State Wildlife Area (see Ride 9, p. 46). Interpretive signage adds extra interest. The trails are natural-dirt paths mixed with crusher fines and are clearly marked, named, and numbered. Mueller is home to eagles, deer, elk, and even bighorn sheep. This outstanding park is ideal for riding.

11 Alderfer/Three Sisters Park

Overall Ride Rating	OOOOOO
Trail Rating	Moderate
Distance	12.5 miles of trails on 1,100 acres
Elevation	7,700 feet–8,450 feet
Best Season	Year-round
Main Uses	Equestrian, hiking, mountain biking
Trailhead Amenities	Loop-around parking adequate for several rigs; bathrooms, kiosk with maps, picnic tables, and shelter available. No water.
Dogs	On leash
Shoes	Recommended
Maps	DeLorme *Colorado Atlas & Gazetteer*, p. 39; National Geographic *Trails Illustrated Map 100, Boulder/Golden*; Jefferson County Open Space map, Alderfer/Three Sisters Park (http://co.jefferson.co.us/openspace)
Contact	Jefferson County Open Space
Fees	None
Regulations	See the Trail Savvy section (p. 12), website and posted regulations for additional information.
Special Notes	Parking lots can be full on weekends

Alderfer/Three Sisters Park has no major water crossings and the climbs are neither steep nor long. The 8.5-mile route crosses Buffalo Park Rd. and picks up either branch of the Wild Iris Loop. Follow this trail east to the Evergreen Mountain Trail West, turn right, and climb Evergreen Mountain to the Summit Trail. The Summit Trail is a balloon loop: You follow the string up, circle the "balloon" portion, and come down to Evergreen Mountain Trail East.

Tall ponderosa pine trees shelter this trail, which offers great views of Mount Evans and the Continental Divide. The route skirts the Evergreen Heights neighborhood before it connects with the Evergreen Mountain Trail and crosses Buffalo Park Rd. at the eastern parking lot. Go through the lot to the Hidden Fawn Trail. Wildflowers abound in the summer. The trail may be snow-covered in places in the winter and spring. After passing the intersection with the Dedisse Trail, riders can either turn right onto a more technical, rocky trail to climb between the rocks in the Three Sisters formation or turn left to stay on the easier side in front of the Brother formation. This trail has several switchbacks, so double-check the tightness of your girth during the ride.

The Sisters Trail connects to the Ponderosa Trail, where riders turn right to a section of the Silver Fox Trail. Turn right again onto the Homestead Trail, which

Directions to Trailhead

Take I-70 going west from Denver and get off at Exit 252 for CO 74/Evergreen. Head south on CO 74 for 8 miles into the main part of Evergreen. Turn right (south) onto CR 73. Go about 0.5 mile to the stoplight at Buffalo Park Rd., turn right (west), and continue 2 miles past Evergreen High School and the first parking lot to the second lot at the western edge of the park.

loops around a rock formation. Returning to the meadow, riders can follow the Bluebird Meadow Trail or the Silver Fox Trail to the parking lot. This area is good for green horses ready to be exposed to people and bikes. After the ride, enjoy a short walk from the parking lot to the Alderfer homestead.

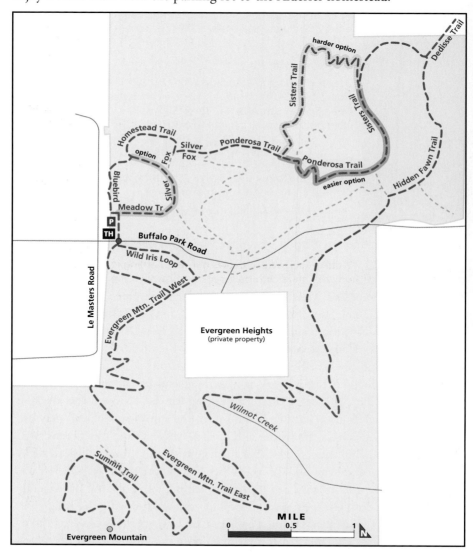

12 Elk Meadow Park

Overall Ride Rating	UUUUU
Trail Rating	Moderate
Distance	13 miles of total trail network on 1,385 acres
Elevation	7,600–9,700 feet
Best Season	Year-round (meadow trails recommended in winter)
Main Uses	Equestrian, hiking, mountain biking
Trailhead Amenities	Loop-around parking lot with room for several large rigs; restrooms, hitching posts, an informational kiosk with park maps, and picnic tables available. No water at the Lewis Ridge Rd. lot, but it is available at the Elk Meadow lot off Stagecoach Blvd.
Dogs	On leash
Shoes	Recommended
Maps	DeLorme *Colorado Atlas & Gazetteer,* p. 39; National Geographic *Trails Illustrated Map 100, Boulder/Golden;* Jefferson County Open Space map, Elk Meadow Park (http://co.jefferson.co.us/ openspace)
Contact	Denver Mountain Parks; Jefferson County Open Space; Colorado Division of Wildlife, Bergen Peak State Wildlife Area
Fees	None
Regulations	See the Trail Savvy section (p. 12), website and posted regulations for additional information.
Special Notes	The Bergen Peak Trail passes through the Bergen Peak State Wildlife Area, which allows hunting. Parking lots can be full on weekends with trails receiving heavy use.

Directions to Trailhead

From I-70 heading west from Denver, take Exit 252 for CO 74/Evergreen. Head south 5 miles on CO 74 past Bergen Park to Lewis Ridge Rd. Turn right (west) and park in the large lot on the right side of the road.

These trails epitomize foothills riding, with beautiful views, diverse plant life, and a nice mixture of ascents and descents. Only minor water crossings occur when snowmelt is running off the hills. A challenging 11-mile route starts on the Sleepy "S" Trail from the parking lot. At the first intersection, turn right on the Elk Ridge Trail, then right again onto the Meadow View Trail in another 0.5 mile. On the forested edges of the trails, snow may linger as late as May.

The next intersection with the Too Long Trail presents a choice. If you're not looking for a difficult ride, turn right and stay on the Meadow View Trail to the Founders Trail or down toward the highway and the Painters Pause Trail past the historic barn and back to the parking lot. Passing mostly through open meadow, these trails offer a relaxed ride. In the winter, you may see elk grazing in the meadow, but do not approach them. In the spring, the ground may be soggy in low areas; stay on the trails in order not to crush tender plants.

If you are looking for a challenge, turn left and follow the switchbacks of the Too Long Trail up the side of Bergen Peak. This trail gains 1,220 feet in 2.4 miles and makes a great tune-up for mountain riding. Watch for a particularly tight spot between boulders as well as a few short rock scrambles— it's wiser to ascend this trail with a horse rather than to descend. If the Too Long Trail is a delight, then take the Bergen Peak Trail 1 mile farther to the peak and soak up the outstanding views stretching from Mount Evans to Pikes Peak. A small hillside meadow below the radio tower makes a good spot for a picnic lunch. Backtrack down the mountain, staying right on the Bergen Peak Trail another 2.7 miles to the Meadow View Trail. Here, turn right to return to the lower-elevation meadows. A left turn onto the Sleepy "S" Trail will return you to the parking lot.

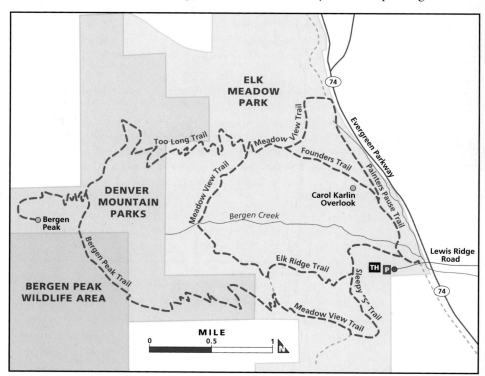

13 Lair O' the Bear Park

Overall Ride Rating	UUUUU
Trail Rating	Easy
Distance	4.3 miles of trails on 320 acres, with 3 miles open to equestrians
Elevation	6,400–6,700 feet
Best Season	Year-round (the upper Bruin Bluff Trail not recommended if snow or ice)
Main Uses	Equestrian, hiking, mountain biking, fishing.
Trailhead Amenities	Loop-around parking lot large enough for five to six rigs; bathrooms, picnic area, hitching rail, trash receptacles, an informational kiosk with park maps, and a handicap-accessible fishing pier. Horse water is available in the creek.
Dogs	On leash
Shoes	Recommended
Maps	DeLorme *Colorado Atlas & Gazetteer*, p. 40; National Geographic *Trails Illustrated Map 100, Boulder/Golden*; Jefferson County Open Space map, Lair O' the Bear Park (http://co.jefferson.co.us/ openspace)
Contact	Jefferson County Open Space
Fees	None
Regulations	Horses not allowed on the Creekside Loop or the riparian section of the Creekside Trail between the parking lot, the Bear Creek Trail, and Bear Creek. See the Trail Savvy section (p. 12), website and posted regulations for additional information.
Special Notes	Heavy traffic possible on the weekends. There are three trail bridges to cross, but they are wide and sturdy.

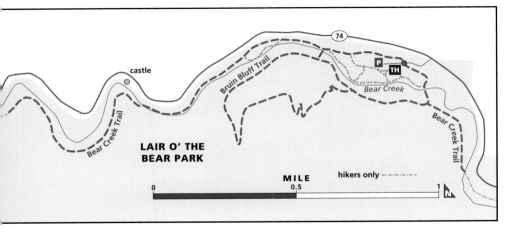

Directions to Trailhead

From C-470, take the CO 8/Morrison Rd. exit and go west through Morrison. At the second stoplight, continue straight onto CO 74 (Bear Creek Canyon Rd.). Continue 4.7 miles; the park entrance is on the left side of the road and is well signed.

Flowering plants and a variety of wildlife abound almost any time of year in this foothills park. In the autumn, the cottonwood and willow trees are dazzling in yellows, reds, and oranges. This suggested 3.6-mile route starts on the Bear Creek Trail to the north side of the parking lot and heads east toward the park entrance, crossing the road. Shortly, you come to the Ouzel Bridge. Cross via the bridge or through the creek and follow the Bruin Bluff Trail to the right. To add another 0.6 mile, stay on the Bear Creek Trail until you reach the Lair O' the Bear park boundary at Little Park and then return.

The Bruin Bluff Trail rises and descends, exposing views into the canyon below until it reaches a Y, where it turns left and ascends in a 1.3-mile loop. This is a nice departure from the creek-side trails and tends to be less crowded. In snowy weather, turn right to follow the Castor Cutoff 0.2 mile to where the Bruin Bluff Trail rejoins. Cross the creek at the Dipper Bridge and reconnect with the Bear Creek Trail west of the parking lot. Turn left to parallel Bear Creek for another 0.8 mile toward the western boundary of Lair O' the Bear, crossing one small feeder creek and another bridge. After the third bridge, the trail narrows considerably as it stays close to the canyon's rock face and passes a beautiful, private stone castle nestled in the rock wall along the north side of the creek. The Bear Creek Trail continues beyond Lair O' the Bear another 5 miles through Corwina Park and O'Fallon Park to Pence Park, all part of Denver Mountain Parks. Return to your trailer by staying on the Bear Creek Trail all the way back.

14 Apex Park and Lookout Mountain Park

Overall Ride Rating	○○○○○
Trail Rating	Moderate to difficult
Distance	5.6 miles one way
Elevation	6,300–7,600 feet
Best Season	Spring to fall
Main Uses	Equestrian, hiking, mountain biking
Trailhead Amenities	Very large paved lot in conjunction with Heritage Square, unlimited parking, restrooms, informational kiosk with trail maps. Nearby Heritage Square shopping center has phones, restrooms, food, shopping, and amusement rides.
Dogs	On leash
Shoes	Recommended
Maps	DeLorme *Colorado Atlas & Gazetteer*, p. 40; Rand McNally *2003 Denver Regional StreetFinder*, maps 2191–2192; National Geographic *Trails Illustrated 100, Boulder/Golden*; Jefferson County Open Space map, Apex Park (http://co.jefferson.co.us/openspace)
Contact	Jefferson County Open Space; Denver Parks and Recreation Department; Denver Mountain Parks
Fees	No fees to ride the trails. Admission to Buffalo Bill Museum is $3 for adults, $2 for seniors over 65, and $1 for children 6 to 15; children under 6 are free. For more information, go online at www.buffalobill.org or call 303-526-0744.
Regulations	See the Trail Savvy section (p. 12), website and posted regulations for additional information.
Special Notes	There are restrooms, water, and food available at the top of Lookout Mountain at the Buffalo Bill Museum and Pahaska Teepee gift shop during business hours. The first Sunday in June is Western Heritage Day and Burial Commemoration, a special event for the Buffalo Bill Riding Club from Jefferson County and educational for all ages.

The Apex Trail starts in the trees on the north side of the parking lot and parallels the Heritage Square shopping center to the west. After a bridge crossing, it climbs Apex Gulch. Horses can drink when the trail crosses it near the top. Prior to that is a 100-foot section of rock that needs to be taken slowly, without crowding others. Cross a few cute wooden bridges and don't forget to look behind at the views of the city and plains.

Directions to Trailhead

Take I-70 west of Denver to US 40 Exit 259. Go north approximately 1 mile to Heritage Square and turn left. Parking is in the lower lot on the north side.

The trail intersects with the Pick N' Sledge and Sluicebox Trails. These switchback up Indian Mountain and can extend the ride if you want. The Enchanted Forest Trail is described on the descent, but you'll pass two intersections for it on the way up. These trails are used by mountain bikers, so be willing to share the trail.

At 2.8 miles, the Apex Trail pops out between houses on Lookout Mountain Rd. If the Buffalo Bill Museum and Grave is your destination, then cross Lookout Mountain Rd. and take the Lookout Mountain Trail on the right side of Colorow Rd. for 1 mile. Watch out for cars, as visibility is reduced and speeds are high. Large groups might send out a rider to stop traffic. Follow the road past the Boettcher Mansion and the Lookout Mountain Nature Center and Preserve. Cross the street one more time and enter Lookout Mountain Park; follow the Buffalo Bill Trail through ponderosa pine forest, past the picnic area, and across the entrance road to the Buffalo Bill Museum. Horses can be tied to trees, away from the grave and parking area. Return to Apex Park along the same route. For a nice change of scenery, turn right on a side trail 1.3 miles through the Enchanted Forest; note that it's steep in places. On the far side of the ridge is a spring where horses can drink. It is said that the water is blessed since it flows from where the Mother Cabrini Shrine is located. The route connects to the Apex Trail at a wooden bridge and follows it back to Heritage Square.

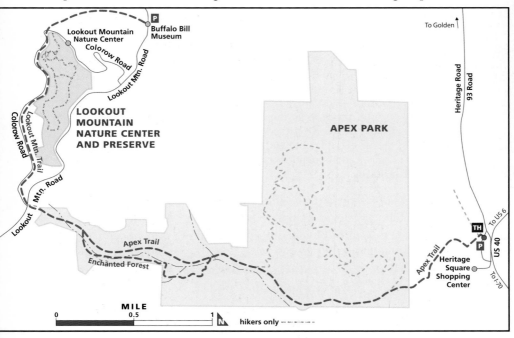

15 Golden Gate Canyon State Park

Overall Ride Rating	UUUUU
Trail Rating	A variety of easy, moderate, and difficult trails
Distance	25-plus-mile trail system
Elevation	7,600–10,400 feet
Best Season	Year-round; call the park for winter riding conditions
Main Uses	Equestrian, hiking, campground camping, fishing, mountain biking, hunting, cross-country skiing, snowshoeing
Trailhead Amenities	Riders should bring their own water. Restrooms, picnic areas with grills, and horse-safe water from pumps are scattered throughout most of the park. Camping with horses is allowed at the Aspen Meadows campground sites 22 and 23 only. There are no facilities for your horses; however, you may high-line, bring your own panels, use an electric fence, or tie to your trailer. A restroom, water pump, and dumpster are also located here. See Directions for individual trailhead information.
Dogs	On leash
Shoes	Recommended
Maps	DeLorme *Colorado Atlas & Gazetteer*, p. 39; National Geographic *Trails Illustrated Map 100, Boulder/Golden*; Golden Gate Canyon State Park Visitor Center map (http://parks.state.co.us)
Contact	Colorado State Parks
Fees	$5 for daily park passes at self-service dispensers. Camping $12 per night plus the daily park fee. For campsite reservations, call 800-678-2267or visit www.ReserveAmerica.com
Regulations	Maximum camping stay is 28 days within a 45-day period. See the Trail Savvy section (p. 12), website and posted regulations for additional information.
Special Notes	Call the visitor center for hunting information. No horse trailers allowed on the upper section of the Mountain Base Rd. due to steep grade.

Directions to Trailhead

Take CO 93 north from Golden 1 mile to Golden Gate Canyon Rd. (also CR 70). Turn left (west) and continue for 13 miles to the park. NOTT CREEK: Turn right at the visitor center and travel approximately 2 miles east to the trailhead, where there is space for approximately four to five trailers depending on parking conditions. Restroom available. KRILEY POND: Turn left (west) at the visitor center and travel 1 mile. There are three trailer spaces, a restroom, and a picnic table. ASPEN MEADOWS: A separate route is necessary to reach the campground area. Take Golden Gate Rd. (CO 46) past the visitor center for 4 miles to CO 119. Turn right (north) on CO 119 and head 3 miles to Gap Rd. (CO 2). Go right (east) to the campground in 3 miles. Once at the campground area, go left at the fork in the road to equestrian sites 22 and 23.

Less than an hour from Denver, Golden Gate State Park boasts 12,000 acres of glorious meadows and dense fir, pine, and aspen forests. Spectacular views of the snowcapped peaks of the Continental Divide, Mount Evans, Longs Peak, and the Indian Peaks stretch as far as 100 miles. In the last 300 years, the park has been home to Cheyenne and Arapaho Indians, trappers and hunters, and miners prospecting the nearby towns of Black Hawk and Central City. Now the land is protected and shelters a vast array of wildlife and flora. Eight trails ranging from 0.7 mile to 6.7 miles in length are open to equestrian users, with one sure to meet every skill level. The entire trail system offers about 25 miles of riding. Blue Grouse, Buffalo, Elk, Mule Deer, and Raccoon are all moderate trails; Burro, Mountain Lion, and Snowshoe Hare are more difficult.

Mostly natural-dirt paths, the trails offer gentle slopes, rockier climbs, stream crossings, and ponds. Opportunities to water your horses and practice your water-crossing skills are numerous. The trails are well signed; red-signed trails allow horses and green are for hikers only. Pick up a detailed large-scale trail map at the visitor center to take along.

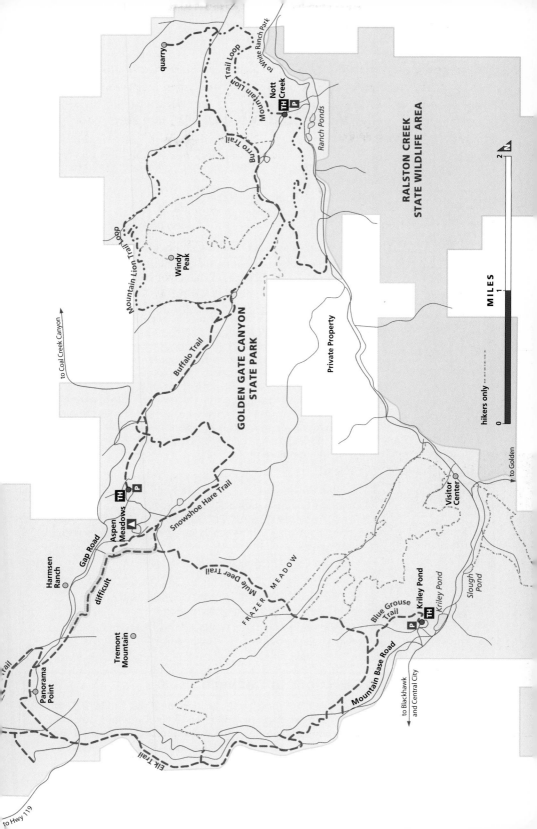

GOLDEN GATE CANYON
STATE PARK

RALSTON CREEK
STATE WILDLIFE AREA

quarry

Trail Loop

Mountain Lion

Nott Creek
TH P

to White Ranch Park

Burro Trail

Ranch Ponds

Mountain Lion Trail Loop

Windy Peak

to Coal Creek Canyon

Buffalo Trail

Private Property

Snowshoe Hare Trail

Aspen Meadows
TH P

Gap Road

difficult

Harmsen Ranch

Mule Deer Trail

F R A Z E R   M E A D O W

Visitor Center

to Golden

Kriley Pond

Kriley Pond

Slough Pond

Blue Grouse Trail

P TH

Tremont Mountain

Panorama Point

Mountain Base Road

to Blackhawk and Central City

Elk Trail

Trail

to Hwy 119

MILES

hikers only

0   1   2

N

16 White Ranch Park

Overall Ride Rating	ʊʊʊʊʊ
Trail Rating	Easy to moderate in the upper park; difficult in the eastern portion
Distance	19.5 miles of trails on 4,390 acres
Elevation	Upper lot, 7,500 feet; lower lot, 6,150 feet
Best Season	Year-round
Main Uses	Equestrian, hiking, backcountry camping, mountain biking
Trailhead Amenities	The more popular upper parking area has two designated pull-through trailer spaces, picnic tables, trash receptacle, informational kiosk with trail maps, round pen, interpretive trail, vault restrooms, and a hitching rail about 0.5 mile away at the picnic area. A much larger, lower parking lot has similar amenities. No water at either trailhead. Camping is available by free permit at the pack-in Sourdough Springs Equestrian Camp. It is a 1.5-mile ride from the upper lot to the 10 sites, which allow up to 3 tents and 8 people per site. The camp is equipped with a vault restroom, hand-pump water hydrant with a drinking fountain, spring-fed water trough, split fire-wood, and two corrals. Each site has a picnic table, fire pit, and a hitching rail. Reservations and permits available at the Open Space office in Golden or on a first-come, first-served basis at the upper parking lot.
Dogs	On leash
Shoes	Recommended
Maps	DeLorme *Colorado Atlas & Gazetteer,* p. 40; National Geographic *Trails Illustrated Map 100, Boulder/Golden*; Jefferson County Open Space map, White Ranch Park (http://co.jefferson.co.us/openspace)
Contact	Jefferson County Open Space
Fees	None
Regulations	See the Trail Savvy section (p. 12), website and posted regulations for additional information.
Special Notes	This is a popular park on weekends and lots can be full. Please be aware that this is bear country.

Directions to Trailhead

To reach the upper lot, take CO 93 north from Golden for about 1 mile to Golden Gate Rd. Turn left (west) and head about 4 miles to CR 57 (Crawford Gulch Rd.). Turn right (north) and go 4 miles to Belcher Hill Rd. and there turn right (east) and continue 0.4 mile to the White Ranch Park entrance. The designated trailer parking is at the end of the gravel entrance road.

To reach the lower lot, take CO 93 1.7 miles north from Golden, passing Golden Gate Rd., to 56th Ave. Turn left (west), go 1 mile to Pine Ridge Rd., and turn right into the park.

This large open space park is unsurpassed for beautiful views and some rugged riding. A short drive from the city brings you to pristine canyons, buttes, and dramatic outcroppings. The well-marked trails vary from easy to strenuous. For surefooted mounts and hearty riders, White Ranch Park is filled with memorable trails.

This suggested 11-mile loop shows off the essential characteristics of the park. From the upper lot, find the Rawhide Trail in the northwest corner. This trail makes a 4.5-mile "U". To see the equestrian campground, turn off on the Waterhole Trail. Continuing on, the Rawhide Trail ends near restrooms, so turn left onto the Longhorn Trail. After 1 mile, the Longhorn Trail tracks left and becomes a difficult shelf trail with boulder-lined sections. This is not a trail for green horses or inexperienced riders. The Shorthorn Trail to the right is an easier, but rocky, alternative. If you take the Longhorn Trail, you eventually meet the New Trail off to the left; this meets up with the Belcher Hill Trail. Turn right on the Belcher Hill Trail to the Mustang Trail. A section of this trail has steps. You'll turn right onto the Sawmill Trail, which returns to the parking lot.

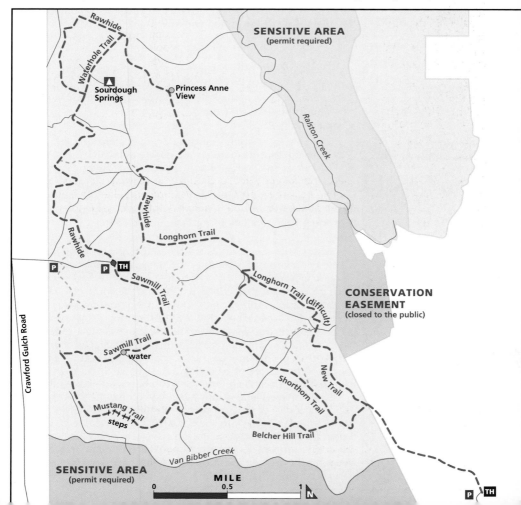

17 Chatfield State Park

Overall Ride Rating	♘♘♘♘♘
Trail Rating	Easy to moderate
Distance	24 miles of trails in 5,300 acres
Elevation	5,500 feet
Best Season	Year-round
Main Uses	Equestrian, hiking, camping, mountain biking, fishing, boating
Trailhead Amenities	Multiple parking areas suitable for trailers inside and adjacent to the park. See directions for main lot descriptions. Trailer parking allowed in lots outside of the road circling the lake, including below the dam. Water is available for horses from the South Platte River, Plum Creek, outlying pond inlets, and outlets. (Note that horses can be kept overnight in the corrals, but riders must camp in the nearby developed campground about 2 miles away. Reservations are recommended and can be made by contacting Chatfield State Park by phone or online.)
Dogs	On leash except in the off-leash dog park below the dam
Shoes	Barefoot okay
Maps	DeLorme *Colorado Atlas & Gazetteer*, pp. 40 and 50; Rand McNally *2003 Denver Regional StreetFinder,* maps 2446, 2447, 2530, and 2531; Colorado State Parks map (http://parks.state.co.us) and entrance brochure
Contact	Chatfield State Park, Douglas County Open Space
Fees	$6 per day May 1 through Labor Day; $5 per day after Labor Day through April 30. Annual state parks pass is $55.
Regulations	Horses not allowed inside the paved park road circling the lake. Some trails by the wetlands-area lakes at the south end of the park and on the west side of the river are for hikers only. Comply with restricted-access signage. See the Trail Savvy section (p. 12), website and posted regulations for more information.
Special Notes	None of the trails in the park are named. A few have old posts that are no longer maintained; horseshoe signs indicate main trails. Large sports competitions such as marathons and triathlons are held here on weekends. Be prepared to find alternative parking and trails during these planned events. Crossing the South Platte River, especially during spring runoff, can be dangerous. If there is any question at all about the safety of a river crossing, do not hesitate to use the car bridge just south of the lake (but watch for cars). Use caution and stay on trails, particularly when riding along Plum Creek, as there are dangerous areas of quicksand due to the constantly shifting streambed and local beaver activity. Beware of the lakeshores: Many are steep and can get deep quite quickly.
Watch for low-flying planes when riding near the model airplane field west of the Roxborough Park Rd. parking lot. In the summertime, ride early to avoid the bugs. Be certain to spray your horses and yourself to ensure a pleasant ride. Blue herons are special residents at Chatfield. From March through September, these giant cranes can be observed nesting high up in the cottonwoods surrounding the South Platte River.

Directions to Trailhead

From C-470 in Littleton, take the Wadsworth exit and proceed about 1 mile south to the park's Deer Creek entrance on the left.

ALTERNATE ENTRANCE: Take US 85 (Santa Fe Drive) south from C-470 to the Titan Rd. exit, head west to Roxborough Park Rd., and turn north. Enter the park and proceed to the Plum Creek entrance.

STABLE-AREA PARKING: From the park's Wadsworth entrance, turn right at the T intersection just beyond the entrance station. Take the next right at the Y, following the park signs to the stables. There is a pull-through parking area large enough to accommodate 15–20 rigs. Restrooms, corrals with seasonal water, and year-round commercial stables are located here. Horses can be kept overnight in the corrals, but people must camp in the developed campground, which is about two miles away.

PLATTE RIVER BRIDGE PARKING: From the park's Wadsworth entrance, turn right at the T intersection just beyond the entrance station. Pass the entrance to the stables and proceed across the river bridge to the first parking area on the right. The lot is a loop with room for approximately six to eight rigs. Restrooms, a drinking fountain, a hitching post, and handicapped river access are available. Another large lot is located near the ponds on the west side of the river. Turn right just prior to crossing the bridge. This lot has a portable toilet and picnic tables.

PLUM CREEK PARKING: From the park's Plum Creek entrance, proceed to the Y and go right. Take the second right to the large lot with restrooms and a picnic area. Do not take the road to the Plum Creek Nature Area, as it is flooded and there is no turnaround.

WATERTON CANYON TRAILHEAD PARKING: This lot and the next are outside of the park and do not require a vehicle entrance fee. There is no charge for walk-in entry to Chatfield State Park.

Proceed south on Wadsworth, passing the park entrance. Turn left onto Waterton Rd. Take the second left, passing the Discovery Pavilion parking lot, and park in the grass area signed for horse trailers on the south side next to the picnic area. Restrooms and picnic tables are available.

ROXBOROUGH PARK ROAD PARKING: Douglas County Division of Open Space and Natural Resources, in cooperation with the Denver Water Board, built a public parking lot to improve access to the Highline Canal (see Ride 18, p. 67) and Chatfield State Park. Follow the directions to the park's Plum Creek entrance, but before reaching the station, turn right into the fenced parking lot just after the canal. Loop-around parking is available for four to five rigs; other amenities include a portable toilet and picnic shelter.

Chatfield State Park's delightful trails meander through the South Platte River basin on the southwest side and the Plum Creek drainage on the southeast side. Due to the numerous parking options, trail selections are varied. Take the time to expand your familiarity with the existing trails inside and beyond this large park. Tall cottonwood trees provide shade in the summer. The foothills are visible to the west, eliminating concerns about getting lost. The footing is generally soft, but there are areas near the river that are rockier and should be ridden with shoes. Elk take up winter residence in the meadow east of the river.

Just south of the Platte River bridge is a river crossing with gently sloping banks. Fences have been installed to channel riders and avoid further impact to the riverbanks and the Preble's jumping mouse habitat. A trail bridge across Plum Creek near the Plum Creek parking area allows access to the eastern side of the park near the railroad tracks. Riding farther south on the west side of the Platte River to the Waterton Canyon trailhead accesses the Waterton Canyon Trail after crossing Waterton Rd. The Highline Canal Trail can be joined easily from the Roxborough Park Rd. lot. Note, however, that the re-entry point at the far south end of the park has a restrictive V opening in the fence too small for most horses.

This park makes an excellent winter ride due to the easy accessibility and churned-up footing—a result of high use from the local boarding stables and the park's commercial stable.

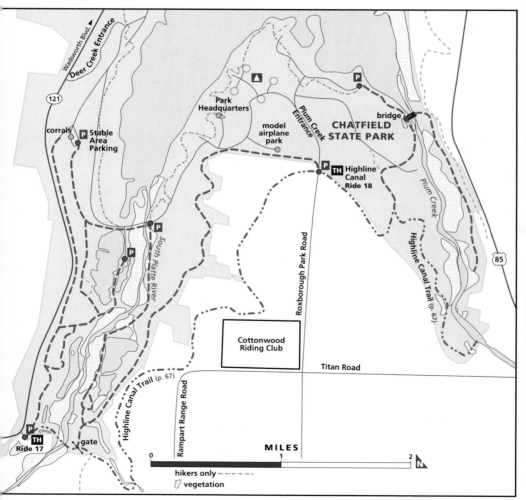

18 Highline Canal Trail
(For Trail Map see p. 66)

Overall Ride Rating	UUUUU
Trail Rating	Easy
Distance	3.5 and 9.5 miles round-trip
Elevation	5,440 feet
Best Season	Year-round
Main Uses	Equestrian, hiking, mountain biking
Trailhead Amenities	A large loop parking area for four to six rigs (depending on size); portable toilet, kiosk, covered picnic table, and trash receptacle are located at the Roxborough Park Rd. trailhead.
Dogs	On leash
Shoes	Barefoot okay
Maps	DeLorme *Colorado Atlas & Gazetteer*, p. 40; Denver Water's "Guide to the Highline Canal Trail;" Douglas County Parks and Trails map, Highline Canal Trail (www.douglas.co.us/openspace)
Contact	Denver Water Recreation Office; Douglas County Parks and Trails; Chatfield State Park
Fees	None
Regulations	See the Trail Savvy section (p. 12), website and posted regulations for additional information.

Directions to Trailhead

From C-470, turn south on US 85 (Santa Fe Dr.) to Titan Rd. and turn right (west). Go 2 miles on Titan Rd. to Roxborough Park Rd. and turn north (right). Continue 1.6 miles to the trailhead on the right.

Originally, the Highline Canal was intended for little more than distributing drinking and agricultural water to the growing population of Denver following the gold rush of 1859. Today, the areas surrounding the canal have become a natural resource for many recreationists and home to an array of wildlife. From the trailhead at Roxborough Park Rd., riders have several choices, with the trail extending east, west, and north into Chatfield State Park.

For a shorter ride, begin heading east/northeast on a level, natural-dirt path along the cottonwood-lined canal. The trail becomes sandy, wide, and unmaintained as it meanders through the Plum Creek drainage. Great horned owls, white-tailed deer, porcupine, and a myriad of other animals live and play in the riparian area here. Occasional glimpses of Castle Rock, Pikes Peak, and Highlands

Ranch are sometimes possible through the trees in the sandy washes. This segment is only 3.5 miles out and back, but it makes an excellent short ride or a nice warm-up.

From the trailhead on the east side of Roxborough Park Rd., riders can also head north to pick up the Chatfield State Park trail system (no fee). The area offers great views of the dam and downtown Denver. Listen for strange buzzing noises from the model airplane field within the park boundary and be aware that this may be an unfamiliar or even frightening sound for your mount. Here you can explore and enjoy 24 miles of equestrian trails (see Ride 17, p. 64).

A longer ride is also available to the southwest. Cross Roxborough Park Rd., which has little to no traffic, and ride southwest along the Highline on a natural-dirt path, passing between two open fields that receive irrigation from the canal. The path continues through the backyard alleys of several neighborhoods, where everyone stops to wave as they see you ride by. The next mile is probably the most enjoyable, as you ride through a rural country setting near the practice areas of the former Denver Polo Club and the Cottonwood Riding Club. Russian olive, large cottonwood, box elder, elm, and willow trees shade the gorgeous setting, and it's wonderful to watch students working and training with their animals in such a beautiful environment.

Riders can continue on from here but will need to cross Titan Rd. and then Rampart Range Rd. (CR 5) as the trail curves to the west and south. Both roads experience a relatively steady flow of traffic, with some development also taking place nearby, so use caution. If you decide to continue, follow the trail south for a glimpse of the red sandstone rock formations of Roxborough State Park and remain on the path bordering the Platte Canyon  Reservoir. The next major road crossing at Waterton Canyon is an extremely busy one with only a difficult bridge and a parking lot ahead. Turn around here rather than crossing, and return to the trailhead for a 9.5-mile round-trip.

19 Deer Creek Canyon Park

Overall Ride Rating	◡◡◡◡◡
Trail Rating	Moderate to difficult
Distance	10.2 miles accessible to horses
Elevation	6,040–7,440 feet
Best Season	Spring to fall
Main Uses	Equestrian, hiking, mountain biking.
Trailhead Amenities	Large, paved, loop-around parking with room for seven to eight trailers on the south side if cars aren't parked in the same spots. Information kiosk with maps, restrooms with water in the sinks, drinking fountain (during warm months), picnic shelter, pay phone, and trash cans also available. There is no water spigot to fill buckets, so bring your own water for horses.
Dogs	On leash
Shoes	Recommended
Maps	DeLorme *Colorado Atlas & Gazetteer,* p. 40; Rand McNally *2003 Denver Regional StreetFinder,* map 2445; National Geographic *Trails Illustrated Map 100, Boulder/Golden*; Jefferson County Open Space map, Deer Creek Canyon Park (http://co.jefferson.co.us/openspace)
Contact	Jefferson County Open Space
Fees	None
Regulations	The Meadowlark, Homesteader and Golden Eagle trails are open to hikers only; please respect this rule. See the Trail Savvy section (p. 12), website and posted regulations for additional information.
Special Notes	For the most part, no water is available for horses along these trails. Sometimes a small spring runs on the right side of the upper Plymouth Mountain Trail just past the Plymouth Creek intersection.

Directions to Trailhead

From C-470, exit Kipling Pkwy. southbound to W. Ute Dr., turn right (west), and follow the 90-degree curve to the south where it becomes S. Owens St. Deer Creek Canyon Rd. joins Owens St. from the left; here Owens St. becomes Deer Creek Canyon Rd. and curves back to the west. Follow this approx. 2 miles and turn left onto Grizzly Dr. at the brown park sign. Follow Grizzly Dr. up a few winding turns past a firehouse to the parking lot entrance on the right.

Deer Creek Canyon Park is a great, nearby day ride for Denver-area residents, with enough parking that even a weekend visit is feasible. Mountain bikers are typically very courteous and patient here. Jefferson County Open Space's trail courtesy campaign has provided a wonderful service by posting signs along the trails describing safe practices for all users. Most trails are wide enough to allow travel in both directions, except for the lower or eastern side of the Plymouth Mountain circuit and the upper part of the Red Mesa Loop.

Start from the parking lot and head past the restrooms and picnic shelter to the Plymouth Creek Trail. Don't forget to pick up a trail map at the kiosk and check out the nearby ground marker indicating the population center of Colorado. The trail begins by winding around the lowest foothill ridges and gulches through thick stands of scrub oak. As you reach the canyon, climbs are steeper and very rocky. Water plays a large part in washing away the dirt cover to expose the rocks that make up the canyon walls and floor. Trail maintenance crews have built steps to help hikers negotiate the steepest and rockiest spots, but they are too narrow to accommodate horses; the equestrian route is clearly marked next to the steps. Once through the narrowest part of Plymouth Canyon, you pass the first intersection with the Plymouth Mountain Trail. Keep going, as the trail is best ridden counterclockwise, heading uphill through the steep, western portion. Additionally, most bikers ride it clockwise, and passing face to face is easier for you and your horse.

Continue past this intersection 0.4 mile to the upper intersection. For horses at a typical 2.8-mph walking pace, there are two possibilities for perfect 11- and 11.5-mile day rides from this point. The first and longest is to take the Plymouth Mountain loop around to the Black Bear Trail. Follow this relatively bike-free trail down through some pretty, wooded gullies and across a couple of small wooden bridges. Follow the neighborhood road to the right and pick up the

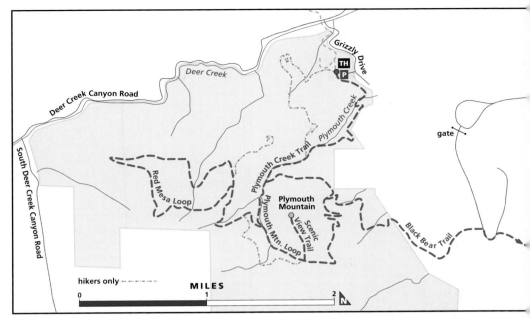

trail again through a large prairie dog colony. Soon riders get an up-close and personal encounter with the striking red rock formations and ledges that make up the west side of the hogback. Find a cool spot for lunch and let the horses enjoy the lush grass. To finish the ride, return up the Black Bear Trail and turn right back onto the Plymouth Mountain Trail. Along this stretch are fantastic views of the hogback and the entire Denver metro area, including Chatfield Reservoir and Marston Lake.

The second trail combination involves continuing on up the Plymouth Creek Trail to the Red Mesa Loop. Pick a direction and follow this easy loop around to the north for some great views. At 7,440 feet, this is the high spot in the park. For some reason, fewer bicyclists use this trail. A meadow intersects the trail at both the upper and lower sections: Either spot is fine for a picnic. Once back on the Plymouth Creek Trail, follow it back down to the upper Plymouth Mountain Trail intersection and go right. At the Scenic View Trail, turn left and follow this 0.4 mile past some fun rock outcroppings and another top pick for a picnic spot. If time is short, this leg can be eliminated.

Continue around the loop back to the Plymouth Creek Trail and return the same way to the parking lot. Unfortunately, there is no way to avoid the dreaded rocky spot to enjoy these wonderful trails. Just slow down, keep a tight rein, and pick them up quickly if a horse should stumble or slip so they can recover. Dismounting and leading them up or down is also an option. In the winter and early spring, this part of the canyon also stays icy throughout the cold season due to the shade—even on those warm 50- and 60-degree days. This makes it too dangerous for horse passage.

20 Indian Creek Trail (No. 800)

Overall Ride Rating	♘♘♘♘♘
Trail Rating	Moderate
Distance	13.5-mile loop
Elevation	7,400–7,900 feet
Best Season	Spring to fall
Main Uses	Equestrian, hiking, trailhead and backcountry camping, mountain biking
Trailhead Amenities	Large loop-around parking accommodating eight to ten trailers with separate parking for cars, vault restrooms, and water hydrant during the season. The separate equestrian campground has seven spaces with no hookups (four pull-through; three back-in), vault restrooms, and four metal hitching rails. Nine pipe panel pens are available on a first-come, first-served basis. Highlines or portable pens are allowed, but be sure to clean up all manure and excess hay. The three back-in spaces do not have trees and are in close quarters so highlines would need to be set up away from your campsite. Tying to trailers is also an option. Water is generally available from hydrants, but the Forest Service well pump is unreliable so bring adequate water for your stay. There is no watering trough available and the nearby stream is protected habitat.

The equestrian campground gate is kept locked by the campground hosts at the adjacent Indian Creek Campground unless someone is using it. Sites are reserved through ReserveUSA.com or had on a first-come, first-served basis. Reservations must be made at least four days in advance. A combination of 10 persons and no more than 4 horses are allowed per site. One vehicle and horse trailer per site. Open from mid-May through Labor Day weekend. |
Dogs	On leash at the trailhead and campground; under voice control on the trail
Shoes	Recommended
Maps	DeLorme *Colorado Atlas & Gazetteer*, p. 50; National Geographic *Trails Illustrated 135, Deckers/Rampart Range*
Contact	Roxborough State Park; Pike National Forest, South Platte Ranger District
Fees	$4 day-use fee; $15 per-night campground fee
Regulations	Horses are not allowed east of the Indian Creek Trail within Roxborough State Park. No overnight camping is allowed in the state park section. See the Trail Savvy section (p. 12), website and posted regulations for additional information.

Directions to Trailhead

Take US 85 (Santa Fe Dr.) south of C-470 to Sedalia. Turn right at the stoplight onto CO 67 and head up Jarre Canyon 10 miles to the trailhead on the right. Go to the upper (second) lot entrance and loop down to park facing out.

This trail was made with equestrian usage specifically in mind. It connects an existing section of trail at the end of Waterton Canyon to the Indian Creek trailhead and equestrian campground to the south. There are also many unsigned trails in the area to explore as well. New directional signs have made the Indian Creek Trail much easier to follow.

Starting from the end of the equestrian campground near the restrooms, the trail descends to cross Bear Creek, then emerges into a meadow. It follows the creek, crossing it again before veering away at about 2 miles.

At this point, the trail climbs out of a gulch. Turn left at the flat area, following the trail sign toward a ridge that offers great views. Before leaving, note the short trail to the left (northwest) that connects to the Colorado Trail (No. 1776) at the Lenny's Rest memorial bench. This is a good access point, bypassing Waterton Canyon, if you are planning a ride on the Colorado Trail. After this intersection, at 4 miles, the trail descends sharply into Stephens Gulch. This is a difficult section, especially when a biker appears around a switchback.

At 5.5 miles, the Waterton Trail branches left and leads to the top of Waterton Canyon, where the east end of the Colorado Trail officially begins. At this point the trail has entered Roxborough State Park. Take note of posted park regulations and abide by them. Look for red raspberry bushes, a special treat during their season, along the path. At the northernmost point, the trail crosses Mill Gulch, a small stream that usually has water for the horses, except during very dry summers or fall. This is a nice place to stop for lunch. Lush fernlike vegetation on damp hillsides along the trail are reminiscent of trails in the Northwest.

The trail soon turns south-southeast and reenters Roxborough State Park. At a well-signed intersection with the Carpenter Peak Trail, stay on the Indian Creek Trail. At 8 miles, the trail returns to Mill Gulch in an area known as Homestead Meadows. Trail users should stay right at another intersection, which leads to a road within Roxborough State Park. The trail climbs up, and at a set of power line towers joins a jeep road, not open to motorized travel, known as the Dump Rd. Follow this road in a southerly direction for 3 miles to a signed intersection where the Indian Creek Trail returns to a single track to the right. This section descends 1.6 miles, returning to the day-use parking lot. The trail to the left is a connector to the Ringtail Trail within Douglas County's Sharptail Ridge Trail System (see Ride 21, p. 75).

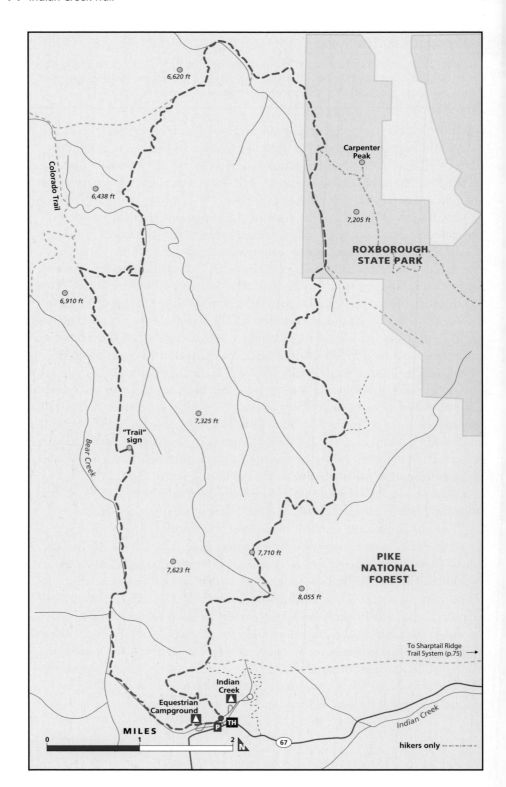

6,620 ft

Carpenter
Peak

Colorado Trail

6,438 ft

7,205 ft

ROXBOROUGH
STATE PARK

6,910 ft

7,325 ft

"Trail"
sign

Bear Creek

7,710 ft

PIKE
NATIONAL
FOREST

7,623 ft

8,055 ft

To Sharptail Ridge
Trail System (p.75)

Indian
Creek

Equestrian
Campground

P TH

MILES

Indian Creek

0   1   2

N

67

hikers only

21 Sharptail Ridge Trail System

Overall Ride Rating	ひひひひひ
Trail Rating	Sharptail Trail, easy; Swallowtail and Ringtail Trails, moderate
Distance	Sharptail Trail, 4.4 miles one way; Swallowtail Trail, 3.3-mile figure-eight loops; Ringtail Trail to Indian Creek Trail, 6.3 miles one way
Elevation	Swallowtail Trail: 5,600–6,400 feet; Ringtail Trail: 8,000 feet; Sharptail Trail: 5,600 feet
Best Season	Year-round as weather allows; see Regulations regarding closures on the Sharptail Ridge Open Space and trailhead parking during fall hunting season.
Main Uses	Hikers and equestrians only on the Sharptail Trail through the Sharptail Ridge Open Space and Roxborough State Park. Mountain bikes are allowed from the Indian Creek Trail to the Ringtail and Swallowtail Trails on the Pike Hill and Nelson Ranch Open Spaces.
Trailhead Amenities	The Sharptail trailhead has a loop-around gravel lot that's large enough for 10–12 trailers. There is a portable toilet, potable water hydrant, an informational kiosk with maps, an emergency telephone, bear-resistant trash receptacles, designated handicapped parking, and large, covered picnic pavilion with adjacent covered hitching rails (a feature unique to Douglas County open space parks).
Dogs	Not allowed at the Sharptail trailhead, on the Sharptail Trail, in the Sharptail Ridge Open Space, or in Roxborough State Park. On leash on the Swallowtail and Ringtail trails within the Nelson Ranch and Pike Hill Open Spaces. Under voice control in Pike National Forest.
Shoes	Not needed on the Sharptail, but recommended on the Swallowtail and Ringtail trails.
Maps	DeLorme *Colorado Atlas & Gazetteer,* p. 50; Douglas County Division of Open Space and Natural Resources Trails brochure
Contact	Douglas County Division of Open Space and Natural Resources; Roxborough State Park; Colorado Division of Wildlife; Pike National Forest, South Platte Ranger District
Fees	None
Regulations	Sharptail Ridge Open Space and the Sharptail Trail and trailhead have closures during fall hunting seasons. The area is managed jointly by the Colorado Division of Wildlife and Douglas County Open Space and Natural Resources. Part of this management includes a hunting season to help manage the deer and elk populations at the Sharptail Ridge State Wildlife Area. See website for yearly posted dates (www.douglas.co.us/openspace/). Users must stay on trails. See the Trail Savvy section (p.12), website and posted regulations for additional information.
Special Notes	Please avoid using the trails while they are muddy. Be aware of summer afternoon lightning storms, as these trails are very exposed. Be cautious of prairie rattlesnakes, mountain lions, and black bears.

Directions to Trailhead

From US 85 (Santa Fe Dr.) south of Denver, turn west on Titan Rd. Go 2 miles to Roxborough Park Rd. (gravel), turn left (south) and follow this 3.7 miles to the trailhead on the left.

To access the Sharptail Trail, equestrians step over a low log in the buck-and-rail fence near the picnic pavilion and pick up the trail near the line of trees. All trails are natural surface at least 4 feet wide and have no water. The route sweeps across grasslands as it climbs to Roxborough State Park, with views of Aurora Rampart Reservoir, Chatfield Lake, the hogback, and Denver. Once in the state park, the trail descends to join a short section of CR 5, then continues through the Nelson Ranch Open Space and becomes the Swallowtail Trail. Scrub oak lines the path. Rest or have lunch at a shaded log picnic table with a nearby hitching rail. A red rock monolith, encircled by one of the Swallowtail loops, dominates the scenery. The two adjoining loops cross large slabs of sandstone and pass along colorful sandstone cliffs. A picnic table and several benches dot the trailside among the rock formations.

The Ringtail Trail departs from the center of the Swallowtail loops and begins a long, steady, 3.5-mile climb south and west over the Nelson Ranch and Pike Hill Open Spaces to the boundary of Pike National Forest. As you climb, the shrublands change to montane forest. At the boundary is a cabin known as "Goldilocks' Cabin." The Indian Creek Trail intersection is another 2.8 miles into the forest. This trail combination would make a great shuttle trip, or you can keep it a day trip by following the Sharptail Trail out, around the figure-eight Swallowtail Trail loops, and back for a great 12-mile ride.

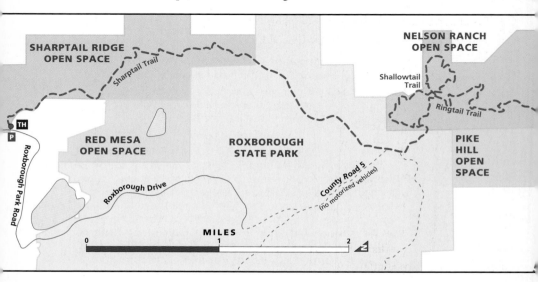

22 Monument Preserve

Overall Ride Rating	∪∪∪∪∪
Trail Rating	Easy
Distance	Approximately 12 total miles of trails
Elevation	7,000–7,400 feet
Best Season	Year-round
Main Uses	Equestrians, hiking, mountain biking
Trailhead Amenities	Loop-around parking for six to seven trailers is separate from car parking, although cars are allowed to park in the loop and frequently do. There is a trailhead sign with minimal information and a trash can. No water is available.
Dogs	Under voice control
Shoes	Recommended
Maps	DeLorme *Colorado Atlas & Gazetteer,* p. 50; National Geographic *Trails Illustrated 137, Pikes Peak/Cañon City;* Recreation Guide Map Co. *Colorado Springs and the Pikes Peak Area Map and Guide No. CO-2*
Contact	Pike National Forest, Pikes Peak Ranger District
Fees	None
Regulations	No public access to the Monument Fire Center. See the Trail Savvy section (p. 12), website and posted regulations for additional information.

This area passes through one of the great reforestation projects of the Pike National Forest, begun in the early 1900s at the foot of Mount Herman. The Monument Nursery was one of the first in the seedling facilities in the forest system and the most important in the Rocky Mountains. In the 1970s, after nearly 60 years producing millions of seedlings annually, it was converted into the Monument Fire Center and now serves as a base for elite firefighting crews.

The Monument Preserve's paths through meadows and stands of ponderosa pine are enchanting at any time of the year because the relatively low elevation and open terrain keep the preserve snow free. The only numbered and named Forest Service trail in this area is No. 715, which is called either the Monument Trail or the Raspberry–Chautauqua Mountain Trail depending on the reference map. It officially starts on the southern side of the Monument Fire Center, with other paths crisscrossing the forest around the fire center buildings and helipads. The easiest way to familiarize yourself with the trails in the vicinity is to follow a simple 4-mile loop that encircles the general area.

Directions to Trailhead

From I-25 in northern El Paso County, take the Monument exit (Exit 161) and drive west 0.7 mile on Second St. until it ends, just across the railroad tracks on the west side of town. Turn left (south) onto Mitchell Ave. and drive 0.7 mile to Mount Herman Rd. Turn right (west) and drive about 0.8 mile, turning left onto Nursery Rd. (also signed for Schilling Ave.) to the Forest Service parking lot for the Monument Preserve/Mount Herman trailhead immediately on the right. The second and third entrances lead to the loop lot.

From the left side of the sign at the end of the car parking lot, follow the trail west into the forest. Almost immediately, another trail crosses your path; continue straight, through an open gate, and down the pine-covered hill. At 0.2 mile, stay on the more heavily used trail to the right and again go straight at 0.4 mile on the wider trail. Turn right at the work center's dirt entrance road at 0.8 mile and find a trail on the opposite side just in front of the closure gate and wood fence.

This next trail section winds through the trees along the hillside. Soon the trail drops into scrub oak where, during the winter, riders catch an initial glimpse of Monument Rock. A towering erosional remnant of the Dawson Arkose, its upper layer contains several hundred feet of coarse gravel and sandstone layers derived from the uplifted Rocky Mountains. Warmer-weather riders must wait until reaching the meadow before viewing it. A small pond at its base acts as a reflecting pool and is the only source of drinking water for horses. As the trail brings you parallel with the rock, it once again passes intersections with lesser-traveled trails to both the left and right, then loops around both sides of the pond to the foot of the landmark. A small outlet stream crosses the trail on the east side of the pond. When circling the rock, take a close look at the jumbled bits of quartz and feldspar pressed together. This formation was molded from the eroding portions of the ancestral Rockies that washed onto the plains about 55 million years ago.

Continue directly west of the monument on a well-used trail into a small stand of pine. At 1.7 miles, the trail swings south and parallels the Mount Herman Rd. while climbing up a ridge. Ice can remain on the upper part of this section during the winter months. When on the ridge, turn left for a panoramic view of the Monument area and the Black Forest farther east. Return back to the original trail and continue south down a gentler slope. A single-track trail to the right leads back to the Mount Herman Rd., but continue straight here.

At 2.5 miles, the trail ends at an access road. To the left, the road enters the fire center and is closed to the public, so riders must turn right. Along the way are several single-track trails worth exploring. Continue on this road all the way to the Memorial Grove at 2.75 miles. The sculptures, as well as the trees planted nearby, commemorate those who have served as Forest Service employees. Please show respect by not taking horses within the memorial area. Several picnic tables in one corner are perfect for a lunch break. After passing the memorial and

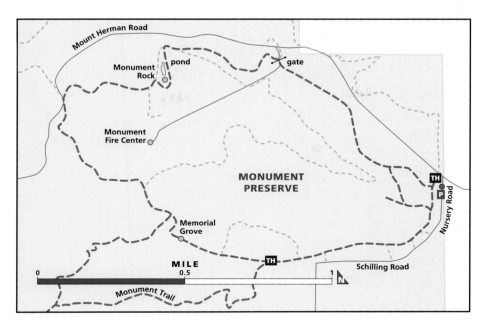

turning east, riders will see more signs of the preserve's historic past, including sprinkler equipment, chimney remains of a caretaker's house, and pine trees growing in neat rows.

Multiple single-track trails to the left lead into the central area of the preserve and are worth exploring. At 3 miles is the official beginning of Trail No. 715, marked by a Carsonite trail sign and a user sign-in box. Part of this scenic trail makes a nice 2.5-mile loop if riders make a right turn before reaching the Mount Herman Rd. crossing and return to the nursery road near the Memorial Grove. The nursery road ends at a gate at 3.25 miles. Riders must turn left onto the single-track trail, track right through the fence, and stay left at the next Y. The trail now travels parallel between the road and the fence. At 3.33 miles is yet another Y that will take you to Schilling Ave.; stay left and go up the hill. Soon after, at a spot very near the road, the trail turns left, passing through the fence and into the preserve, or continues straight, returning directly to the

parking lot at 4 miles. If riders turn left into the meadow, they should bear right at the next three Y intersections. After passing under a set of power lines, turn right in order to return to the parking lot following the same trail.

More good trails are found directly north of the parking lot and across Mount Herman Rd. in a sliver of national forest between the local neighborhoods and the road. Have fun discovering various routes.

23 New Santa Fe Regional Trail

Overall Ride Rating	☺☺☺☺☺
Trail Rating	Easy
Distance	15 miles, plus a 2-mile connection to Greenland Open Space
Elevation	5,995 feet
Best Season	Year-round
Main Uses	Equestrian, hiking, mountain biking
Trailhead Amenities	Trailheads at Monument, Palmer Lake, and Baptist include restrooms, water, and picnic tables. CO 105 and North Gate have parking areas only.
Dogs	On leash
Shoes	Barefoot okay
Maps	DeLorme *Colorado Atlas & Gazetteer*, pp. 50 and 62; El Paso County Parks and Recreation map, Santa Fe Regional Trail (http://adm.elpasoco.com)
Contact	El Paso County Parks and Recreation
Fees	None
Regulations	See the Trail Savvy section (p. 12), website and posted regulations for additional information.

Directions to Trailhead

All trailheads for the New Santa Fe Regional Trail tend to fill early, particularly on weekends. Arrive early and position your rig for an easy out at the end of your ride. THE NORTH GATE LOT: Take Exit 156B from I-25 and go west over the freeway on North Gate Blvd. for approximately 0.25 mile. The parking area is on the right (north) side of the road just before the entrance to the US Air Force Academy. This is a nice, gravel lot with room for six to eight trailers.

THE CO 105 PARKING LOT: Take Exit 161 from I-25 and go west over the freeway. Stay to the right on CO 105 for approximately 0.75 mile; as the road curves, the parking will be on your right. It has room for six to eight short trailers facing nose in and would be problematic for more than a two-horse rig.

THE MONUMENT LOT: Head west from Exit 161 for 0.4 mile to N. Jefferson St. Go right (north) on Jefferson and make another right onto 3rd St. The trailhead will be just ahead on your right with parking for two to three rigs.

THE BAPTIST LOT: Take Exit 158 off I-25 and head west over the freeway to the trailhead, on the right side of the road at approximately mile 0.3. This lot has room for two to three trailers.

THE PALMER LAKE LOT: Take CO 105 west for approximately 4.5 miles through the town of Palmer Lake. At County Line Rd. go right (east) to the Palmer Lake Recreation Area parking. This small lot only has room for one or two trailers. You may want to just use the trailhead as a picnic/rest stop on your journey.

The New Santa Fe Regional Trail is a wonderful 15-plus-mile urban trail that presents excellent opportunities for fall, winter, and spring riding. It can be a little warm during the summer months due to the lack of shade. The footing is a wide, sandy, dirt-and-gravel path that is well marked and features some interpretive signage. Enjoy views of Elephant Rock, the Front Range, and the prairies. The trail now also connects at its northernmost trailhead to the Douglas County Greenland Open Space.

From the Palmer Lake trailhead, ride southeast over the gently rolling landscape toward the CO 105 trailhead 3.1 miles away. Pike National Forest and the abandoned Atchison, Topeka and Santa Fe Railroad right-of-way is not far to the west, and the Monument trailhead lies just 0.4 mile south. Monument Lake and Mount Herman are the dominant landmarks at this point. Continue riding south for 2.6 miles to reach the Baptist trailhead and another 3 miles to arrive at the North Gate trailhead. Note that an easement agreement granted by the US Air Force Academy restricts recreationists from going off the trail during the 6.9-mile segment through the Air Force property. From the North Gate trailhead, continue south for another 8.5 miles to reach the end of the Santa Fe Trail, the City of Colorado Springs Pikes Peak Greenway, and the Monument Creek Trail.

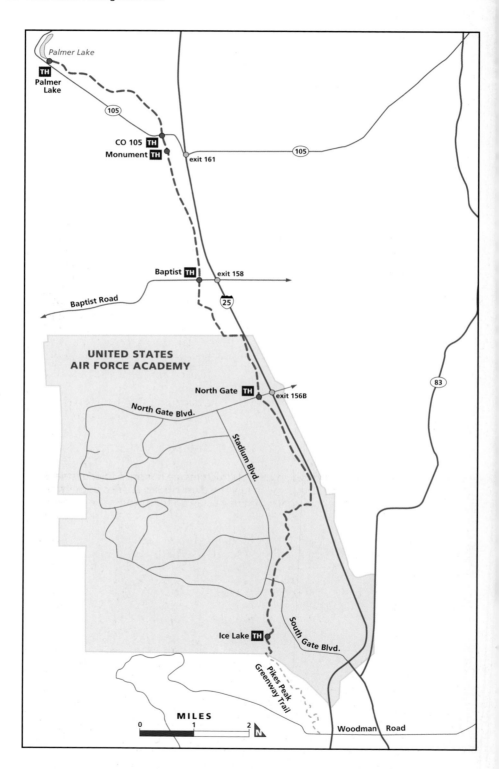

24 Barr Lake State Park

Overall Ride Rating	UUUUU
Trail Rating	Easy
Distance	9-mile loop, plus 1-mile Prairie Welcome Trail
Elevation	5,400 feet
Best Season	Year-round
Main Uses	Equestrian, hiking, mountain biking, fishing, boating, bird-watching, waterfowl hunting.
Trailhead Amenities	Horse trailers should park in the large, signed, mowed field to the right of the park road next to the canal and picnic area before reaching the nature center parking lot, which has two access drives. There are heated bathrooms, picnic tables (some with shelters and grills), and a nature center with limited hours. A large group picnic shelter is available by reservation. Potable water from a hydrant is available seasonally. Alternative parking for trailers is at the paved boat ramp lot, but is discouraged in order to give space to boaters. Restrooms, picnic tables with grills, and horseshoe pits available at the boat ramp lot.
Dogs	On leash; prohibited in the wildlife refuge from the nature center bridge south
Shoes	Barefoot okay
Maps	DeLorme *Colorado Atlas & Gazetteer*, p. 41; Colorado State Parks map, Barr Lake State Park (http://parks.state.co.us)
Contact	Barr Lake State Park
Fees	$5 per day; $55 for an annual state parks pass
Regulations	The road across the top of the dam (Crest Trail), the dam face, and any irrigation control structures are not open to equestrians. Please use the trail below the dam. Horses are not permitted on the boardwalks and must stay on trails within the wildlife refuge; no one is allowed between the trail and the lake from the gazebo boardwalk south and west toward the railroad tracks. The refuge is a protected bald eagle nesting habitat, and penalties for leaving the trail are very high. Please yield the right-of-way to personnel and equipment from the irrigation companies on and along the trails. Trails near the dam are closed on waterfowl hunting days (Wednesdays and Saturdays from October through February). See the Trail Savvy section (p. 12), website and posted regulations for additional information.
Special Notes	An arching pedestrian bridge over the canal accesses the lake trail from the nature center parking lot. If crossing is a problem, follow the road back to the boat ramp road over the canal for easier trail access. The trail closely parallels very busy railroad tracks in two places along the northwest side of the lake for 1.5 miles total. The second, longer section is quite gravelly and can be rough on unshod feet. The trains run frequently, so riders often choose to turn around and return, making this an out-and-back trip. Flying bugs can be particularly annoying during warmer months. Bring binoculars to watch seasonally for bald eagles and other birds. A portable toilet is available seasonally at the gazebo boardwalk entrance.

Directions to Trailhead

Follow I-76 northeast from Denver, taking exit 23 onto Bromley Lane. Go east approximately 1 mile to Picadilly Rd., then south less than 2 miles to the park entrance on the right. After entering the park, turn left to the nature center parking lot. Alternate Route: Take E-470 to the 120th Ave. exit. Proceed east on 120th to the first traffic light. Turn left onto Tower Rd. This road takes a right-hand, 90-degree turn after a mile and becomes 128th Ave. After 2 miles, turn left onto Picadilly Rd., where 128th becomes a dirt road. Proceed for about 0.3 mile and look for the signed park entrance on the left. After entering the park, turn left to the nature center parking lot.

This is an easy, flat ride at low altitude on roads wide enough to ride side by side. If you plan to turn around at the railroad tracks (see Special Notes), it makes the most sense to turn left after crossing the bridge at the nature center and go 3.5 miles through the wildlife refuge along the south end of Barr Lake.

A short loop called the Fox Meadow Trail sweeps closer to the lakeshore and returns to the main trail. Here, bald eagles can swoop so close, you can hear their wings. There are no water crossings, but there is another shorter bridge to cross.

You can also try the Prairie Welcome Trail, a mowed, 1-mile-loop warm-up ride across the meadow that starts next to the group picnic shelter at the nature center, heads through the Cottonwood Picnic Area along the canal, and back to the nature center picnic area next to the equestrian parking area. To minimize impact to the picnic areas, riders should stay around the outer perimeter. This 2,600-acre park is a good place for tune-ups, exercising, and conditioning.

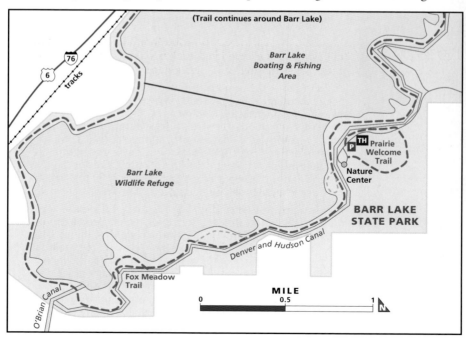

25 Bear Creek Lake Park

Overall Ride Rating	○○○○○
Trail Rating	Easy
Distance	9.5 miles
Elevation	5,560–5,780 feet
Best Season	Year-round
Main Uses	Equestrian, hiking, fishing, mountain biking, swimming, boating, bird-watching, wildlife viewing, archery, windsurfing
Trailhead Amenities	Parking is available for numerous large rigs. White Tail is the largest lot and the area preferred by management for horse trailers. The second preferred lot is the area at the equestrian arena. Parking is also available in smaller lots at Muskrat and Cottontail. Drinking water, restrooms, covered picnic tables, grills, trash receptacles, kiosks, and water spigots are throughout the park.
Dogs	On leash at all times and owners must clean up after their dogs; rules are strictly enforced
Shoes	Barefoot okay
Maps	DeLorme *Colorado Atlas & Gazetteer,* p. 40; City of Lakewood map, Bear Creek Lake Park (www.lakewood.org)
Contact	Bear Creek Lake Park, City of Lakewood
Fees	$4 per day
Regulations	Stay on marked trails. Riding prohibited on the dam, the Fitness Trail, the Owl Trail, the Cottonwood Trail, and the Fisherman's Trail. Horses not allowed in the lakes, swim beaches, or campgrounds. See the Trail Savvy section (p. 12), website and posted regulations for additional information.
Special Notes	Rental horses are available at the stable for nature rides, hay rides, lessons, summer camps, and evening rides from April to October by calling 303-697-9666. The equestrian arena is open to the public.

Directions to Trailhead

From C-470, take the Morrison Road exit, then go right (east) for 0.25 mile to the park entrance on the right (south). After the entry booth on your left, the road splits; stay to the left to access the parking areas.

This park's proximity to the metro area gives riders a chance to experience nature with their equine partner without driving for hours. One can explore over 2,500 acres of riparian woodlands, ravines, and grasslands stretching nearly 3 miles. Water is abundant: Big Soda Lake and Little Soda Lake are the result of earlier limestone quarries, while Bear Creek and Turkey Creek meander through the park, flowing into Bear Creek Reservoir and providing ample opportunities to water your horses and practice water-crossing skills. The park is home to an array of wildlife, including snakes, birds, coyotes, prairie dogs, birds of prey, and deer. The trails are mostly flat, earthen paths with occasional gentle slopes, making it ideal for the barefoot horse. Shaded areas are few but appreciated along this mostly open trail. This park connects to the Bear Creek Greenbelt and the Kipling Equestrian Trail to the east.

There are three interconnecting loop trails in the park. The Mount Carbon Loop is a 6.9-mile multiuse loop running almost the entire length of the park. It begins at the lakes on the west end and connects to the entire trail network, looping around the reservoir and climbing to the highest point in the park. The Cowen Trail is a short, 1.4-mile loop extending from the Mount Carbon Loop south of the horse arena and reservoir. The North Park Trail extends 2.2 miles from the Mount Carbon Loop to the northern edges of the park and then to the Greenbelt Plateau Trail that lies to the east.

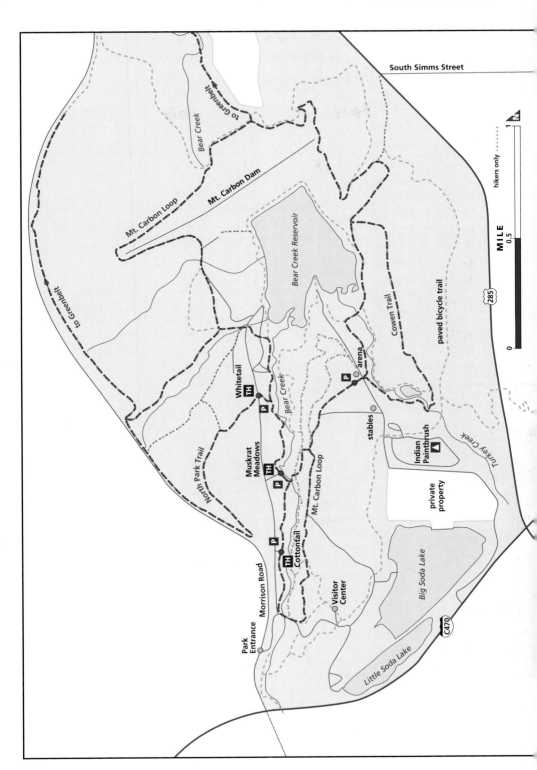

South Simms Street

Bear Creek

to Greenbelt

Mt. Carbon Loop

Mt. Carbon Dam

Bear Creek Reservoir

Cowen Trail

paved bicycle trail

285

to Greenbelt

Whitetail

North Park Trail

Bear Creek

arena

stables

Muskrat Meadows

Mt. Carbon Loop

Indian Paintbrush

Turkey Creek

private property

Cottontail

Visitor Center

Morrison Road

Big Soda Lake

Park Entrance

C470

Little Soda Lake

hikers only

N

M I L E

0   0.5   1

26 Cherry Creek Regional Trail

Overall Ride Rating	ՍՍՍՍՍ
Trail Rating	Easy
Distance	17 miles one way; will be 24 miles one way when completed
Elevation	5,700–6,100 feet
Best Season	Year-round
Main Uses	Equestrian, mountain biking, road biking, rollerblading, hiking.
Trailhead Amenities	Multiple trailheads are available and suitable for equestrian access. See Directions for descriptions.
Dogs	On leash
Shoes	Barefoot okay
Maps	DeLorme *Colorado Atlas & Gazetteer,* p. 41; Rand McNally *2003 Denver Regional StreetFinder,* maps 2453, 2537, 2621, and 2705; Douglas County Division of Open Space and Natural Resources map, Cherry Creek Regional Trail (www.douglas.co.us/openspace)
Contact	Town of Parker; Arapahoe County Public Works and Development; Douglas County Division of Open Space and Natural Resources
Fees	None
Regulations	See the Trail Savvy section (p. 12), website and posted regulations for additional information.
Special Notes	This is a very urban, 8-to-10-foot-wide, concrete trail with an occasional parallel, unpaved path. If there is no path, equestrians must ride on the narrow shoulder, usually alongside a fence and often blocked by directional signs. Please take the time to kick manure off to the side on paved sections. Closures and detours due to development are not always signed at the trailheads. Large machinery could be operating along the trail and erosion control in the form of long, black, plastic sheets may be installed along the ground and across the trail. Be prepared to turn back due to hazardous situations that you may not be comfortable with.
	Because the trail is paved, bicyclists ride very fast, rarely slowing down for other users. Watch out for the many runners with jogging strollers. Some underpasses have low clearance or are narrow, so riders should be prepared to dismount and lead their horses. There are several long but wide bridges that riders must take due to unmaintained or deep creek crossings. Quicksand occurs in some areas of the creekbed. Several livestock gates must be opened and closed behind you on the southern part of the trail.

Directions to Trailhead

From I-25 south of Denver, take Exit 193 at Lincoln Ave., go east 5 miles to CO 83 (Parker Rd.) and the town of Parker. From here, you have six trailhead options.

COTTONWOOD PARK: From CO 83 (Parker Rd.) and Lincoln Ave., proceed north on CO 83 1.5 miles, passing the E-470 intersection to Cottonwood Rd. Turn left at the stoplight and go west on Cottonwood Rd. across Cherry Creek to the parking lot on the left. Gravel, loop-around parking available for three to four rigs separated from paved car lot (use caution when exiting due to concrete curbing and small radius), with restrooms, emergency phone, and bicycle rack.

BAR CCC PARK: From Lincoln Ave., proceed south on CO 83 1.25 miles to the intersection of Parker Rd. and E. Main St. and go right. At 0.5 mile, turn left on Twenty Mile Rd. Parking facilities are on the right side with room for multiple trailers. Do not block any public works access gates. The exit back onto Twenty Mile Rd. is very steep but short, with a right turn only permitted due to the road's center median. Trail access is between concrete barriers on the far north side of the lot, then down a hill to the concrete Sulphur Gulch Trail and left toward the Cherry Creek Trail at a bridge. No restrooms; only picnic tables in the park.

SALISBURY EQUESTRIAN PARK: From CO 83 and Lincoln Ave., head south 1.25 miles to the intersection of Parker Rd. and Mainstreet. Go west on Mainstreet 1.2 miles to Motsenbocker Rd. Turn south on Motsenbocker and go 2.1 miles. Salisbury Park is on the east side of Motsenbocker, north of Parker's public works facility. This 130-acre park provides grassy parking areas at both arenas large enough to accommodate trailers at a horse show. Seasonal restrooms and a portable toilet, a water hydrant (next to the public works facility), large ball field complex, two equestrian arenas, playground, and covered picnic pavilion are some of the amenities. To access the trail, ride east past the white fenced arena either down the hill and across a covered bridge or across the pond dam toward the creek. The small loop trails in the field between the trail and the developed portion of the park are used for a cart-driving obstacle course.

EAST BANK PARK: From CO 83 and Lincoln Ave., head south 2.5 miles to the intersection of Parker Rd. and Indian Pipe Rd. Turn right at the stoplight onto Indian Pipe and make an immediate right into the parking lot for East Bank Park. Loop-around parking is available for two to three rigs, with restrooms and picnic tables available.

PINERY TRAILHEAD: From Lincoln Ave., go south on CO 83 5.5 miles to Pinery Pkwy. Turn west onto the road toward the sewage treatment plant and take the left Y to the trailhead lot. A gravel loop-through lot accommodates three to four rigs, with a portable toilet, picnic table, and trailhead informational sign.

HIDDEN MESA TRAILHEAD: From CO 83 and Lincoln Ave., go south on CO 83 8 miles to the Hidden Mesa entrance immediately north of the Grange Hall on the right. A gravel loop-through lot accomodates six to seven rigs in designated trailer parking, with a portable toilet; large, covered picnic shelter; seasonal water hydrants and an informational sign.

When this trail is completed, it will connect Cherry Creek State Park (p. 93) on the north end to Castlewood Canyon State Park on the south. Currently the two ends are not connected to their final destinations, but this still leaves 17 contiguous miles open for riding. From the Cottonwood trailhead, riders can turn north and pass under Cottonwood Rd. The local homeowners association has signed this area and the bridge over the creek closed to horses in an attempt to keep horses out of their community park. But trail managers for the Town of Parker have assured us that closing any section of the trail to horses is not their intent and that the signs are improperly placed. As an alternative, riders can follow the sand trails east of the concrete trail, cross through the creek, and then use the second bridge, which is signed for horses. Soon after this bridge are more sand trails between the paved trail and the creek, which weave around the willows. Riders encounter one more easy creek crossing where a new bridge has just been installed. On the other side is a trailhead sign with several picnic tables spread out beyond. The trail does not go much further in Arapahoe County before it ends at private property.

From the Cottonwood trailhead south, the first segment passes through a section of new multifamily housing where the original trail has been rerouted. This area is tight for horses and caution is needed. Soon after, the trail corridor opens up, crosses a small bridge, and passes a wetlands area created by the construction of E-470. The crossing under this interstate is quite good. On the south side, the Cherry Creek Trail intersects the E-470 Trail. There is still a large amount of open space and riding is easy from here all the way south past Challenger Regional Park and the recreation center. After heading under Lincoln Ave., cross the creek again (the channel is deep, especially in the spring, so the bridge might be the best option), continue past the Parker Fire Department training grounds, and go under Mainstreet (limited visibility due to a curve and willows) to the Bar CCC Park and the Sulphur Gulch Trail intersection. Here, the trail crosses the creek back to the west side where equestrians must take the bridge. The trail corridor remains wide open farther south past the Salisbury Equestrian Park, where it crosses the creek again to access the East Bank Park. This section has some broad fields and enjoyable dirt trails that loop over to the giant cottonwood trees to the west. The local neighborhood children love to hike and play in this area along the creek.

At the Stroh Rd. underpass, the trail becomes very narrow as it clings to the bank between the river and the adjacent backyards. Dogs, although contained

in their yards, can easily scare horses on the closely bordering trail. This underpass also has lower head clearance. Signs recommend riders to dismount and walk their horses underneath. On the other side of Stroh Rd., the trail corridor remains narrow until it gets closer to the Pinery trailhead. There is an emergency phone along this stretch. Riders encounter two more creek crossings in tight, fenced areas. Be aware that bicycles crossing these bridges at

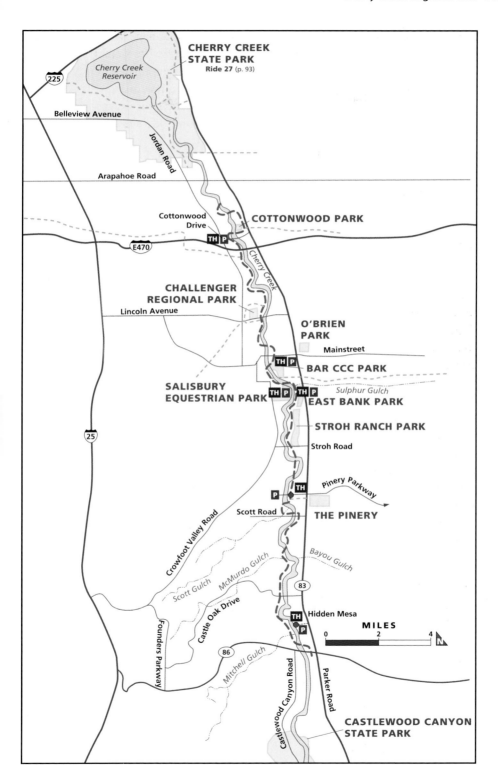

CHERRY CREEK STATE PARK Ride 27 (p. 93)

Cherry Creek Reservoir

225

Belleview Avenue

Jordan Road

Arapahoe Road

Cottonwood Drive

COTTONWOOD PARK

TH P

E470

Cherry Creek

CHALLENGER REGIONAL PARK

Lincoln Avenue

O'BRIEN PARK

Mainstreet

TH P

BAR CCC PARK

Sulphur Gulch

SALISBURY EQUESTRIAN PARK

TH P   TH P

EAST BANK PARK

STROH RANCH PARK

Stroh Road

25

P   TH

Pinery Parkway

Scott Road

THE PINERY

Crowfoot Valley Road

Scott Gulch

McMurdo Gulch

Bayou Gulch

83

Castle Oak Drive

Founders Parkway

TH

Hidden Mesa

P

MILES

0   2   4   N

86

Mitchell Gulch

Castlewood Canyon Road

Parker Road

CASTLEWOOD CANYON STATE PARK

high speeds make a strange, rumbling sound, often spooking horses. The trail corridor improves before reaching the Pinery trailhead, where it intersects a trail that will take you to the parking lot and farther east into an open meadow before crossing under Parker Rd. and into the Pinery subdivision. This is a nice out-and-back side trail, but do not bother going through the narrow underpass as there is not trail on the other side, only a neighborhood sidewalk.

Just south of the trailhead, the trail crosses the creek again. Either take the bridge or cross through the water. This is a good place to let your horse drink. Once you reach Scott Rd., trail users must follow the road east across the bridge and turn right to get around the boarding stables. Scott Rd. and the driveway are lightly traveled, but are gravel and can be "ouchy" on bare hooves. Once at the development, the trail turns back west and follows a drainage ditch along the neighborhood. This is a very narrow area and the section of trail past the swimming pool and clubhouse can stay icy in the shade on the north side.

Once back on track along Cherry Creek, the trail opens up again and is a pleasant ride to another creek crossing. Soon, you reach another underpass at Bayou Gulch Rd., a low area with river rock lining the trail until it climbs back up and along the side of a meadow. Farther south, at Castle Oaks Dr., riders must turn west and follow the road about one block to regain the trail. The next segment passes through Douglas County and Castle Rock's Hidden Mesa Open Space and associated trails, which connects with the Cherry Creek Trail. The new Hidden Mesa trailhead is next to the Pikes Peak Grange Hall along Parker Rd. and a trail to the left (toward the creek) connects with the new parking area.

The trail passes through a field that is thick with prairie dogs. Riders should stay on the paved trail in this area to avoid the holes. After passing a nice-sized private lake, the trail reaches the cul-de-sac on Walker Rd. To complete the last section, turn left and follow the road to the curve, then continue straight ahead through the fenced easement, heading south into a pretty wooded area behind Franktown. The trail crosses Cherry Creek again before passing under CO 86, where it continues for another 2.5 miles and requires one more creek crossing, ending at Castlewood Canyon State Park. This trail is worth exploring for local riders, who will discover their own favorite sections and trailheads.

27 Cherry Creek State Park

Overall Ride Rating	ʊʊʊʊʊ
Trail Rating	Easy
Distance	Approximately 16 total miles on 4,200 acres
Elevation	5,600 feet
Best Season	Year-round
Main Uses	Equestrian, hiking, camping, mountain biking, fishing, boating, swimming, off-leash dog area, shooting range, model airplane field
Trailhead Amenities	Horse trailer parking available at any of the park's designated lots if there is room. See Directions for descriptions of two of the larger areas. Camping with horses at the park can be arranged in the designated group campground at the group rate. Reserve by calling the park office at 303-699-3860, ext. 721. No corrals available. Horses can be tied to trailers or kept in personal pens but cannot be tied to trees or highlined.
Dogs	On leash except in the Twelve Mile South Area from the parking lot north approximately halfway to the park road, west to Cherry Creek, and south to the park boundary. Prohibited in the wetlands preserve on both sides of the creek north of E. Lake View Rd. and at the swim beach.
Shoes	Barefoot okay
Maps	DeLorme *Colorado Atlas & Gazetteer,* pp. 40–41; Rand McNally *2003 Denver Regional StreetFinder,* maps 2283, 2284, 2367 and 2368; Colorado State Parks map, Cherry Creek State Park (http://parks.state.co.us)
Contact	Cherry Creek State Park
Fees	$6 per day May 1 through Labor Day or $5 day after Labor Day through April 30 plus $1 daily, year-round Cherry Creek Basin Water Quality Authority fee. Annual state parks pass is $55 plus $3 Cherry Creek Basin Water Quality Authority sticker.
Regulations	Horses are not allowed in the well-signed wetlands preserve, at the swim beach, near the group picnic shelters, or in the campground except in the group area as campers. Due to high use during weekends and holidays, park entrance is limited when attendance reaches a maximum number. New users are only allowed in as others leave. See the Trail Savvy section (p. 12), website and posted regulations for additional information.
Special Notes	This park has nearly 1.5 million visitors yearly. Watch out for the many runners with jogging strollers who frequent the trail. This is also a very popular area for dog-walking and the number of dogs can sometimes be overwhelming. In fact, the undeveloped southern portion is often referred to as "the dog park." The designated off-leash area is not contained and includes the trails, creek crossings, and the one bridge equestrians can utilize to get from parking areas on the east side of the park to the lesser-used and safer west side. The only alternative is to follow the paved road around the southern end of the lake where the traffic is heavy, with relatively high speeds and no shoulder room.

Directions to Trailhead

From I-225, take CO 83 (Parker Rd.) Exit 4 and go south on Parker Rd. to either E. Lehigh Ave. (1 mile) or Orchard Rd. (4 miles). For 12 Mile House, turn west into the park at the light at E. Lehigh Ave. and follow the entrance road to the entrance station. Turn left at the first Y and left again at the intersection. Follow E. Lake View Rd., passing the park office entrance; take the next left to the 12 Mile House picnic area and park on the loop. There is room for four to five rigs depending on the level of use; restrooms and picnic tables also available.

For the Twelve Mile South Area, turn west on Orchard Rd. and then immediately right into the park on a rough dirt road. If needed, purchase a pass at the self-pay station and pass the first parking area (normally very full) to the fenced grass area on the left in front of the rental stable office. Pull-through parking available for 10 or more rigs, with a portable toilet, commercial stables, and picnic table nearby.

Cherry Creek State Park, Denver's backyard playground, offers varied trail opportunities within a natural prairie environment of gentle, rolling hills anchored by an 880-surface-acre lake. Like Chatfield State Park, trails are not signed and many are not on the park map. Because of the urban surroundings and openness of the park area, however, it is impossible to become lost. If riders start from the stables, trails lead north toward the administration building, which offers a hitching rail, picnic tables, and restrooms (available when the office is open). Plenty of deer frequent this area to browse on their preferred diet of grasses and forbs, as well as on the sagebrush and mountain mahogany prevalent on the hillside. Continuing north, riders need to cross Shop Creek at a moderately deep pool where horses can drink. In the winter, ice can force riders to cross at a bridge on the park road farther west. Use caution, as this road is very busy, with minimal shoulder space.

On the east side of the road, higher up the hillside and near the Paint Horse Stable's old location, you'll find another hitching rail, picnic table, and benches on a high spot called Slagle Hill. This is a great opportunity to photograph friends with the lake, Denver, and the mountains in the background. Trails now track both east and west of the entrance station and around the campground. In the far northeast corner, a concrete trail leaves the park under Parker Rd. and along E. Hampden Ave. At the dam, riders must turn back as there is no access to the west side.

Also from the Twelve Mile parking area, riders can go directly west and cross the creek, if it is not too high, at one of several crossings that the stables use. This is a good place to let your horses drink. You can also ride farther south and use the bridge. While traveling on trails near the creek, riders should watch for pheasant and other large birds that seek protection in the thick grasses. Once on the west side, a variety of trails allow you to explore every corner of the park. Trails that track through the trees near the creek can be icy or muddy in the winter and spring. Cross now-closed Jordan Rd. and pick up a trail to Cottonwood Creek by using a new bridge. There are marshy areas and downed barbed wire in the vicinity, so it is best to stay on the trails. This urban drainage has been rerouted and structure added in a restorative effort to more closely simulate the natural flow of a stream. Transplanted native willow and cottonwood and a small pond will rejuvenate this area and improve wildlife habitat. After crossing a low concrete bridge, the trail shortly becomes concrete and

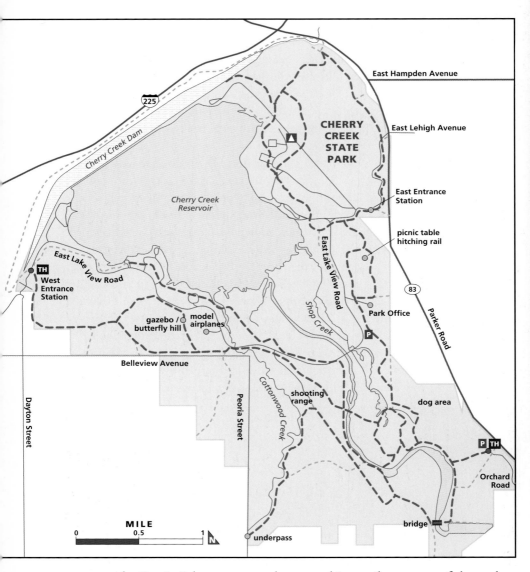

crosses under Peoria Rd. at a new underpass, taking trail users out of the park to Greenwood Village and their growing greenway trail system.

The park's large, lesser-developed western portion is also open to equestrians. Its open-meadow trails cover the higher ground north of Belleview Ave. and west of the lake all the way over to the west entrance at Union and Dayton Streets. Included in this area and worth visiting are Butterfly Hill and a nearby gazebo, which has signboards documenting the Pope's World Youth Day visit in 1993. Loops of several miles can be made throughout the area, but return access back east to the trailers is still limited to the road, the creek or bridge crossing and through the off-leash dog area.

28 The Greenland Trail

Overall Ride Rating	❍❍❍❍❍
Trail Rating	Easy
Distance	8.2-mile loop, plus 1.8-mile connection to New Santa Fe Regional Trail
Elevation	6,740–7,450 feet
Best Season	Year-round
Main Uses	Equestrian, hiking, mountain biking
Trailhead Amenities	Horse-friendly trailhead features ample parking for approximately 20 large rigs. Restrooms, a covered picnic pavilion seating up to 48 people, hitching rails, water spigot, kiosk, and trash receptacles. Overflow parking for group rides is available by arrangement with Douglas County.
Dogs	On leash and strictly enforced
Shoes	Barefoot okay
Maps	DeLorme *Colorado Atlas & Gazetteer*, p. 50; Douglas County Division of Open Space and Natural Resources map, Greenland Trail (www.douglas.co.us)
Contact	Douglas County Division of Open Space and Natural Resources
Fees	None
Regulations	See the Trail Savvy section (p. 12), website and posted regulations for additional information.

Directions to Trailhead

Take I-25 to the Greenland exit (Exit 167 on the west side of the freeway), travel west for 0.25 mile on Noe Rd. and turn south. Curving to the south, continue 0.5 mile to the well-signed entrance at the south end of the historic Greenland townsite.

The Greenland Trail lies within the Greenland Open Space, which boasts 3,600 pristine acres of the overall 33,000 acres dedicated to the South I-25 Conservation Corridor Project. Located not too far east of the Denver & Rio Grande Railroad, Greenland was once a thriving little village and shipping

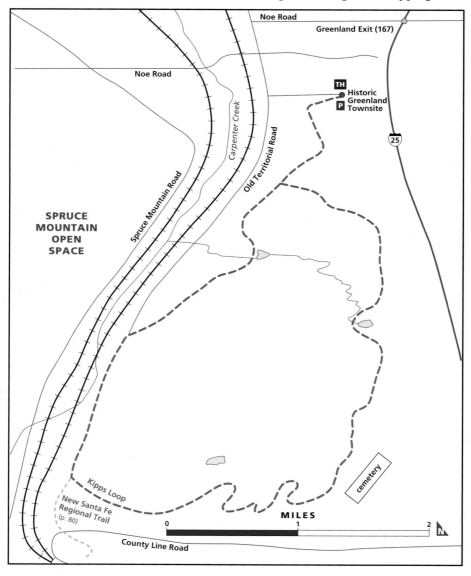

center in the 1870s. It laid claim to two general stores, a post office, a school, and possibly a saloon. Ranching continued here even after the town's demise, and today the magnificent landscape has been preserved for its recreational, resource, and historical value.

Traveling south from the well-designed trailhead on the wide, natural-dirt path mixed with crusher fines, riders will enjoy the gently rolling grasslands and far-reaching views. Follow the path parallel to the Old Territorial Rd. that runs between the trail and the railroad until it forks. If you take the right fork, you reach the Palmer Lake trailhead of the New Santa Fe Regional Trail, adding approximately 1.8 miles to your trip. By taking the left fork, you head east on the Kipps Loop for an 8.2-mile loop that returns you to the trailhead.

After the left fork, the loop heads east past private property to the south. The trail curves to the north, taking you through scattered scrub oak and pine. Be sure to look for the final resting place of eight of Greenland's previous residents, including Mr. Edward Thomas Kipps for whom the trail was named. His gravestone will tell you that he is not dead, just sleeping. Past the sight of the old cemetery are three nice picnic spots with hitching rails. The grassy meadows and several small ponds attract a variety of wildlife, including elk, mule deer, coyote, black bear, and many species of birds. Greenland is a wonderful place to ride and an excellent spot for conditioning, training, and group rides.

29 Homestead Ranch Park

Overall Ride Rating	⋃⋃⋃⋃⋃
Trail Rating	Easy
Distance	3.25 miles
Elevation	7,220 feet–7,400 feet
Best Season	Year-round
Main Uses	Equestrian, hiking, mountain biking
Trailhead Amenities	Large, level, gravel parking area accommodates 6 to 10 rigs depending on size and other cars (watch out for the high curbs); extremely nice restrooms, drinking fountains, a park kiosk, and a playground. A windmill-fed stock water tank on the trail supplies drinking water for horses when operational. Bring water for horses just in case.
Dogs	On leash
Shoes	Barefoot okay (a few, minimal rocky spots)
Maps	DeLorme *Colorado Atlas & Gazetteer,* p. 51; El Paso County Parks and Recreation map, Homestead Ranch Park (http://adm.elpasoco.com)
Contact	El Paso County Parks and Recreation
Fees	None
Regulations	See the Trail Savvy section (p. 12), website and posted regulations for additional information.

Directions to Trailhead

From Colorado Springs, go east on CO 24 to Elbert Rd. Travel north 5 miles to Sweet Rd. and then east for 2.5 miles on to Gollihar Rd. Proceed north 0.5 mile on Gollihar to the park entrance on the left.

Originally a homestead settled in 1874, this park features two loops that are perfect for a short morning or afternoon ride or for conditioning, training, or ponying. Beginning at the parking area, ride to the left (southwest) of the main building and follow the wide, gentle, uphill, natural-dirt and granite path. The trail will briefly curve toward the 1.5-acre spring-fed pond, which often attracts deer, coyote, pronghorn, fox, and waterfowl. It is sometimes empty in the dry summers. Continue west toward the trees to make the upper portion of the first loop, which features far-reaching vistas of the Front Range and the Sangre de Cristos.

Each loop is 1.2 miles, though you might consider riding the two loops in a figure-eight pattern via the 0.26-mile connector trail between them. At the connector segment is a windmill-fed watering tank for horses. You should bring your own water, though, as this source is not always operable. From here, continue around the scenic bluff of Rattlesnake Butte, the dominant landmark of the park. The downhill side of this loop can be a little more challenging in wet, icy, or snowy conditions. Proceed back to the connector trail and take the lower portion of the first loop back to the trailhead. The gentle, rolling terrain—a mix of open space and tree cover—and interesting bluffs make for an excellent half-day outing.

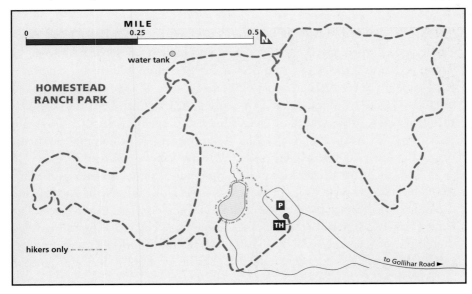

Chapter 2

Central Region

Panoramic vistas abound on the Colorado Trail.

The Central Region is the heart and soul of the magnificent Colorado Rockies, where the horseback riding and scenery are second to none. There are endless miles of wonderful trails to explore within this chapter (DeLorme *Colorado Atlas & Gazetteer* maps 37–38, 47–49, and 59–61). The notable 483-mile Colorado Trail and many of its trailheads lie at the core of this geography, as do several of Colorado's and the nation's highest mountain peaks. The area boasts 23 of Colorado's 56 fourteeners, in addition to hundreds of peaks above 12,000 feet in elevation, all soaring above treeline.

The riding is best here during the summer and fall due to the significant elevations, though some trails at lower elevations may be rideable in the late spring depending on weather conditions. Afternoon thunderstorms in the Rockies are almost a daily occurrence and are often accompanied by severe lightning. One should plan to start early and finish early. Horses will definitely require thorough conditioning before attempting trails at higher elevations or trails with significant elevation gains.

Traveling the Colorado Rockies from the back of your favorite horse promises awe-inspiring views and unforgettable experiences amidst some of the most pristine country in the nation. Enjoy the ride!

Accommodations

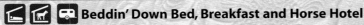 Beddin' Down Bed, Breakfast and Horse Hotel

10401 CR 160
Salida, CO 81201

719-539-1815; 1-800-470-1888
www.beddindown.com

Your friendly hosts Carolyn and Jerry Sparkman are the owners of this lovely facility catering to horses and their owners. Beddin' Down is conveniently located on CR 160 just 10 miles west of Salida off US 285, 3 hours from Denver, and 1.5 hours from Colorado Springs. This beautifully decorated log home sits on 24 acres, with 360-degree views and a variety of wonderful, nearby trails for your riding pleasure. The ranch offers five spacious guest rooms and clean, large, covered, separated, and safe accommodations for the horses. They will provide the feed or you can provide your own for a reduced fee. The ranch also offers an outdoor arena and round pen. RV and living-quarter or camper rigs are also welcome to overnight at sites with or without hookups. One site has 30-amp power, water, and sewer; the other has 30-amp power and water. Additional sites are available for self-contained units with no hookups. Call for pricing and availability and be sure to make a reservation, as you won't want to miss the fabulous breakfast and warm hospitality.

Breckenridge Equestrian Center

710 Wellington Road
Breckenridge, CO 80424

970-453-7971

The Breckenridge Equestrian Center is owned by the Town of Breckenridge. They offer four partially covered 12-by-48-foot runs, nine 12-by-36-foot outdoor runs, and six 12-by-24-foot outdoor runs, plus an arena and two round pens. Guests traveling with their horses are welcome to stable at the center overnight. Horse owners are required to provide their own feed, buckets, clean up, and current health records. The center is a nonprofit organization that supports the 4-H program. For directions, availability, and reservations call Sharon Hinkles at 970-453-7971.

M Lazy C Ranch

P.O. Box 461
Lake George, CO 80827

1-800-289-4868
www.mlazyc.com

The M Lazy C Ranch is a real working cattle ranch with thousands of acres of the Pike National Forest accessible from the property. It is located just west of Colorado Springs, 0.75 mile off US 24. The ranch offers cabins, seven RV sites (four with full services and three with electric and water only), and a primitive camping area for larger groups, with teepees, wall tents, and RV sites. For the equestrian guest, they offer 16-by-16-foot uncovered stalls, unlimited access to trails, and a 40-foot round pen. Guests are required to provide their own feed;

current vaccinations and proof of ownership. The ranch caters to a variety of activities, such as weddings, meetings, hunting, team building, catering, shooting, cattle drives, horseback riding, and hay rides.

Mount Princeton Riding Stables & Equestrian Center

13999 CR 162
Nathrop, CO 81326   719-395-6498

This nice equestrian center provides overnight stabling, trail rides, pack trips, riding lessons, and guide services. It also caters to riding clubs, rodeos, gymkhanas, training, and other equestrian events. Self-contained campers and living-quarter rigs can park in their large lot overnight (no hookups). A small convenience store/gift shop is located on site. The center is conveniently situated between Salida and Buena Vista outside of the small town of Nathrop, just 2 miles east of US 285 on CR 162, with access to miles upon miles of excellent trails and magnificent scenery. Browns Creek, Little Browns Creek, Wagon Loop, and the Colorado Trail are just a few of the trails that can be ridden or driven to from this location. Mount Princeton Equestrian Center can accommodate up to 17 guest horses with covered stalls at $20 per night per horse including hay and fresh water.

Rides

Bailey
30 Ben Tyler Trail (No. 606) 105
31 Brookside McCurdy Trail
   (No. 607) 108
Bruno (Buno) Gulch Area 111
   32 Abyss Lake Trail (No. 602) ... 112
   33 Burning Bear Trail (No. 601) 115
   34 South Park Trail (No. 600) ... 117
35 Craig Park Trail (No. 608) 120
36 Payne Creek Trail (No. 637) 121

Buena Vista/Salida
37 Browns Creek Trail (No. 1429) 123
38 Colorado Trail (No. 1776)
   from Browns Creek Trailhead 126
39 Colorado Trail (No. 1776) from
   Avalanche Trailhead............. 128
40 Little Browns Creek Trail
   (No. 1430) 132

Breckenridge/Frisco
41 Meadow Creek Trail (No. 33) .. 134
42 Lily Pad Lake Trail (No. 34) 136

Cañon City
43 Shelf Road Recreation Area ... 138

Lake George/Florissant
44 Goose Creek Trail (No. 612).... 143
45 Platte River Trail (No. 654) 146

30 Ben Tyler Trail (No. 606)

Overall Ride Rating	UUUUU
Trail Rating	Moderately difficult
Distance	11.4 miles one way
Elevation	9,550–11,650 feet
Best Season	Summer to early fall
Main Uses	Equestrian, hiking, dispersed and backcountry camping, fishing
Trailhead Amenities	The Ben Tyler Trail has two trailheads. The northern trail access on US 285 is closest to Denver, but does not have an actual parking lot. Parking here with a trailer is highly discouraged due to a narrow shoulder, high-speed traffic, no room for longer trailers, and no room to tie horses at a trailer. The safest access is from the Rock Creek trailhead just off Lost Park Rd. This spur road lacks maintenance and is subject to gullies and ruts, so use caution. Pull off the road in any of the meadows and park along the aspen. Dispersed camping is also allowed, with plenty of room for large groups. There is no water for horses up on this ridge, but there is water in the valley below, about 0.5 mile away. Fishermen have access to beaver ponds along the four-wheel-drive road leading to the trail and the wilderness.
Dogs	On leash in the Lost Creek Wilderness
Shoes	Recommended
Maps	DeLorme *Colorado Atlas & Gazetteer,* p. 49; National Geographic *Trails Illustrated 105, Tarryall Mts./Kenosha Pass;* Pike and San Isabel National Forests map
Contact	Pike National Forest, South Platte and South Park Ranger Districts
Fees	None
Regulations	Maximum of 15 people and 10 stock per group in the Lost Creek Wilderness. Animals must be tethered and kept overnight more than 100 feet from water or trails. See the Trail Savvy section (p. 12), website and posted regulations for additional information.

Since this trail is better accessed from the Rock Creek trailhead, this description will follow the trail from south to north. From the meadows, continue to follow the main dirt road north and down to another meadow below. OHV owners use this area along Rock Creek quite heavily, so there are many roads that lead to nowhere. Once alongside the creek, follow it in a northerly direction to the signed entrance to the Lost Creek Wilderness. Fortunately, most folks don't wander too far from their vehicles, so after a rather hectic beginning, especially on weekends, the trail quickly becomes peaceful.

Directions to Trailhead

From US 285 south of Denver, cross Kenosha Pass. At 1.5 miles south of the pass, turn left onto CR 56 (Lost Park Rd.). Proceed 6.5 miles down this rough, gravel road to FR 133 (Rock Creek Rd.) and turn left (north). Drive about 0.5 mile through the trees to the meadows beyond and find a pretty place to pull off.

The route continues to follow Rock Creek upstream for close to 2 miles. This is a lovely section of trail, passing willows when close to the water and then moving into heavily shaded pine and spruce forest. There are several great back-country camping spots in the area, with brook trout in the creek. Soon after the trail leaves the creek, it ascends at a quicker pace to reach the high point, breaking out of treeline onto a ridge just east of South Twin Cone Peak between the Platte River and Kenosha mountain ranges. As with all above-treeline trails, the views are breathtaking. If the winds are not too brisk, plan to find a rock for a lunch break or photo op.

While traversing the alpine willow field, the trail becomes faint. Follow the rock cairn markers in a northeast direction. If they become difficult to find, continue through the willows and look for a marker post on the other side. Most trail users do not follow the same path through the willows, but it is not difficult to pick up the trail on the other side. Day riders often turn around at this midway point anyway. If continuing on, you now begin your descent into Ben Tyler Gulch. Gentle at first, it becomes more of a mad dash downhill after crossing Ben Tyler Creek. Not long after, the Craig Park Trail (see Ride 35, p. 120) ends at its signed intersection with the Ben Tyler Trail. The next section after the Craig Park Trail junction is a series of long, descending switchbacks that, when traveling east, offer spectacular views down Ben Tyler Gulch. In 1903, a 3,000-

acre fire burned up and out of the end of Ben Tyler Gulch, making room for the huge aspen grove dominating the valley. At this point, the trail gradient increases again and the valley tightens. There are few areas along this section suitable for camping. Finally, the trail levels somewhat down to a crossing of Ben Tyler Creek, after which the steep switchbacks resume all the way down to the northern Ben Tyler trailhead at US 285.

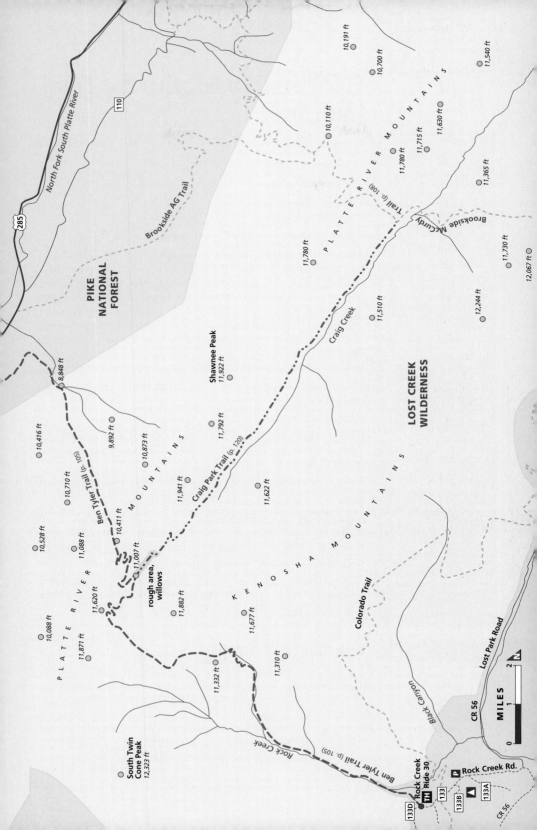

31 Brookside McCurdy Trail (No. 607)

Overall Ride Rating	⬤⬤⬤◯◯
Trail Rating	Difficult
Distance	15 miles one way
Elevation	8,000–11,600 feet
Best Season	Summer to early fall
Main Uses	Equestrian, hiking, dispersed and backcountry camping
Trailhead Amenities	Parking trailers at the signed Payne Creek/Brookside trailhead lot is not practical. A long drive leads to a relatively small lot, making it hard to see if there's space and virtually impossible to turn around if there isn't. If you do want to park there despite the small size, make sure to face out, as rigs could easily get blocked in. Better parking is available in a small field between two county roads just past the trailhead entrance to the right. Dispersed camping is allowed here, with good grass for grazing and portable pens, as well as some trees for highlining.
Dogs	Under voice control until the Lost Creek Wilderness boundary; on leash after that
Shoes	Recommended
Maps	DeLorme *Colorado Atlas & Gazetteer*, p. 49; National Geographic *Trails Illustrated 105, Tarryall Mts./Kenosha Pass*; Pike and San Isabel National Forests map
Contact	Pike National Forest, South Platte and South Park Ranger Districts
Fees	None
Regulations	Maximum of 15 people and 10 stock per group in the Lost Creek Wilderness. Animals must be tethered and kept overnight more than 100 feet from water or trails. See the Trail Savvy section (p. 12), website and posted regulations for more information.
Special Notes	The Brookside McCurdy Trail is 32.6 miles total one way; this description only covers the northern half from the Bailey-area trailhead south to the Colorado Trail junction in Lost Park.

Directions to Trailhead

Take US 285 south of Denver to the west edge of Bailey. Turn left onto CR 64 (FR 110). A lumberyard and post office stand near the corner, with a gas station on the opposite side of US 285. CR 64 crosses the South Platte River immediately and curves to the right. Go left at the Y, staying on CR 64 (now gravel); turning right returns you to US 285. Continue 2.5 miles, passing the trailhead turnoff, to a Y and veer right down a connection road to Old Stage Coach Rd. Park along the road (on the wide, dirt shoulder) or pull into the grass where the ditch isn't too deep.

Ride west back to CR 64 (through an opening in the trees) until you see a brown sign indicating hiking and equestrian use. Cross here and pick up a single-track feeder trail that goes uphill and joins the official trail within 0.5 mile. Turn right when you reach an old two-track trail. Follow this peaceful trail through stands of tall ponderosa pine. A trail goes to a meadow to the right, but stay left, following the trail marker. The Platte River Mountain Range will pop into view, giving glimpses of the saddle that the trail crosses at the top. At a little over 1 mile, the trail splits; Payne Creek Trail (see Ride 36, p. 121) heads to the left and the Brookside McCurdy Trail tracks right.

Not long after this intersection, the trail crosses a meadow with lush mountain grass that horses will pull to dive their noses into. Cross the small stream and enter a dense forest. At this point, the seemingly easy trail starts to increase in difficulty, traveling up and down valley sides to cross several brooks, including the larger stream through Brookside Gulch. Guide your mount safely along. At 3 miles, the trail enters the Lost Creek Wilderness and joins a rocky logging road. The Brookside AG Trail splits off to the right at a ridge. Riders can take a lunch break prior to this intersection on the rock outcropping to the right, which provides outstanding views.

Now the trail begins a serious, switchbacking climb to the ridge. Adding to the challenge is a wet drainage that washes away the dirt cover, revealing rock at every trail crossing. Downed trees are also a problem on this steep hillside, always seeming to land squarely across the trail. After cresting the ridge, the trail takes a steep, straight-down approach to Craig Park. Turn left at the intersection with the Craig Park Trail (see Ride 35, p. 120) and continue down to cross Craig Creek. This creek is reported to be the longest tributary, uninterrupted by humans, draining into the North Fork of the South Platte River.

After an easy creek crossing, the trail enters a boggy area requiring caution. Hikers have laid out a series of stepping-stones that, unfortunately, do not benefit equines. If riders wish to continue, this marsh must be crossed in some form or another. The first two or three riders can probably hustle safely across, but do not dally. After the initial earth crust has been broken, additional riders may want to try a different route. Now the trail begins its climb over the Kenosha Mountain Range. This mountainside has weepy, wet places that cause short detours in the trail, depending on the amount of water flow. Watch the map and trail evidence to keep on track. At the ridge, the high spot on this section, the trail becomes much easier as it meanders between high-mountain meadows. Watch for elk in this subalpine environment. After the trail crosses an idyllic mountain stream, it drops quickly to merge with the Colorado Trail along the North Fork of Lost Creek within Lost Park. A left turn will take you to the North Fork trailhead, about 2 miles southeast.

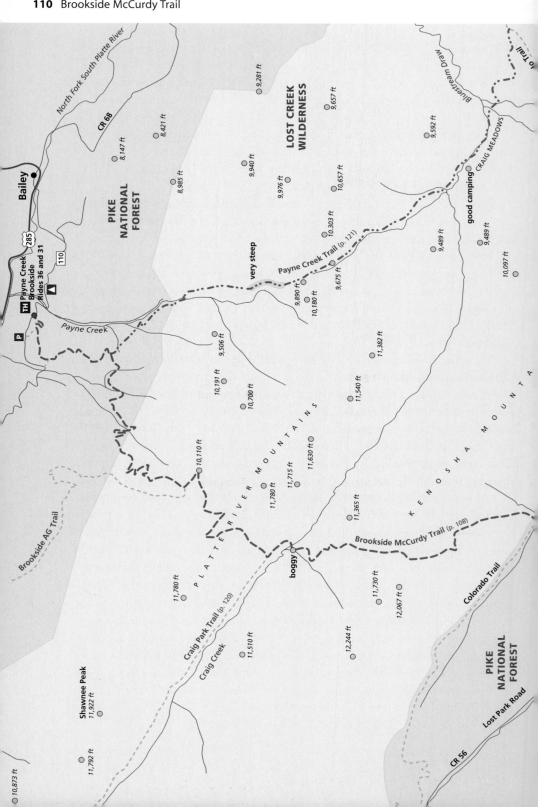

North Fork South Platte River

CR 68

Bailey

285

110

Payne Creek
Brookside
Rides 36 and 31

TH

P

Payne Creek

PIKE
NATIONAL
FOREST

LOST CREEK
WILDERNESS

Blusestream Draw

to Trail

CRAIG MEADOWS

good camping

very steep

Payne Creek Trail (p. 121)

8,147 ft

8,421 ft

8,985 ft

9,940 ft

9,281 ft

9,657 ft

9,592 ft

9,976 ft

10,657 ft

10,303 ft

9,489 ft

9,489 ft

10,097 ft

9,890 ft

9,675 ft

10,180 ft

11,382 ft

9,506 ft

10,191 ft

10,700 ft

11,540 ft

11,715 ft

11,630 ft

11,780 ft

10,110 ft

11,365 ft

Brookside McCurdy Trail (p. 108)

Brookside AG Trail

P L A T T E   R I V E R   M O U N T A I N S

K E N O S H A   M O U N T A

boggy

11,780 ft

Craig Park Trail (p. 120)

Craig Creek

11,510 ft

11,730 ft

12,067 ft

12,244 ft

Colorado Trail

PIKE
NATIONAL
FOREST

Lost Park Road

CR 56

Shawnee Peak
11,922 ft

11,792 ft

10,873 ft

32–34 Bruno (or Buno) Gulch Area

Bruno Gulch—or Buno Gulch, as it appears on Pike National Forest's official map—lies on the south side of Guanella Pass. The larger area is also known as Geneva Basin, with Geneva Creek cutting through it. According to the South Platte Ranger District, a fellow by the name of Buno operated a lumber mill here, hence the national forest's official name. Rangers are insistent that the other map companies have misspelled the original name, though most users of the area call it Bruno Gulch, so for consistency we'll refer to it as Bruno Gulch, too.

This is a large, heavily used dispersed camping area with water for horses in Bruno Creek and four nice, wood-pole corrals. The corrals are almost always occupied, especially on weekends, but there is plenty of room to set up pens and trees to erect highlines. Several beautiful trails are easily accessed without driving from the base area. An old pond within the fenced area to the east appears to have fish and might be worth throwing out a line. Unfortunately, the larger Geneva Creek is polluted from mines farther upstream and does not support fish at this time. **Note**: If you are seeking a place to "get away from it all," this is not it. On a given weekend, you may encounter ATVs, dirt bikes, loud music, barking dogs, shooting, and possibly even all of the above.

Directions to Trailhead

Take US 285 southwest from Denver to the small town of Grant. Turn right (north) onto CR 62, also signed as the Guanella Pass Scenic Byway. Follow this road 6.5 miles, including approximately 3 miles of rough, washboardy, gravel road, to FR 118A on the left. Turn here, where the large culverts carry Geneva Creek under the road. Slowly follow this rough road almost 1 mile west to find an appealing spot to camp. Equestrians generally stick to the right side near the corrals. This area is also accessible from I-70 at Georgetown, but at this writing, the road is under major construction and the complete condition for towing trailers from Georgetown to Guanella Pass is unknown.

32 Abyss Lake Trail (No. 602)

Overall Ride Rating	♡♡♡♡♡
Trail Rating	Very difficult
Distance	8.8 miles one way
Elevation	9,600–12,600 feet
Best Season	Summer to early fall
Main Uses	Equestrian, hiking, backcountry and dispersed camping, fishing
Trailhead Amenities	Large parking lot that should accommodate four to five trailers either backing in or parking parallel with the road. Many more could park, depending on the number of cars. Riders have camped in this lot and pastured their horses across the street, but most go to Bruno Gulch (see p. 111) approximately 1 mile farther down CR 62 (Guanella Pass Rd.) and near the end of FR 118A. There is no water at the trailhead, but stream water for horses is available on the trail. Water for humans is available at the Burning Bear Campground (no horses allowed).
Dogs	On leash in Mount Evans Wilderness
Shoes	Required
Maps	DeLorme *Colorado Atlas & Gazetteer*, p. 39; National Geographic *Trails Illustrated 104, Idaho Springs/Georgetown/Loveland Pass*; Pike and San Isabel National Forests map
Contact	Pike National Forest, South Platte Ranger District
Fees	None
Regulations	Visitors to the Mount Evans Wilderness are required to fill out a permit at the trailhead, keeping the heavier paper copy with them. See the Trail Savvy section (p. 12), website and posted regulations for additional information.

From the trailhead parking, pass through the 4-foot gate in the center of the buck-and-rail fence and head up the hill to the wilderness registration box. Please register your group as required. Continue on a wide path, originally a road before the area was designated as wilderness. The footing in this early section of the trail varies between smooth sand suitable for trotting out, and rough cobbles when the track becomes a fall-line drainage. At close to 2 miles, the trail crosses a small creek and shortly after crosses Scott Gomer Creek for the first time. Enjoy this easy section with the emerging views of the surrounding ridges and shoulders of Mount Bierstadt and Mount Evans, the two fourteeners closest to Denver.

After crossing Scott Gomer Creek again, the Abyss Lake Trail turns to a gnarly mass of boulders and rock steps that take you to and beyond the third creek crossing. Beaver ponds now dot the creek grade, but the trail continues its rocky

Directions to Trailhead

Take US 285 southwest of Denver to the small town of Grant. Turn right (north) onto CR 62, also signed as the Guanella Pass Scenic Byway. Follow this road 4.8 miles including about 3 miles of rough, washboard gravel and a set of steep, paved switchbacks to the Abyss Lake trailhead parking on the right, just after crossing a cattleguard.

For directions to the Bruno Gulch corrals, see p. 111. To ride the 3 miles to the Abyss Lake trailhead from the corrals, go south and cross Bruno Creek. Quite often there are folks camped right on the creek—just find a good crossing and go around them. Once you cross the creek, you will come to a nearby old fence; keep an eye out for downed wire. Head toward the trees and pick up what appears to be a cow trail. Turn left and follow this path southeast along and then around the end of a mountain. The trail heads across a willow and potentilla meadow to cross Burning Bear Creek at what is known locally as Cowboy Flats, then quickly joins the Burning Bear Trail. Turn left and follow the single track out to Guanella Pass Rd. (CR 62) and left to the Abyss Lake parking lot and trailhead, using the gate to bypass the cattleguard.

climb. In approximately 3.6 miles, a signed intersection for the Rosalie Trail (No. 603) appears on the right. If you want to try this equally beautiful trail, do not turn here: It heads across a beaver pond impassable to horses. Instead, con-

tinue on the Abyss Lake Trail across the now much calmer Scott Gomer Creek to a point just before the trail starts its climb up Mount Bierstadt. Look for a small rock cairn on the right at about 0.6 mile past the official signed intersection and turn right, following the creek down the hill to the official Rosalie Trail.

Those wanting to stay on the Abyss Lake Trail will start following switchbacks up the mountainside to a bowl close to treeline. Watch for approaching afternoon storms in this high-exposure terrain. After a brief break, the grade becomes steep again until arriving at an unnamed alpine lake at 11,730 feet. Many riders use this as a turnaround point, but for those die-hards looking for more, the trail continues its final 2 miles by crossing the lake at the outlet end. Hikers have placed rock steps on the mud bank, but horses must ford the water. A long stretch of willow and marsh lies ahead where the Lake Fork spreads after draining out of Abyss Lake. Take some time and search the rocky area for the best

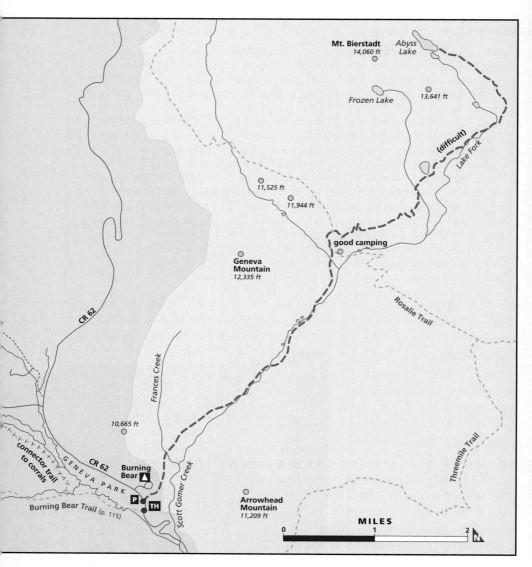

crossings. Once through this area, the trail turns in a more northwestern direction and climbs the last pitch among ever-larger boulders to the glacial cirque, where the lake lies encircled by Mount Bierstadt, the Sawtooths, and Mount Evans.

Although the immediate impression is that no person has set foot here before, the truth is that a surprising number of backpackers have called this bowl home, even if for just one night. The human signs they leave behind are clear enough when you look. After drinking in your fill of the surrounding beauty, it is time for the return trip, backtracking every inch of altitude previously gained. Once down to Scott Gomer Creek, there are some lovely backcountry camping areas along the beaver ponds; they are very popular, though, so keep an eye out for alternative spots.

33 Burning Bear Trail (No. 601) (For Trail Map see p. 119)

Overall Ride Rating	UUUUU
Trail Rating	Moderate
Distance	5.5 miles one way
Elevation	9,600–10,700 feet
Best Season	Summer to fall
Main Uses	Equestrian, hiking, dispersed and backcountry camping, mountain biking
Trailhead Amenities	Parking for the Burning Bear Trail is at the Abyss Lake trailhead (see Ride 32, p. 112). Water for horses is available at two creek crossings, at the beginning of the ride and approximately one-third of the way in. Water for humans is available at the Burning Bear Campground.
Dogs	Under voice command
Shoes	Recommended
Maps	DeLorme *Colorado Atlas and Gazetteer*, pp. 39 and 49; National Geographic *Trails Illustrated 104, Idaho Springs/Georgetown/ Loveland Pass*
Contact	Pike National Forest, South Platte Ranger District
Fees	None
Regulations	See the Trail Savvy section (p. 12), website and posted regulations for additional information.
Special Notes	The official trailheads for the Burning Bear Trail are on CR 62 (Guanella Pass Rd.) on the east and Hall Valley (FR 120) to the southwest. There is also a very good access trail from Bruno Gulch (see p. 111).

From the Abyss Lake parking lot, pass through the gate along the road on the south side. Follow the road, watching out for cars, about 0.2 mile to the gate on the west side. The beginning of this trail is the focus of a large improvement project to raise it up out of the marsh and water. The first 200 feet are a raised dirt-and-gravel turnpike, the next 200 feet are still under construction, and the last 200 feet sport a 4-foot-wide raised boardwalk made out of planks to support horses. This section can be slick when wet and can cause concern for horses. A wheelchair "bumper" has been installed on each side to help keep horses from slipping off. Please use caution and let the horses take their time.

At the end of the boardwalk is a bridge crossing the creek for pedestrian use only. Equestrians continue straight ahead to cross the creek at a nice, shallow spot. Although the creek is heavily mineralized due to past mining activities farther upstream, it is safe for horses to drink. After crossing the creek, turn

Directions to Trailhead

Follow the directions for the Abyss Lake trailhead on p. 113. The trail from the Bruno Gulch corrals joins the Burning Bear Trail just after crossing Burning Bear Creek at Cowboy Flats. If you are planning a shuttle ride, take US 285 3.5 miles farther south past Grant. Turn right at FR 120 (CR 60) and go 2.5 miles to the trail intersection and park along the road.

left and cross another short boardwalk to rejoin the trail. At about 0.5 mile is one more muddy section also slated for repair. The trail emerges from the trees at about 0.7 mile and a spur trail goes off to the right. This is the access trail from Bruno Gulch. Continue left and soon another unmarked trail comes in from the left. This is a trail used by the local dude ranch and has not been explored. Stay right and continue along Burning Bear Gulch. Cross the creek two times and come to the remains of a trapper's cabin at 2.5 miles. The trail has now left Burning Bear Creek and begun its ascent to the highest point on the ridge before dropping down into Hall Valley along CR 60 and Lamping Creek, a tributary to the North Fork of the South Platte River, which has its headwaters at the top of this valley. This road is where your trailers will be parked if you planned a shuttle ride, or you will need to return to either the Abyss Lake trailhead or Bruno Gulch.

34 South Park Trail (No. 600)

Overall Ride Rating	⛰⛰⛰⛰⛰
Trail Rating	Moderately difficult
Distance	6 miles one way
Elevation	10,100–11,600 feet
Best Season	Summer to fall
Main Uses	Equestrian, hiking, dispersed and backcountry camping, mountain biking
Trailhead Amenities	Room for many rigs along Geneva Creek Rd. just east of the signed trailhead on the north side. Dispersed camping is allowed here. Creek water is available from Geneva Creek along the south side of the road.
Dogs	Under voice command
Shoes	Recommended
Maps	DeLorme *Colorado Atlas and Gazetteer*, pp. 38 and 39; National Geographic *Trails Illustrated 104, Idaho Springs/Georgetown/ Loveland Pass;* Latitude 40° *Summit County Trails*
Contact	Pike National Forest, South Platte Ranger District
Fees	None
Regulations	See the Trail Savvy section (p. 12), website and posted regulations for additional information.
Special Notes	The South Park Trail (No. 600) officially starts at Guanella Pass. The additional 5.7-mile section from the pass down to FR 119 (Geneva Creek Rd.) is very steep and hard to follow in many places, and we determined that the difficulty for horses is beyond the scope of this book.

If starting at the Geneva Creek Rd. trailhead, head south at the Carsonite trail marker. The whole meadow area up to Geneva Creek is marshy and can be impassable in the early summer. It is hard to find a consistent trail here, as users wander around looking for the best passage. As riders approach the creek, a wide, muddy path appears between the willows. Yes, this is the trail. It is usually equally muddy on the other side of the creek. After the quagmire, the trail becomes considerably easier. Follow it just short of 1 mile to a trail intersection and bear right. Because of heavy use in the area, there are several "social" trails. These often make nice combinations for short rides with a little exploration. Soon you come across a second intersection marked with blue diamonds intended for cross-country skiers. This is one of the access points to and from Bruno Gulch. Bear right once again.

Directions to Trailhead

Take US 285 south of Denver to Grant. Turn right (north) onto CR 62, also signed as the Guanella Pass Scenic Byway. Follow this road 6.8 miles, including approximately 3 miles of rough, washboardy, gravel road, to FR 119 (Geneva Creek Rd.). Turn left, passing both the Geneva Creek Campground and Duck Creek Picnic Area, and follow this road 2.5 miles to parking on the right and trailhead a little farther on the left.

From the Bruno Gulch corrals, you have two riding options:

OPTION 1: Take 118A back toward Guanella Pass Rd. 0.5 mile to the large meadow on the left. Go north through this meadow, bearing to the left. Soon after entering the trees, a single-track trail appears and passes west of the Geneva Creek Campground. Several of the campsites and a restroom are visible from the trail. Soon the trail curves west and follows the base of a small mountain for 2 miles until its junction with the South Park Trail. This trail avoids the marshy area at the beginning of the South Park Trail (see Description).

OPTION 2: Follow 118A south toward Bruno Creek and continue west along the creek, passing a big, steel trail barrier. Be careful here as there are sharp edges. From this point on, motorized travel is prohibited. Continue to follow Bruno Gulch west slightly over 2 miles to the South Park Trail intersection. Since this is an old road, the dirt is washed away and river cobbles are exposed. The beaver ponds along the creek afford a great opportunity to spot a big bull elk in the late afternoon. Combining the two alternative access points to and from Bruno Gulch with the South Park Trail makes for an easy 8-mile loop.

At approximately 2.3 miles, the trail crosses a pretty little stream in Kirby Gulch, then begins an ascent up to a ridge at 11,200 feet and back down again into the Bruno Gulch drainage. Here is another intersection that leads from the Bruno Gulch camping area. Continue west-southwest across Bruno Creek. Soon after this crossing, the idyllic mountain trail becomes much more difficult, but is still beautiful and well worth it. At almost 5 miles, the trail encounters a hill-

side bog that is not difficult if riders are willing to leave the trail and climb about 100 feet to find an opening in the vegetation (cut by trail volunteers) where it is not so wet. Immediately after crossing the bog, a well-worn trail appears and continues as if nothing had been amiss.

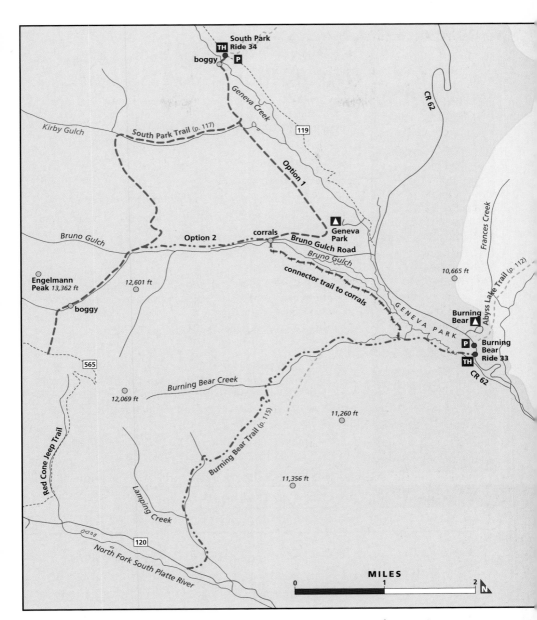

You face one more stream crossing and a steep ascent as the terrain opens up on the way to the ridge. At the end of the South Park Trail is the Red Cone four-wheel-drive road. To get a great view, turn left and follow the road until it turns to drop into a valley. At this point, you're on a two-track path signed for no motor vehicles; follow this up to the ridge and catch the views to the east of Mount Evans and the surrounding peaks.

35 Craig Park Trail
(No. 608) (For Trail Map see p. 110)

Overall Ride Rating	∪∪∪∪∪∪
Trail Rating	Difficult (due to difficulty of access trails)
Distance	6 miles one way
Elevation	10,900–11,600 feet
Best Season	Summer to early fall
Main Uses	Equestrian, hiking, dispersed and backcountry camping
Trailhead Amenities	See Ben Tyler Trail (Ride 30, p. 105) or Brookside McCurdy Trail (Ride 31, p. 108)
Dogs	On leash
Shoes	Recommended
Maps	DeLorme *Colorado Atlas & Gazetteer*, p. 49; National Geographic *Trails Illustrated 105, Tarryall Mts./Kenosha Pass*; Pike and San Isabel National Forests map
Contact	Pike National Forest, South Platte Ranger District
Fees	None
Regulations	Maximum of 15 people and 10 stock per group in the Lost Creek Wilderness. Animals must be tethered and kept overnight more than 100 feet from water or trails. See the Trail Savvy section (p. 12), website and posted regulations for additional information.
Special Notes	This trail has no trailhead. It is reached from either the Ben Tyler Trail or the Brookside McCurdy Trail.

Directions to Trailhead

See the Ben Tyler or Brookside McCurdy Trails (pp. 105 and 108)

This description starts from the Brookside McCurdy trailhead, though the Ben Tyler Trail is equally good riding. From the intersection with the Brookside McCurdy Trail at the lower end of Craig Park, the trail heads northwest, staying on the north side of Craig Creek. The park is between the Platte River Mountains and Kenosha Mountains. Beaver ponds produce abundant brook trout. Be aware of marshy conditions.

Finding a good camping spot is difficult; this side of the park stays steep once the trail reaches the trees. Access to water is also a consideration. Two small drainages emerge from the north for watering horses. The trail is faint and obscured by trees as it reaches the head of the park. The trail ends at the junction with the Ben Tyler Trail after a fast, 600-foot descent over 1 mile.

36 Payne Creek Trail
(No. 637) (For Trail Map see p. 110)

Overall Ride Rating	⛉⛉⛉⛉⛉
Trail Rating	Difficult
Distance	9.8 miles one way
Elevation	8,000–9,900 feet
Best Season	Late spring to early fall
Main Uses	Equestrian, hiking, dispersed and backcountry camping, fishing
Trailhead Amenities	See Brookside McCurdy Trail (Ride 31, p. 108)
Dogs	Under voice control until the Lost Creek Wilderness boundary; on leash after that
Shoes	Recommended
Maps	DeLorme *Colorado Atlas & Gazetteer,* p. 49; Rand McNally *2003 Denver Regional StreetFinder,* maps 2690 and 2689; National Geographic *Trails Illustrated 105, Tarryall Mts./Kenosha Pass;* Pike and San Isabel National Forests map
Contact	Pike National Forest, South Platte Ranger District
Fees	None
Regulations	Maximum of 15 people and 10 stock per group in the Lost Creek Wilderness. Animals must be tethered and kept overnight more than 100 feet from water or trails. See the Trail Savvy section (p. 12), website and posted regulations for additional information.
Special Notes	This trail would make a great shuttle ride in conjunction with the Colorado Trail to the Rolling Creek trailhead. For the shuttle vehicle drop-off, turn east on CR 68 at Bailey and then right (south) onto FR 543 (Wellington Lake Rd.) to the trailhead parking on the right.

Directions to Trailhead

See Brookside McCurdy Trail (Ride 31, p. 108)

The Payne Creek Trail shares the first mile with the Brookside McCurdy Trail. At the signed junction, take the left track and meander through the trees, into the wilderness, and toward Payne Gulch. After crossing Payne Creek, the trail joins an old logging road. Unfortunately, the road follows the fall line straight up, causing the dirt to wash out and exposing a very rocky trail tread. There are a few short switchbacks to give some relief, but otherwise, this is a long, steep haul. Take some time to rest your horses as needed. Just as it seems you've reached the top, there is one more climb ahead. For riders doing an out-and-back trip, this is a good time to remember that what goes up, must come down. After crossing the saddle, you'll see that all the effort was worth it. Stands of aspen as far as the eye can see are reminiscent of a Bev Doolittle painting. Try this trail in the early fall for a stunning visual reward.

Once the trail emerges from the aspen groves, the view into Craig Meadows is equally breathtaking. And you're in luck, because the trail takes riders to that exact spot. As the trail drops to Craig Creek at roughly mile 7, watch for a dangerously eroding edge where riders should go high and to the left of a lone ponderosa. At 7.3 miles, where the trail crosses the creek, you'll find a perfect place to camp. This is a high-impact area, so try to leave it better than you found it and be sure to pack out trash. The stream and nearby beaver ponds are teeming with brook trout, but the bankside willows make fishing a bit of a challenge.

Trail No. 637 continues its journey alongside Craig Creek to the southeast until they diverge where Bluestem Draw comes in, with the stream taking a sharp left as the trail veers right. This crossing is the last chance for stream water. The last mile ascends to the junction with the Colorado Trail just west of the Rolling Creek trailhead.

37 Browns Creek Trail (No. 1429)

Overall Ride Rating	○○○○○
Trail Rating	Moderate to difficult
Distance	5.9 miles one way; can also be looped with the Little Browns Creek Trail (see Ride 40, p. 132) for an approximately 14-mile ride
Elevation	8,970–11,290 feet
Best Season	Summer to fall
Main Uses	Equestrian, hiking, dispersed and backcountry camping (see Special Notes)
Trailhead Amenities	The circular, pull-through trailhead offers ample parking for several large rigs and has restrooms with vault toilets. Bring your own drinking water and water horses at the trailhead and while camping. The trail has ample water for the horses.
Dogs	On leash at the trailhead; under voice and sight control in the national forest
Shoes	Required
Maps	DeLorme *Colorado Atlas & Gazetteer*, p. 60; National Geographic *Trails Illustrated Map 130, Salida/St. Elmo/Shavano Peak;* San Isabel National Forest Service map
Contact	San Isabel National Forest, Salida Ranger District
Fees	None
Regulations	Groups of 75 or more must contact the Salida Ranger District and apply for a group-use permit. See the Trail Savvy section (p. 12), website and posted regulations for more information.
Special Notes	Camping is not permitted at the trailhead or along Little Browns Creek due to erosion of stream banks and damage to the stream. Campers are encouraged to use one of the many nice dispersed campsites farther south on CR 272. The best camping area for horseback groups is located approximately 1.5 miles south of the trailhead on the west side of the road and offers plenty of space for setting up portable electric fence corrals. (See the Trail Savvy section on p. 12 for additional containment methods to ensure low-impact camping.) Do not attempt the Browns Creek/ Little Browns Creek loop if there is any possibility of inclement weather or if you and your horse are not experienced back-country trail users in excellent condition.

Directions to Trailhead

From US 285 midway between Poncha Springs and Buena Vista, take CR 270 west for 1.5 miles to a four-way intersection. From the stop sign, continue traveling west. The road continues as CR 272. Stay on CR 272 for approximately 2 miles. A sign at the cattle guard indicates your entrance to the San Isabel National Forest. At an intersection at the 2-mile point, follow CR 272 left (south) for 1.5 miles to the Browns Creek trailhead. Parking is permitted across from the trailhead and toilet facilities.

The Browns Creek Trail, located just 15 miles southwest of Buena Vista, offers equestrians an unforgettable journey into the heart of Colorado's Rockies. The trail leaves the trailhead parking area heading west and climbs aggressively at first. At 0.25 mile, watch to your right and make an easy-to-miss hard right and continue climbing. The natural inclination here is to continue on the straight path, but going straight will take you down along the creek on a trail that is extremely challenging, wet, and overgrown. Making the right turn allows you to follow the higher and easier path as it meanders through the Browns Creek drainage at the southern foothills of 13,667-foot Mount White. You are soon rewarded with spectacular views of Mount Antero, which lies just to the north of Mount White at a lofty elevation of 14,269 feet.

At 1.5 miles, you come to the junction with the Colorado Trail, which can be ridden to the north or to the south (see Rides 38 and 39, pp. 126 and 128). Shortly after the trail junction, the path crosses Little Browns Creek and then Browns Creek. Don't forget to pack the fishing rod and enjoy some time with the trout. Numerous creek crossings provide plenty of water for the horses and add adventure to an already fabulous ride. The lower portion of the trail begins in a ponderosa pine environment and gradually changes to lodgepole and spruce forest, while the higher elevations offer pristine meadows with colorful wildflowers during summer months. About halfway up the trail, watch for the cascading falls marked by a barely legible wooden sign. The trail surface is sandy and wide in places, but also includes many narrow and rocky portions—nothing to be concerned about as long as the trail is not too wet and you have a trustworthy mount. This would not be a trail for a beginner horse or rider, however.

The crystal waters of Browns Lake lie just before the end of the trail tread. Here, at 5.9 miles, you can decide to return via the same path or make a loop back to the parking area by connecting to the Little Browns Creek Trail. To do the loop, continue west and then north on the four-wheel-drive road FR 278, which reaches an elevation of 12,858 feet not too far from the summit of Mount White. FR 278B takes you east from FR 278, putting you onto the Little Browns Creek Trail. The loop totals about 13.9 miles and at its highest point reaches a rocky slope of Mount White above treeline. Thunderstorms and severe lightning are common at these elevations. If a storm is approaching, move down to a lower elevation quickly to avoid lightning and other related hazards. Only very experienced backcountry trail riders and accomplished, well-conditioned trail horses should attempt making the loop. Do not attempt the loop portion if there is any possibility of inclement weather. Just enjoy the Browns Creek portion and then return to the trailhead.

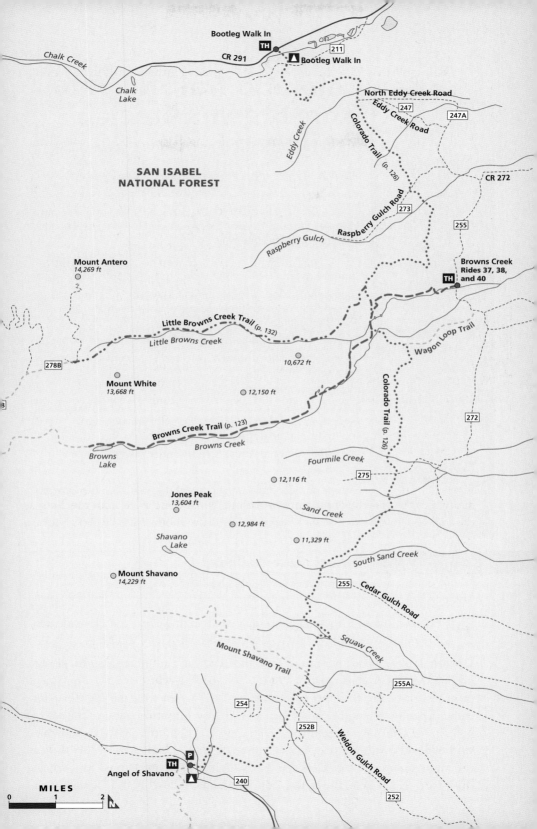

Bootleg Walk In

CR 291

Chalk Creek

Chalk Lake

211

Bootleg Walk In

North Eddy Creek Road

Eddy Creek Road

247

247A

Eddy Creek

Colorado Trail (p. 126)

CR 272

SAN ISABEL
NATIONAL FOREST

Raspberry Gulch Road

273

255

Raspberry Gulch

Raspberry Gulch

Mount Antero
14,269 ft

Browns Creek
Rides 37, 38,
and 40

TH

Little Browns Creek Trail (p. 132)

Little Browns Creek

Wagon Loop Trail

278B

10,672 ft

Mount White
13,668 ft

12,150 ft

Colorado Trail (p. 126)

272

Browns Creek Trail (p. 123)

Browns Creek

Browns
Lake

Fourmile Creek

275

12,116 ft

Jones Peak
13,604 ft

Sand Creek

12,984 ft

Shavano
Lake

11,329 ft

Mount Shavano
14,229 ft

South Sand Creek

255

Cedar Gulch Road

Mount Shavano Trail

Squaw Creek

255A

254

252B

Weldon Gulch Road

P

TH

Angel of Shavano

240

252

MILES

0   1   2

N

38 Colorado Trail (No. 1776) from Browns Creek Trailhead (For Trail Map see p. 125)

Overall Ride Rating	⋃⋃⋃⋃⋃
Trail Rating	Moderate
Distance	Browns Creek trailhead to Chalk Creek, 6.5 miles one way, plus 1.5-mile loop spur; Browns Creek trailhead to Angel of Shavano trailhead, 9.5 miles one way
Elevation	8,970–10,160 feet
Best Season	Summer to fall
Main Uses	Equestrian, hiking, dispersed and backcountry camping (see Special Notes for Browns Creek Trail, Ride 37, p. 123), mountain biking
Trailhead Amenities	See information for Browns Creek trailhead (see Ride 37, p. 123)
Dogs	On leash at trailhead; under voice and sight control in national forest
Shoes	Highly recommended
Maps	DeLorme *Colorado Atlas & Gazetteer,* p. 60; National Geographic *Trails Illustrated Map 130, Salida/St. Elmo/Shavano Peak;* San Isabel National Forest Service Map
Contact	San Isabel National Forest, Salida Ranger District
Fees	None
Regulations	Groups of 75 or more must contact the Salida Ranger District and apply for a group-use permit. See the Trail Savvy section (p. 12), website and posted regulations for more information.

Directions to Trailhead

See directions for Browns Creek Trail (Ride 37, p. 123)

Head west out of the parking area on a steady uphill climb for approximately 1.5 miles to reach the signed junction with the Colorado Trail.

Option 1: Take a hard right onto the Colorado Trail and proceed north, always keeping Mount Antero's soaring 14,269-foot peak at your left side. This is a great place to enjoy a trot or canter on the 2- to 4-foot-wide natural-dirt path through gently sloping meadows scattered with evergreen and aspen. The color is brilliant almost any time you go, thanks to fragrant wildflowers in the summer and turning aspen leaves in the fall. Just 2.5 miles to the north lies the intersection with CR 273 (Raspberry Gulch Rd.), a little-used four-wheel-drive road. From here, the trail continues on a fairly level path in a northwest direction to the intersection with FR 274 and FR 274A, which form a small tri-angle around a lovely meadow. (By taking this to the east on your return you can add an extra 1.5 miles, creating a small loop.) Proceed around the base of an unnamed 11,000-foot peak, noting views of lofty Mount Princeton (14,197 feet). Cross Eddy Creek and ride the switchbacks uphill to end at Chalk Creek. Across CR 291, the white crumbly Chalk Cliffs rise steeply and abruptly from the base of Mount Princeton.

Option 2: Turn left (south) at the Colorado Trail junction for some wonderful views of the lower Arkansas headwaters. You reach the junction with the Browns Creek Trail to the west and, shortly after, the Wagon Loop Trail to the east. The next landmarks are the creek crossing at Fourmile Creek and then the intersection with FR 275 (N. Fourmile Rd.). Pass Sand Creek, South Sand Creek, and FR 255 (Cedar Gulch Rd.), and follow the trail as it crosses Squaw Creek at 10,160 feet and continues to descend. Approximately 0.5 mile after crossing Squaw Creek, the Mount Shavano Trail forks to the right at the base of Mount Shavano (14,229 feet) and Tabeguache Peak (14,155 feet). Within the next 0.25 mile, CR 252 (Weldon Gulch Rd.) ends where it reaches the Colorado Trail. This access point is known as Blank Cabin. From here, the trail follows the base of Mount Shavano into the North Fork drainage to the Angel of Shavano Camp-ground. This is an excellent segment for a shuttle ride if you can plan for a trailer to pick you up at Angel of Shavano. Depending on the size of the rig and car parking, the lot can accommodate two to three trailers.

Colorado Trail (No. 1776) from Avalanche Trailhead

Overall Ride Rating	ⵔⵔⵔⵔⵔ
Trail Rating	Moderate
Distance	8.75 miles one way south to Mount Princeton Rd.; 3 miles one way north to N. Cottonwood Rd.
Elevation	9,400–11,900 feet
Main Uses	Equestrian, hiking, dispersed and backcountry camping, mountain biking south of CR 306 (outside of the wilderness)
Trailhead Amenities	The large, paved parking area will accommodate numerous rigs of any size. There are restrooms but no water or other amenities. Camping is prohibited at the trailhead; however, on the south side of CR 306 across from the trailhead are several camping spots for horse trailers, in addition to numerous backcountry campsites.
Dogs	On leash at trailhead; under voice and sight control in the national forest
Shoes	Highly recommended
Maps	DeLorme *Colorado Atlas & Gazetteer*, p. 59; National Geographic *Trails Illustrated Map 129, Buena Vista/Collegiate Peaks* and *Map 128, Maroon Bells/Redstone/Marble;* San Isabel National Forest Service map
Contact	San Isabel National Forest, Salida Ranger District
Fees	None
Regulations	See the Trail Savvy section (p. 12), website and posted regulations for additional information.

Directions to Trailhead

From the intersection of US 24 and CR 306 (Cottonwood Pass Rd.) in the center of Buena Vista, go west at the one and only traffic light. The Avalanche trailhead is located on the north side of the road as you curve around the mountain pass. Slow down and prepare for an easy-to-miss, hard right-hand turn at 7.7 miles.

From the trailhead, you can head either north or south on the Colorado Trail for exceptional scenery and riding.

Option 1: Beginning at the Avalanche trailhead, travel southeast out of the parking lot. Be extremely careful, as you will need to cross Cottonwood Pass Rd., a curved road with fast-moving traffic. Once on the other side, pick up the trail at Cottonwood Creek, climbing significantly for 1 to 2 miles on a fairly rocky and narrow path. Beautiful Rainbow Lake lies on private property just beyond

the wildflower-lined path. A forest dense with aspen and evergreen is a delight. The resident beavers have been hard at work building numerous, sizeable dams across the creek.

The route continues in a southeastern direction, bisecting CR 344 (S. Cottonwood Rd.) and CR 343 (S. Cottonwood Cutoff Rd.) and Cottonwood Creek at 2 miles. Here, a welcome wider, sandy path gently climbs to remarkable views of the impressive Collegiate Peaks. You experience Mother Nature at her finest on this journey, as dense quaking aspen and an assortment of mature pines offer a shady escape from Colorado's intense summer sun. Cross Maxwell Creek at 6 miles and Dry Creek at 7.5 miles. At 8.75 miles, the trail joins the Mount Princeton Rd., where a signboard explains the next 5 miles of trail. Unfortunately, from here on, the trail borders the road to Chalk Creek. Although breathtaking, the area around Chalk Cliffs is an extremely high-traffic area with fast-moving vehicles. It is here that the horse-safe portion of this segment ends! A better option for riders who would like to continue riding the Colorado Trail would be to return to the Avalanche trailhead and ride north or try the segments that begin at the Browns Creek trailhead (see Ride 37, p. 123).

Option 2: From the trailhead, ride north into the Collegiate Peaks Wilderness. The Colorado Trail begins an uphill journey paralleling Hughes Gulch Creek for the first mile, with the summit of Mount Yale towering only 2 miles away at a lofty 14,196 feet. The trail itself eventually reaches 11,900 feet. Continuing north, parallel Silver Creek for another 1.75 miles before crossing it on the climb to the North Cottonwood Creek drainage and CR 365 (N. Cottonwood Rd.), where this segment ends.

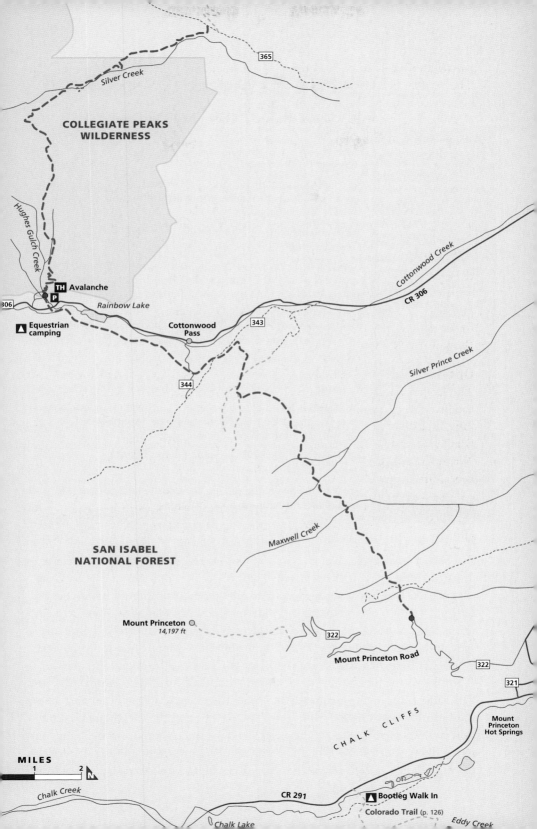

COLLEGIATE PEAKS
WILDERNESS

Silver Creek

365

Hughes Gulch Creek

Cottonwood Creek

CR 306

TH Avalanche

P

306

Rainbow Lake

Silver Prince Creek

Equestrian camping

Cottonwood Pass

343

344

Maxwell Creek

SAN ISABEL
NATIONAL FOREST

Mount Princeton
14,197 ft

322

Mount Princeton Road

322

321

CHALK CLIFFS

Mount Princeton Hot Springs

MILES

1   2

N

Chalk Creek

CR 291

Bootleg Walk In

Colorado Trail (p. 126)

Chalk Lake

Eddy Creek

40 Little Browns Creek Trail (No. 1430) (For Trail Map see p. 125)

Overall Ride Rating	☺☺☺☺☺
Trail Rating	Difficult
Distance	5.5 miles one way, including 1.5 miles each way from the parking lot to the trailhead; also connects to the Browns Creek Trail for a 13.9 mile loop
Elevation	8,800 feet (Browns Creek trailhead)–12,400 feet
Best Season	Summer to fall
Main Uses	Equestrian, hiking, dispersed and backcountry camping (see Special Notes for the Browns Creek Trail, p. 123), fishing
Trailhead Amenities	The circular, pull-through trailhead at Browns Creek offers ample parking for several large rigs and restrooms with vault toilets. No water at the trailhead. See Special Notes for the Browns Creek Trail (Ride 37, p. 123) for camping information.
Dogs	On leash at trailhead; under voice and sight control in national forest
Shoes	Required
Maps	DeLorme *Colorado Atlas & Gazetteer*, p. 60; National Geographic *Trails Illustrated Map 130, Salida/St. Elmo/Shavano Peak*; San Isabel National Forest Service Map
Contact	San Isabel National Forest, Salida Ranger District
Fees	None
Regulations	See the Trail Savvy section (p. 12), website and posted regulations for additional information.

Little Browns Creek is an older trail that's no longer maintained by the Forest Service and thus challenging in many ways. The trail is not always clear of downed timber and is steep, narrow, and rocky in a number of places. Only experienced trail horses and riders in excellent condition should undertake the difficult, 3,600-foot elevation gain. Additionally, horses should be given frequent rest breaks. Although it is not recommended for equestrians, hikers often use a spur of the trail to access the 14,269-foot summit of Mount Antero to the north.

Begin by riding west from the Browns Creek trailhead parking area for 1.5 miles to the junction of the Colorado Trail and turn right (north) onto the Colorado Trail. In approximately 0.5 mile, the Colorado Trail heads east where the Little Browns Creek Trail begins. The elevation at this clearly marked junction is 9,600 feet. Watch for the brook trout in the stream or bring along your rod and test your fishing skills. The trail climbs aggressively upward as it follows the rugged drainage of Little Browns Creek through various ecosystems, beginning

Directions to Trailhead

See directions to Browns Creek trailhead (p. 123).

in a forest of aspen and lodgepole pine and ascending to spruce and fir. Occasional rock outcroppings interrupt the landscape before you reach treeline.

The trail tread ends 5.5 miles from the parking area at FR 278B. You can return on the same path you've traveled or take the four-wheel-drive road west around Mount White and across alpine tundra, reaching nearly 12,000 feet (with very rocky conditions). Continue until you intersect FR 278 and descend south and then east to connect with the Browns Creek Trail. By riding the Browns Creek Trail east (see Ride 37, p. 123) back to the parking area, you will have completed an advanced 13.9-mile journey with significant portions above treeline. Keep in mind that severe lightning is common at these elevations and storms can gather rapidly during summer afternoons. With the first sign of thunder or lightning, move quickly to a lower elevation. Only very experienced backcountry trail riders and accomplished trail horses in excellent condition should attempt making the loop. Do not attempt this loop if there is any possibility of inclement weather or if you and your horse are not experienced backcountry trail users.

43 Shelf Road Recreation Area

Overall Ride Rating	ＵＵＵＵＵ
Trail Rating	Easy
Distance	More than 30 miles of trails
Elevation	6,500–8,000 feet
Best Season	Year-round
Main Uses	Equestrians, hiking, dispersed camping, mountain biking, rock climbing, motorized vehicles (OHV and ATV)
Trailhead Amenities	Parking available for large rigs and groups on both a wood-fenced, gravel lot and on dirt and grass. Dispersed camping options include corrals with wood fencing (one large, one medium, one small, and one very small). There is a larger holding area and a small pasture built with wood posts and field fence topped with barbed wire. These are typical old cattle-loading facilities that have been slightly renovated to allow horse use. Nearby junipers are not suitable for highlining, but there is ample room for portable corrals or electric fences. Bring water for horses and humans.
Dogs	Under voice control
Shoes	Recommended
Maps	DeLorme *Colorado Atlas & Gazetteer*, p. 62; National Geographic *Trails Illustrated Map 137, Pikes Peak/Cañon City*
Contact	Bureau of Land Management, Royal Gorge Field Office
Fees	None
Regulations	If the area is too wet, the gate at the corrals may be closed to motor vehicles. Trailers can park in the gravel lot on the south side of the road. Horses can be walked over the metal bar in the fence line to access the corrals and trail. The BLM has restricted the dispersed camping area in the meadow next to the corrals. Please park within the Carsonite signs. See the Trail Savvy section (p. 12), website and posted regulations for additional information.
Special Notes	In the warm months rattlesnakes can be out, including at the corrals. Some horses may be sensitive to the abundant weeds at the corrals. There is no water in the area for humans or animals, even at the two developed BLM campgrounds. Windmills are situated along the trails, but they have been disabled and any water in the tanks is strictly due to rain collection. Due to the renewed use of the area for cattle grazing, there is one water tank currently operated by a solar-powered pump. It is located in a meadow along Trail T5820D just before it intersects with Trail T5820E.

Directions to Trailhead

From US 50 on the east side of Cañon City, turn north onto Dozer Ave. just west of Wal-Mart. After several blocks, Dozer curves west and becomes Central St. At the stop sign, turn north (right) onto Field Ave. On the far north end of town, Field Ave. joins Red Canyon Rd. This is now signed as the Gold Belt Tour or Scenic Byway. Continue north, passing the Garden Park Fossil Area and Red Canyon Park. At 8.7 miles, the pavement ends. Continue another 1.1 miles, passing the Sand Gulch Campground sign, until you reach a BLM sign for The Bank at 9.8 total miles and turn left. A large gravel lot is immediately on the left and the corrals are on the right as you drive across a cattle guard. Do not go past the Shelf Rd. sign, as vehicle length is restricted.

This vast and complex trail network on BLM land includes four-wheel-drive roads, old ranch roads, and single-track paths. There are literally thousands of acres and many miles worth exploring. Current maps, including GPS receivers, do not show any trail detail, so a natural sense of direction for at least one group member is helpful, and, as always, you should include a very detailed topographical map in your pack. A GPS turned on to "track" should show you how to follow your track back if needed.

The terrain varies from large, open meadows to abrupt, rocky canyons. Juniper, piñon pine, and scrub oak will swap with ponderosa pine and aspen in moister valleys, but the overall feeling is that of high desert. This description details two routes that make very nice day rides. Many of the trails are numbered, but some are not, so pay close attention as you're riding.

Option 1: This is an out-and-back course that makes an 18-mile round-trip if followed in its entirety. From the corrals, head toward the west end of the meadow to a wooden signpost with trail number T5820. This track parallels a section of the road leading to the Bank Campground. When the trail ends partway up the hill, riders will need to follow the road the remainder of the way. Because of the cattle guards at the campground, bear left on the trail along the fence and pass through the gate. At the Y, follow the main road to the right into Trail Gulch. Watch along the right side of the road for rock climbers on the wall. Alongside the road on the left are two large, shallow caves dug out of the rock wall for mining exploration.

At 2.75 miles is a windmill with a possibility of rainwater in the stock tank during the spring months. Soon after passing the windmill, the trail intersects T5820A to the left. To follow this route description, bear right. At 3.3 miles, you encounter a major unmarked intersection. The road to the right rejoins the Shelf Rd., but you will want to bear left. At the intersection with T5820B, take the left route marked for hikers, bikers, and equestrians. You pass another windmill at 4.6 miles, but this one will also have little or no water. Soon after the windmill, at the intersection with T5820C, which goes left, turn right and start a moderate altitude-gaining ascent. The massive scar of the Cripple Creek &

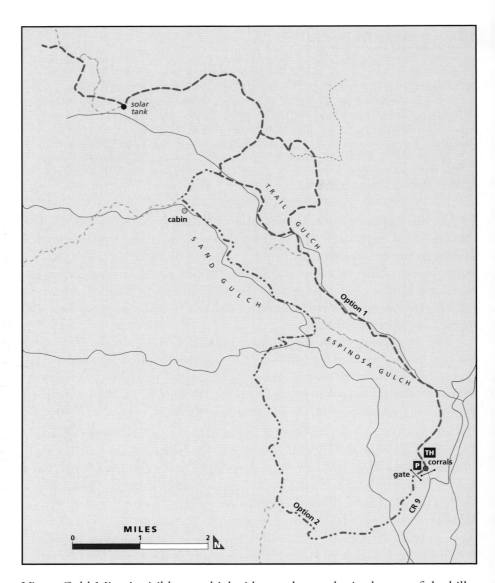

Victor Gold Mine is visible on a high ridge to the north. At the top of the hill, follow T5820D through the gate into the meadow. Use caution when passing through the gate, as the BLM plants short posts to discourage motorcycles and ATVs that are hard for horses to see. They may either trip over them or see them at the last minute and veer to the side, forcing your leg into the gatepost. Many riders dismount to allow their horses to safely navigate the obstacle alone.

Beyond the gate is a picturesque meadow known locally as the Lost City. Stories are told of Irish immigrants settling here and farming potatoes as they had in their homeland. The remains of stone foundations lie along the side of the rock cliff ahead and to the right of the meadow. This is a peaceful lunch and rest place and a possible turnaround point, depending on the length of ride desired. To extend the ride a few miles farther, continue through the meadow on the trail. At 6.7 miles, on the left, is the stock tank with a well powered by a solar collector (see Special Notes). Just beyond the tank, at an intersection with T5820E, turn right. Once again, you have a variety of trail options, including the possibility of a long loop on T5820E. The next intersection is with T5820F and T5808B; stay on T5820D by going straight. At just under 7 miles, take trail T5808B, which is open to hikers and horses, but closed to bicycles. At this point, the trail becomes narrow and rocky as it descends into a valley. At just under 7.5 miles the trail makes a hard left and switchbacks on down the hill. At 8.6 miles is a future intersection with a new trail built to connect to another trailhead, called Booger Red, several miles northwest on High Park Rd. (The Rocky Mountain chapter of Back Country Horsemen of America volunteers are currently working on the project with the BLM.) Continue straight through the meadow on the single track, cross a check dam, and veer right. There is a permanent survey benchmark on a berm to the right. After a left turn, follow the fence line on the right along a small gulch. Turn right and go through an opening in the fence.

At this point, you've gone roughly 9 miles and private property lies ahead, so this is the turnaround point. Backtrack on the same route past the Lost City and through the gate all the way to the second windmill and trail intersection with T5820C. Turning right here is an alternative to repeating the whole route on the return trip and adds a negligible amount of mileage that is worth the change of scenery. At the bottom of the hill is another red gate where trail T5820E turns right. Note the intersection, as it's included in the narrative for Option 2. For this route, remain on T5820C until it rejoins the road at the first windmill. Follow the road back past the Bank Campground to the parking area.

Option 2: An 11-mile loop, suitable for a shorter second day of riding, starts at the 4-foot red gate across the road from the corrals. Cross the large meadow heading toward the entrance road for the Sand Gulch Campground and pick up the BLM road that continues south toward the neighboring ranches. Several four-wheel-drive roads, including 5825B and 5825C, cut right toward the cliffs and are used for dispersed campsites. Stay on the main road through a red gate and down a hill into a rock and sand gully where you'll find a stock tank intermittently fed by an artesian spring. When we rode, the water was fresh and drinkable for the horses in the early season, but by late summer and fall had grown full of algae and moss and did not look very desirable. At 1 mile, the road forks and 5825D goes left along the base of the cliff; turn right toward a canyon. The road begins switchbacking up the face of the cliff and the broadening views of Garden Park below are marvelous. Along the ascent is a dilapidated gate across the road with a BLM sign instructing visitors to close it as they pass. Just past the gate is a Carsonite sign informing users that motor vehicles are not allowed. Continue on the main road.

At just under 2.5 miles, you come across the remains of a mine, possibly the Blue Nugget, fenced for safety. After ascending several ridges and descending into the gulches between them, you reach an intersection where 5830 goes east while you stay on 5825. At an intersection with T5825A, approximately 0.75 mile farther, turn left. Soon you'll see signs and a series of large boulders placed to keep ATV traffic off the single-track trail. Use caution when negotiating this obstacle. In the open meadow, the trail is less evident. When you see the check dam, go left to cross the dam, then turn right onto a more visible trail to enter Sand Gulch. Notice the vegetation change from piñon pine and juniper to trees with higher moisture requirements, such as ponderosa pine, Douglas fir, and aspen. Follow this peaceful gulch up to a quaint log cabin and shed, possibly remnants from homesteading days. The essential outhouse completes the picture. Unfortunately, others have exploited the area and left reminders of contemporary use (i.e. trash). If you stop here for lunch, pack out everything you use and perhaps some of what others have uncaringly left.

After a refreshing respite and photo op break, continue through the small meadow into the trees, crossing the dry creek bed. At the T intersection with T5820E, turn right, leaving the valley and climbing over a ridge. At the top of the hill is another trail marker for T5820F, but stay on T5820E. At 8 miles is the red gate mentioned in Option 1. This is where T5820E ends. Go through the gate cautiously, watching for another short post in the ground in the middle of the opening. Turn right on T5820C, returning to road T5820 near the first windmill and following this again past the Bank Campground and down to the corrals.

44 Goose Creek Trail (No. 612)

Overall Ride Rating	❂❂❂❂❂
Trail Rating	Easy to moderate
Distance	9.4 miles one way
Elevation	8,200–10,140 feet
Best Season	Summer to fall
Main Uses	Equestrian, hiking, dispersed and backcountry camping, fishing, hunting
Trailhead Amenities	Parking for trailers at a loop signed "Horse Unloading Ramp." Dispersed camping is also allowed here, with room for four to eight rigs among the trees, depending on parking expertise and desired privacy. There are remains of a single-pole, round corral as well as an old-fashioned truck-unloading ramp, but no other amenities. Do not park or leave a horse in the vicinity of the standing, dead snags. Do not drive down the road to the official trailhead, as turning around could be difficult in the long, narrow lot.
Dogs	On leash
Shoes	Recommended
Maps	DeLorme *Colorado Atlas & Gazetteer*, p. 49; National Geographic *Trails Illustrated 105, Tarryall Mtns./Kenosha Pass*; Pike and San Isabel National Forests map
Contact	Pike National Forest, South Platte Ranger District
Fees	None
Regulations	Maximum of 15 people and 10 stock per group in the Lost Creek Wilderness. Animals must be tethered and kept overnight more than 100 feet from water or trails. See the Trail Savvy section (p. 12), website and posted regulations for additional information.
Special Notes	The first 0.5-mile section of the Goose Creek Trail travels through the 2002 Hayman Burn area. Be aware of standing dead snags that can fall without warning, especially on windy days. The 3.5-mile section of trail to the historic buildings is extremely popular and usage is heavy on summer weekends.

Directions to Trailhead

From Lake George, head west on US 24 about 1 mile to CR 77 (Tarryall Rd.). Turn north (right) and proceed 9 miles to CR 211 (Matukat Rd.). Turn right (northeast) and follow this gravel road 11.5 slow, winding miles to the Goose Creek trailhead turnoff. Turn left and follow unsigned FR 558 1.5 miles to the parking area on the right, signed for a horse-unloading ramp.

From the lower part of the parking area, a two-track path leads 0.5 mile to the official trailhead near the car parking lot. Across the lot, the trail immediately enters the Lost Creek Wilderness, descending through a heavily burned area to cross Hankins Creek. At the trail junction, turn right to follow Hankins Creek downstream while the Hankins Pass Trail (No. 630) heads off to the left. After leaving the burn area and reaching Goose Creek, the trail veers left and follows the large mountain creek upstream. Ride past the metal footbridge about 100 feet and cross the creek beyond. Watch for brook trout in the cool water. Continuing upstream, you'll come across several fantastic places to set up camp and do some fishing in the nearby beaver ponds. Arrive early, as these are popular spots on warm, summer weekends.

After this point, the creek drops away as the trail climbs, offering views of the stunning granite spires and arches that draw so many to the area. At 3.5 miles, a sign marks the trail to the historic buildings and shafthouse where employees of the Antero and Lost Park Reservoir Company attempted to dam Lost Creek. Follow the trail in the front of the buildings between some boulders to another popular campsite. Farther down the hill reveals the final time Lost Creek emerges from its underground creek bed; here it is renamed Goose Creek. Taking the spur trail signed "Shafthouse" affords riders a chance to get up close and personal with those gigantic boulders on their way to the spot chosen over 100 years ago for a possible reservoir. All that remains are a steam wench and a boiler. Returning to the Goose Creek Trail, you begin to gain elevation rapidly before dropping down into Watkins Gulch. The trail heads back up again in a generally northwesterly direction, intersecting with the McCurdy Park Trail (No. 628) at a high point overlooking the valley. The Goose Creek Trail bears right up to a saddle east of a granite tower before descending into Wigwam Park and terminating at its intersection with the Wigwam Trail (No. 609). Across Wigwam Creek there is a backcountry campsite near beaver ponds.

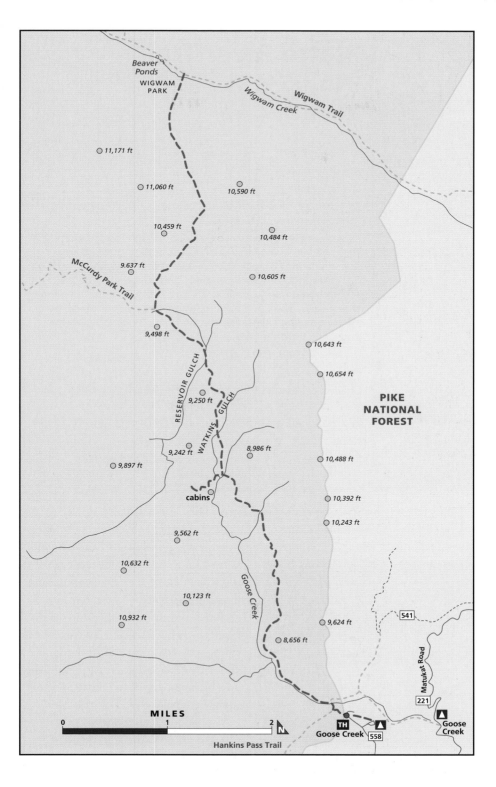

Beaver
Ponds
WIGWAM
PARK

Wigwam Creek

Wigwam Trail

11,171 ft

11,060 ft

10,590 ft

10,459 ft

10,484 ft

McCurdy Park Trail

9.637 ft

10,605 ft

9,498 ft

10,643 ft

RESERVOIR GULCH

10,654 ft

WATKINS GULCH

9,250 ft

PIKE
NATIONAL
FOREST

9,242 ft

8,986 ft

9,897 ft

10,488 ft

cabins

10,392 ft

10,243 ft

9,562 ft

10,632 ft

Goose Creek

10,123 ft

541

10,932 ft

9,624 ft

8,656 ft

Matukat Road

221

MILES

0   1   2

Goose Creek TH 558

Goose
Creek

Hankins Pass Trail

45 Platte River Trail (No. 654)

Overall Ride Rating	♘♘♘♘♘
Trail Rating	Difficult
Distance	4 miles one way
Elevation	7,800–8,400 feet
Best Season	Spring to fall
Main Uses	Equestrian, hiking, backcountry camping, fishing, mountain biking, floating or tubing
Trailhead Amenities	Parking at the trailhead is only large enough for a few cars. Trailer parking is available at several fishermen's parking areas on the right side of the road before and after the Happy Meadows Campground. These are pull-through parking lots and will accommodate up to three to six rigs, with the largest parking area found approximately 1 mile past the campground. There are no other facilities available. Bring drinking water; horses may drink from the river.
Dogs	Under voice control
Shoes	Recommended
Maps	DeLorme *Colorado Atlas & Gazetteer*, p. 49; National Geographic *Trails Illustrated 137, Pikes Peak/Cañon City*
Contact	Pike National Forest, South Park Ranger District
Fees	None
Regulations	See the Trail Savvy section (p. 12), website and posted regulations for additional information.

This route is for the trail-riding angler, so make sure you pack a pole. After saddling up, ride north along CR 112 to the signed trailhead on the left side of the road. The trail starts with a gentle climb, bypassing private property

that now lines the banks of the South Platte River below. The large rocks along and in the trail need to be carefully negotiated and result in this trail's difficult rating. A horse can easily trip while stepping through, down, and over some of the tricky spots. Take it easy, hold the horse's head up, and watch knee and foot clearance to make this trail passable.

After about 2 miles, at the end of the neighborhood, the trail descends

Directions to Trailhead

From Lake George, take US 24 west approximately 1 mile. Turn right (north) onto CR 77 (Tarryall Rd.) and proceed 2.5 miles to CR 112. Turn right toward the Happy Meadows Campground. Park at any of the fishermen's pull-offs on the right (one before the campground and two more after).

back down to the river as it starts into the mouth of the canyon. Here, the trail is sandy, flat, and easy as it meanders alongside the picturesque river—it's a scene worthy of the movie *A River Runs Through It*. Camping and fishing opportunities are abundant on both sides. For riders who don't care to fish, remove your hot riding boots and cool your toes in the clear, rushing water. Enjoy the calm solitude of the river now, as it soon starts its crashing journey through the rocky canyon farther below. As the river starts to drop, the trail climbs and the rock obstacles return. If passage becomes too rough, turn around, as eventually the trail reaches a place that is definitely unsafe for horses and riders, struggling upward to intersect the Platte Springs Trail (No. 626) via a set of rock steps. Don't bother trying them: There's no need, since the best part of this trail is had on the gorgeous South Platte River.

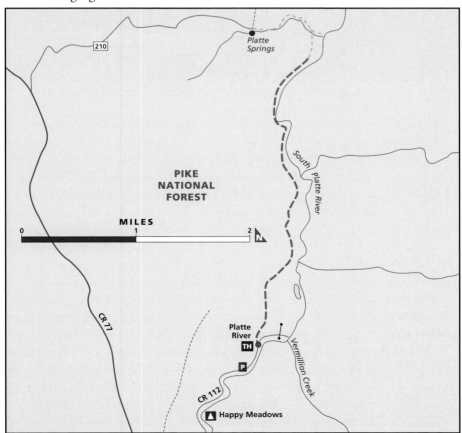

Chapter 3

North-Central Region

The Jacks Gulch Equestrian Campground and trails make for great family excursions.

This is truly an exceptional and horse-friendly area of Colorado, encompassing numerous city and county parks, many open space areas, two state parks, three national forests, and one national park, and offering hundreds, if not thousands, of miles of excellent equestrian trails for every skill level. One of the best-developed equestrian campgrounds in the state is located here, along with an impressive selection of overnight accommodations for horses and their owners. These range from family-oriented horse hotels to delightful bed-and-breakfasts.

The scenery varies significantly in the north-central region, primarily due to the substantial elevation range (5,150–11,350 feet) and the diversity of ecosystems. At lower elevations near metropolitan areas, the landscape is comprised of short- and midgrass prairies often bordered by varying types of brush and gambel oak. Lower mountain ranges and foothills decorated in juniper and piñon pine offer unique rock outcroppings and fabulous views. The upper elevations of the region feature deep river canyons and majestic mountain peaks veiled by assorted evergreen and aspen. The almost desertlike plains are home to raptors, colonies of prairie dogs, coyotes, pronghorns, and many species of birds, while moose, deer, elk, beavers, and mountain lions favor the higher elevations. The north-central region can be referenced on DeLorme *Colorado Atlas & Gazetteer* maps 17–20 and 27–30.

Accommodations

 Beaver Meadows Resort

100 Marmot Drive, Unit 1	970-881-2450; 1-800-462-5870
Red Feather Lakes, CO 80545	www.beavermeadows.com

Wonderful Beaver Meadows Resort is a recreational wonderland, with plenty of parking, a riding stable for rental horses, restaurant, bar, gift shop, picnic tables, fishing ponds, public restrooms, meeting rooms, sauna/showers, paddle boats, horseshoes, volleyball, 50-foot round pen, guides services, and catering. The resort offers a variety of overnight accommodations to suit nearly anyone's style and budget, including lodge rooms, condominiums, log cottages, family cabins, 10 tent campsites, and 14 RV sites with vault toilets (no electricity, water, or sewer hookups). There are also three riverside sites (24, 25, and 26). Electric fences or portable panels can be used. Water is available for horses at the creek or at the base facilities. Three outside paddocks (16 by 16 feet) are available at the barn.

 Copper Top Acres

4625 Kiva Drive	970-221-4382
Laporte, CO 80535	E-mail: lljtc4x4149@cs.com

Lee and Lora Lee Carter are the warm and friendly host and hostess of this charming equine bed-and-breakfast. Located 6 miles northwest of Fort Collins at the intersection of CR 54G and US 287, Copper Top is just minutes from Horsetooth Mountain Park, Lory State Park, and numerous other riding opportunities. Copper Top's beautiful new barn offers three 12-by-12-foot stalls with 12-by-42-foot runs and a 120-by-90-foot arena and wash rack. Hay is available for a fee. The bed-and-breakfast allows RV hookup with electrical and water or can provide an air-conditioned bedroom and bath in the home as well as a delicious homemade breakfast. Call for directions, pricing, and reservations.

 Cross Creek Ranch

8050 W. CR 80	970-219-1569
Livermore, CO 80536	www.cross-creek-ranch.com • E-mail: alan@cross-creek-ranch.com

Similar to an equine bed-and-breakfast but without the breakfast, Cross Creek Ranch lets you experience a little piece of history when you overnight here. Enjoy the beautifully decorated original homestead log cabin, complete with two single beds, a sofa bed, and private bath, or hook up your living-quarter RV or camper at the barn for water and electric. For the horses, Cross Creek offers nice, clean, large paddocks with loafing sheds that are large enough to be shared; box stalls; an arena; and a round pen. Cross Creek is just 20 miles north of Fort Collins, conveniently located 3 miles from the new Eagle's Nest Open Space and Red Feather Lakes Rd. (CR 74E) for access to many excellent trails.

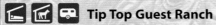

Tip Top Guest Ranch

Rist Canyon Road • P.O. Box 176   970-484-1215
Bellvue, CO 80512   www.tiptopranch.com

This is a lovely, remote, historic working ranch with overnight accommodations for horses and their owners, open from May through October. Rental horses with guides and overnight, dinner, or lunch rides are available. Overnight accommodations for personal horses are available in portable panel stalls, with water for horses accessible at the office. Owners are required to supply their own feed, valid health certificates, and Coggins test. Three rustic, historic, nonsmoking cabins with full kitchens and electricity (but no plumbing or bathroom facilities) are available for overnight stays. Dry camping is available for up to five campers (no electric or water hookups). The riding possibilities are practically unlimited on this 7,000-acre hidden gem of a ranch.

Rides

Estes Park and Rocky Mountain National Park
46 Bulwark Ridge Trail (No. 928) .. 151
47 North Fork Trail (No. 929) 153
48 Lawn Lake Trail 154
49 Ypsilon Lake Trail 157

Fort Collins/Loveland
50 Bobcat Ridge Natural Area.... 158
51 Eagle's Nest Open Space 160
52 Horsetooth Mountain Park ... 163
53 Lory State Park 166
54 Pineridge Natural Area 169
55 Vespers Trail 172

Jacks Gulch Campground and Trails at Pingree Park 173
56 Fish Creek Trail (No. 1009) 174
57 Flowers Trail (No. 939) 178
58 Jacks Gulch Trail/Cutoff Trail .. 180

Red Feather Lakes Area
59 Beaver Meadows Resort Ranch 182
60 North Lone Pine Trail (No. 953) 184

46 Bulwark Ridge Trail (No. 928)

Overall Ride Rating	♡♡♡♡♡
Trail Rating	Difficult
Distance	6 miles one way to the summit of Signal Mountain
Elevation	7,680–11,260 feet
Best Season	Summer through early fall
Main Uses	Equestrian, hiking, trailhead and backcountry camping
Trailhead Amenities	A nice equestrian trailhead with one horse corral that could accommodate one to two horses, restrooms with vault toilets, and an emergency phone. Parking is ample for large rigs. Self-contained units can overnight at the trailhead. There is no water, so bring your own for horses and humans.
Dogs	On leash
Shoes	Required
Maps	DeLorme *Colorado Atlas & Gazetteer*, pp. 19 and 29; National Geographic *Trails Illustrated Map 101, Cache la Poudre/Big Thompson* and *Map 200, Rocky Mountain National Park*
Contact	Roosevelt National Forest, Canyon Lakes Ranger District
Fees	None
Regulations	See the Trail Savvy section (p. 12), website and posted regulations for additional information.
Special Notes	There is no water on trail; make sure to tank up before leaving the trailhead.

The trail access is at the northern end of the parking area and doubles as the trailhead for the Signal Mountain Trail. The route ascends sharply on a rocky path about 18 inches wide for the first 0.75 mile, where it intersects the Indian Trail (No. 927). For the first 1.5 to 2 miles, it switchbacks steeply through dense forest, then levels off and opens up to meadows decorated with purple lupine, bluebells, and Indian paintbrush among yellow wildflowers. Riders can then begin a challenging climb for 2-plus miles and traverse the Comanche Peak Wilderness boundary to the top of Signal Mountain.

This is a warm, south-facing slope with spectacular views in all directions. The elevation gain is a significant 3,582 feet, so make sure that you and your horse are in good shape, take plenty of water, tank up before leaving the trailhead, and allow frequent rest breaks. The journey is 12 miles round-trip if you ride to the summit of Signal Mountain, so bring a picnic lunch.

Directions to Trailhead

From Loveland (exit 257B at I-25), travel 21 miles west on US 34 to Drake. At Drake, bear right (west) at the fork in the road toward Glen Haven traveling 6.4 miles on CR 43. Turn right onto CR 51B (Dunraven Glade Rd.) before you get to the little town of Glen Haven. You will see a Forest Service sign here. Travel approximately 2.25 miles northwest to the end of this well-maintained dirt-and-gravel road, where you'll find the trailhead.

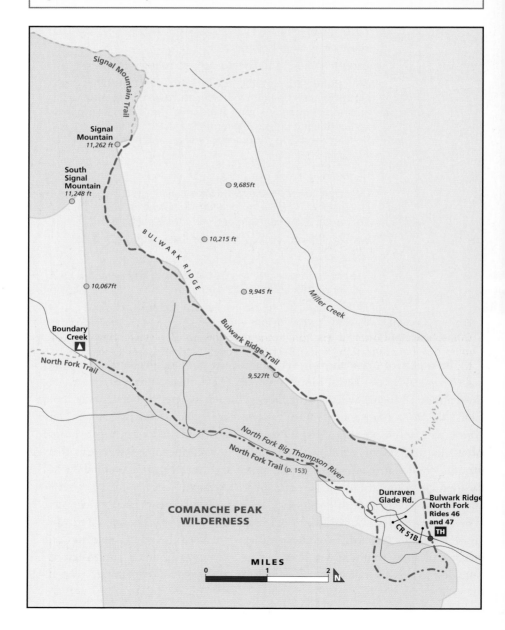

47 North Fork Trail
(No. 929) (For Trail Map see p. 152)

Overall Ride Rating	○○○○○
Trail Rating	Easy
Distance	4.5 miles one way
Elevation	8,010–8,880 feet
Best Season	Summer through early fall
Main Uses	Equestrian, hiking, trailhead and backcountry camping
Trailhead Amenities	See trailhead amenities for the Bulwark Ridge Trail (Ride 46, p. 151). There is water for the horses along the North Fork Trail.
Dogs	On leash
Shoes	Recommended
Maps	DeLorme *Colorado Atlas & Gazetteer*, pp. 19 and 29; National Geographic *Trails Illustrated Map 101, Cache la Poudre/Big Thompson* and *Map 200, Rocky Mountain National Park*
Contact	Roosevelt National Forest, Canyon Lakes Ranger District
Fees	None
Regulations	See the Trail Savvy section (p. 12), website and posted regulations for additional information.
Special Notes	There is no water on the trail.

Directions to Trailhead

From Loveland (exit #257B at I-25), travel 21 miles west on US 34 to Drake. At Drake, bear right (west) at the fork in the road toward Glen Haven traveling 6.4 miles on CR 43. Turn right onto CR 51B (Dunraven Glade Rd.) before you get to the little town of Glen Haven. You will see a Forest Service sign here. Travel about 2.25 miles northwest to the end of this good dirt-and-gravel road.

This trail begins on the northwest side of the lot, dropping abruptly to the North Fork of the Big Thompson River and crossing the stream many times. After the first mile or so, you leave the Comanche Peak Wilderness and enter private land owned by Cheley Colorado Camps. Please be respectful and stay on the designated trail through this area. Shortly after, you reenter the wilderness and pass several campsites. Continue on to find the remains of a 1913 cabin. Five more campsites can be found uphill from here.

Now the trail begins to leave the river and wind its way 1.5 miles to the border of Rocky Mountain National Park. If you want to extend your ride, you can continue past the park boundary another 5.5 miles to Lost Lake, just below the Continental Divide. The minimal elevation gain and 2-to-3-foot-wide dirt path makes this a fairly easy trail for the first 4.5 miles.

48 Lawn Lake Trail

Overall Ride Rating	∪∪∪∪∪
Trail Rating	Moderate
Distance	5.75 miles one way
Elevation	8,540–11,000 feet
Best Season	Summer through fall. Call the park for weather conditions, as snow is possible as late as July and as early as September.
Main Uses	Equestrian, hiking, backcountry camping, fishing
Trailhead Amenities	Parking for four to five large rigs, with picnic tables, hitching posts, and a stock-loading ramp. Restrooms are located just a short distance west of the trailhead and parking area. No water is available at the trailhead, but streams provide water for horses on the trail. People should bring their own drinking water.
Dogs	Not allowed on trails in Rocky Mountain National Park and must be on leash in picnic areas, campgrounds, along roadsides, and in developed areas
Shoes	Recommended
Maps	DeLorme *Colorado Atlas & Gazetteer*, p. 29; National Geographic *Trails Illustrated Map 200, Rocky Mountain National Park;* Rocky Mountain National Park map (www.nps.gov/romo/pphtml/maps.html)
Contact	Rocky Mountain National Park
Fees	$20 vehicle pass required; valid for up to seven days
Regulations	Stay on marked trails. Permits are required for backcountry camping, which is allowed with horses for groups of 10 riders or less. Camp a minimum of 200 feet from any trails or water source. See the Trail Savvy section (p. 12), website and posted regulations for additional information. Certified weed-seed-free hay or processed/pelletized feed is required for stock.
Special Notes	There is heavy traffic in the park. Many park visitors may not be familiar with the needs of equestrians. Please understand and help by communicating to other park users. This is a high-altitude trail, so use care when planning your trip. Riding this trail in wet or cold weather is not recommended.

Directions to Trailhead

Take US 34 west from Loveland to Estes Park, or follow US 36 north and west from Boulder and turn left onto US 34 at Estes Park. Follow US 34 into Rocky Mountain National Park via the Fall River entrance station. You will receive a map at the park entrance. At this point, US 34 is also known as Trail Ridge Rd. Follow the road 2.2 miles to the Lawn Lake trailhead within Horseshoe Park and just past Sheep Lakes. Use the equestrian parking lot, which is about 0.25 mile west of the Lawn Lake trailhead on the left.

From the parking lot, cross Fall River Rd. The Lawn Lake Trail is a steady climb from start to finish, so be sure to give your horse a breather whenever he needs one. As you climb up the face of Bighorn Mountain, you are rewarded with gorgeous views of West Horseshoe Park and Sheep Meadow. The trail is mostly narrow and rocky. It is often best to give your horse his head and let him pick his way. Soon you overlook the Roaring River at Horseshoe Falls. At about 0.3 mile, you need to negotiate a set of switchbacks on your way to the junction with the Ypsilon Lake Trail at 1.5 miles (see Ride 49, p. 157). Stay on the Lawn Lake Trail by continuing along the Roaring River drainage to the right. The flora is as diverse and multicolored in the autumn as it is in the summer and the views get better with each bit of elevation gained. Riders will pass several designated backcountry campsites, Horseshoe Lake and Ypsilon Lake, along the way. The Black Canyon Trail joins the Lawn Lake Trail at 5 miles. The Lawn Lake Trail becomes the Crystal Lake/Saddle Trail at 5.8 miles as you reach beautiful Lawn Lake itself. The terrain is rocky and the pines become sparse as treeline nears. A marvelous view of Longs Peak is a fitting finale to this gorgeous ride.

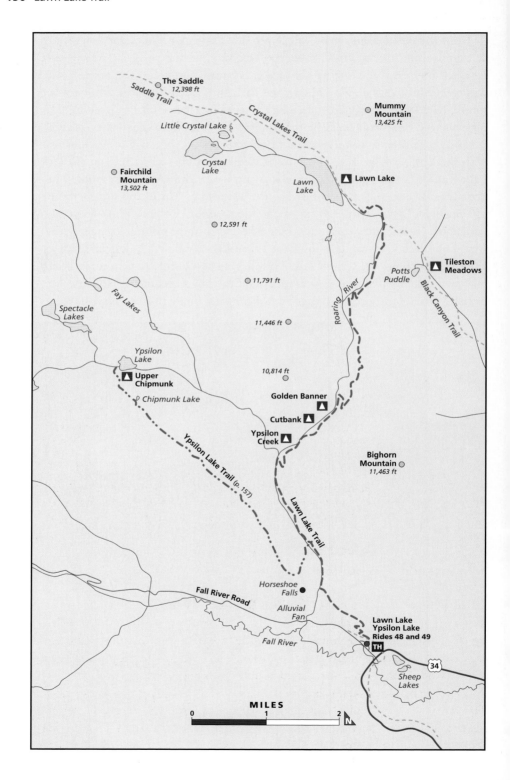

The Saddle
12,398 ft

Saddle Trail

Crystal Lakes Trail

Mummy
Mountain
13,425 ft

Little Crystal Lake

Crystal
Lake

Fairchild
Mountain
13,502 ft

Lawn
Lake

Lawn Lake

12,591 ft

11,791 ft

Fay Lakes

Spectacle
Lakes

Roaring River

Potts
Puddle

Tileston
Meadows

Black Canyon Trail

11,446 ft

Ypsilon
Lake

Upper
Chipmunk

Chipmunk Lake

10,814 ft

Golden Banner

Cutbank

Ypsilon
Creek

Bighorn
Mountain
11,463 ft

Ypsilon Lake Trail (to 157)

Lawn Lake Trail

Fall River Road

Horseshoe
Falls

Alluvial
Fan

Lawn Lake
Ypsilon Lake
Rides 48 and 49

TH

34

Fall River

Sheep
Lakes

MILES

0   1   2   N

49 Ypsilon Lake Trail

(For Trail Map see p. 156)

Overall Ride Rating	booboo
Trail Rating	Moderate
Distance	4.5 miles one way
Elevation	8,540–10,750 feet
Best Season	Summer through fall; call the park for weather conditions
Main Uses	Equestrian, hiking, backcountry camping, fishing
Trailhead Amenities	See trailhead amenities for the Lawn Lake Trail (Ride 48, p. 154)
Dogs	Not allowed on trails in Rocky Mountain National Park, and must be on leash in picnic areas, campgrounds, along road-sides, and in developed areas
Shoes	Recommended
Maps	DeLorme *Colorado Atlas & Gazetteer,* p. 29; National Geographic *Trails Illustrated Map 200, Rocky Mountain National Park;* Rocky Mountain National Park map (www.nps.gov/romo/pphtml/maps.html)
Contact	Rocky Mountain National Park
Fees	$20 vehicle pass required; valid for up to seven days
Regulations	Stay on marked trails. Permits are required for backcountry camping, which is allowed with horses for groups of 10 riders or less. Camp a minimum of 200 feet from any trails or water source. See the Trail Savvy section (p. 12), website and posted regulations for additional information. Certified weed-seed-free hay or processed/pelletized feed is required for stock.
Special Notes	There is heavy traffic in the park. This is a high-altitude trail, so use care when planning your trip. Don't ride this trail in wet or cold weather.

Directions to Trailhead

See directions for the Lawn Lake Trail (Ride 48, p. 154)

From the parking lot, cross Fall River Rd. To access the Ypsilon Lake Trail, begin on the Lawn Lake Trail and turn left after the first 1.5 miles at a clearly signed intersection. Give your horse rest when needed on this steadily climbing segment. At the Ypsilon Lake Trail junction, cross the Roaring River just below the walking bridge. The entry, exit, and creek bed are very rocky.

The trail then makes a sharp turn and begins a long climb via stair steps. This narrow, rocky trail is steep; proceed another 2.5 miles toward Chipmunk Lake. The forest is dense here. Be careful with your mount, as the trail can be tricky. Keep an eye out for wildlife. Ypsilon Lake lies 0.5 mile beyond at a slightly lower elevation than Chipmunk Lake.

50 Bobcat Ridge Natural Area

Overall Ride Rating	♻♻♻♻♻
Trail Rating	Easy, moderate, and difficult trails
Distance	12 miles of trails total: 5 miles opened in fall 2006; an additional 7 miles is projected to open in late 2007
Elevation	6,000–7,500 feet
Best Season	Year-round
Main Uses	Equestrian, hiking, mountain biking. A portion of the trail is handicap accessible.
Trailhead Amenities	Parking is available for six rigs, with portable toilet, picnic area, informational signage, and water for horses. Bring your own drinking water.
Dogs	Not allowed
Shoes	Recommended
Maps	DeLorme *Colorado Atlas & Gazetteer,* p. 30
Contact	City of Fort Collins Natural Areas
Fees	None
Regulations	Riders must stay on or within 10 feet of trails. See the Trail Savvy section (p. 12), website and posted regulations for additional information.
Special Notes	Be watchful of bear and elk.

Directions to Trailhead

From I-25 take US 34 at the Loveland exit west for 10.6 miles to CR 27. A directional sign at the intersection reads Masonville/Big Thompson Elementary School. Turn right (north) on CR 27 for approximately 4 miles and turn left (west) onto CR 32C. This turn is hidden behind a cluster of trees and is very easy to miss. The turn is just before the Masonville post office. (If you get to the T intersection in Masonville where CR 27 turns west and the Mercantile store is on your right hand, or southeast corner, you have missed the turn. Turn around and go back 0.5 mile south.) The parking area for Bobcat Ridge Natural Area is 0.5 mile beyond the turn at 32C.

ALTERNATE DIRECTIONS: From Denver, take I-25 north to the Harmony Road/Timnath exit (Exit 265) and turn left (west) on Harmony Road. Continue 7 miles to the Taft Hill Rd. intersection, where the road becomes CR 38E. Continue around the southern end of Horsetooth Reservoir to the small town of Masonville and turn left (south) on CR 27 at Masonville Mercantile and continue for 0.5 mile. Then turn right (west) on CR 32C, the trailhead is 0.5 mile ahead. It is easier to see the turn at CR 32C from this direction. However, this route will require traveling on steeper, windy grade around the reservoir.

Saddle Up, Colorado! was given the opportunity to visit this new Natural Area in its developmental stages and prior to its official opening. As such, changes may occur between the parks conceptual phase and its final installation. However, with significant improvements and future additional miles of trails, this open space park promises to be a premier park for equestrians. The Bobcat Gulch forest fire of 2000 burned many trees, providing natural clearings with exceptional views from within the park. At the same time, many areas remain untouched by the fire, leaving behind mature ponderosa pine trees and a wide variety of brush and shrubs. Among the park's unique features are fabulous rock outcroppings to the north. The easy prairie sections of trail have an earthen base and are gentle for bare hooves. The land was recently a working ranch, so you'll find several nice roads for trotting and galloping your horse safely. The easier valley loop trail could prove to be a good training place for both horses and riders.

Wild turkey and deer frequent the gently rolling hillsides and the wet-season water crossings. On the more difficult Ginny Trail, a ridge trail that makes a loop, the footing is rocky and a bit rough. When open in 2007, the upper section of trails will provide more challenges for the seasoned horse and rider. The Ginny Trail will be the most difficult, climbing the rockiest and most challenging ridge to Mahoney Park. If you can only make a couple of trips with your horse this season, put Bobcat Ridge on your must-ride list. You are certain to enjoy every minute of the time you spend here.

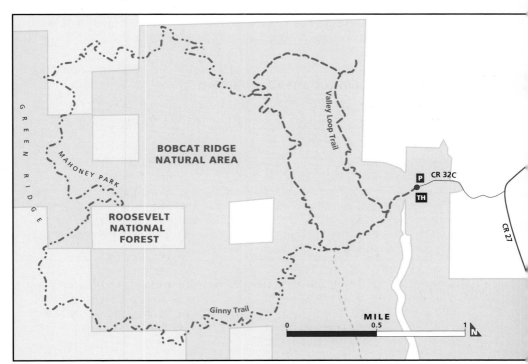

51 Eagle's Nest Open Space

Overall Ride Rating	●●●○○
Trail Rating	Easy
Distance	4.8 miles consisting of two connecting loops
Elevation	8,660 feet
Best Season	Year-round
Main Uses	Equestrian, hiking
Trailhead Amenities	Nice large loop trailhead with designated horse trailer parking for four to six rigs, depending on size. Restrooms and trash service are available, but no water. Bring your own for horses and humans.
Dogs	On leash
Shoes	Barefoot okay
Maps	DeLorme *Colorado Atlas & Gazetteer*, p. 20; Larimer County Parks and Open Lands map, Eagle's Nest Open Space (www.co.larimer.co.us/parks/eagles_nest.htm)
Contact	Larimer County Parks and Open Lands
Fees	None
Regulations	Rock climbing, fires, firearms, bicycles, motorized vehicles, fireworks, and camping are prohibited. See the Trail Savvy section (p. 12), website and posted regulations for additional information.
Special Notes	This is a day-use only park closed from sunset to sunrise. The "dusk-to-dawn" gate at the trailhead opens and closes automatically—please time your ride accordingly. The OT Trail is closed from February 1 to July 15 to accommodate eagles during their annual nesting period at Eagle's Nest Rock.

Directions to Trailhead

Take US 287 north from Fort Collins to Livermore. Turn west (left) at CR 74E (Red Feather Lakes Rd.) at the Forks Restaurant and continue approximately 0.25 mile to the Eagle's Nest Open Space entrance, just past the fire station on the left (south) side of the road. Follow the entrance road for about 1 mile and across two cattle guards to the trailhead parking area.

This scenic journey across former ranch lands promises fantastic and far-reaching views of the Laramie foothills. The land is home to many species of wildlife, but gets its name from the nesting golden eagle that has used the rocky face of the monolith for some 100 years. The gently sloping natural terrain begins as a single-track trail, leaving the trailhead in a southwestern direction on the 3-Bar Trail. You need to dismount three times as you open and close swinging gates. This is due to the livestock grazing rights in the area. These gates close automatically, so please use caution and don't let go until your horse has safely passed through. The land is a mix of prairie and riparian areas trimmed in summer wildflowers or flanked by cottonwood washes. Colorful layers of rock form high, mountainous ridges.

The 3-Bar Trail connects with the OT Trail via a significant and horse-safe bridge over the North Fork of the Cache la Poudre River, which is a nice place to water the horses. This can also be a good fishing spot, but please respect the seasonal closures from February to mid-July (see Special Notes) to protect the eagles' nesting habitat. The return trip back toward the trailhead becomes a double-track trail, which presents a nice opportunity for side-by-side riding or a terrific place to practice your trot and canter. This open space park is also an excellent place for ponying or training a young horse.

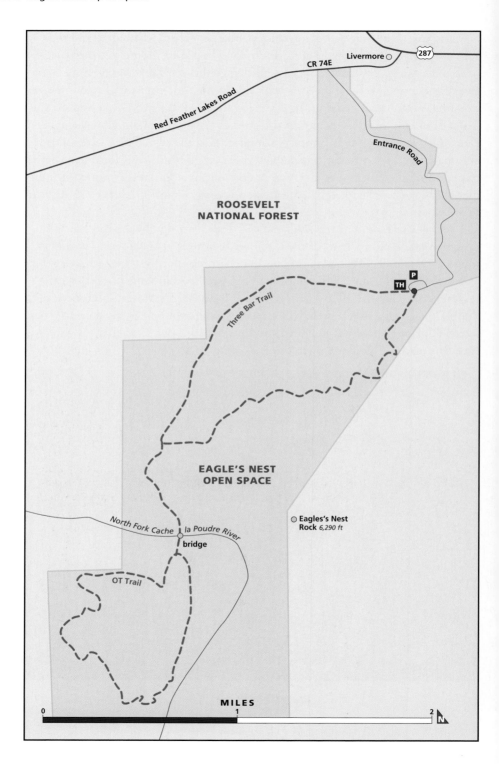

Livermore

CR 74E

287

Red Feather Lakes Road

Entrance Road

**ROOSEVELT
NATIONAL FOREST**

P

TH

Three Bar Trail

**EAGLE'S NEST
OPEN SPACE**

○ **Eagles's Nest
Rock** *6,290 ft*

North Fork Cache

la Poudre River

bridge

OT Trail

MILES

0   1   2

N

52 Horsetooth Mountain Park

Overall Ride Rating	UUUUU
Trail Rating	Easy, moderate, and difficult trails
Distance	29 miles of connecting trails and loops
Elevation	5,430–7,230 feet
Best Season	Year-round
Main Uses	Equestrian, hiking, backcountry camping, mountain biking
Trailhead Amenities	A fairly large loop-around parking area with eight designated pull-in spots for horse trailers at the north end. The lot can be a little tight for larger rigs, especially on weekends, but it can be managed. Plan to arrive early. There are also covered picnic tables, a kiosk map, restroom, water fountain, water spigot, hitching rails, barbeque grills, and trash receptacles.
Dogs	On leash
Shoes	Required
Maps	DeLorme *Colorado Atlas & Gazetteer*, p. 20; Larimer County Parks and Open Lands map, Horsetooth Mountain Park (www.co.larimer.co.us/parks/Htmp.htm)
Contact	Larimer County Parks and Open Lands
Fees	Park permits are $6 daily or $65 yearly for county residents ($75 for non-residents). The fine for not acquiring a permit is $50. The park passes are currently valid at Horsetooth Reservoir, Horsetooth Mountain Park, Carter Lake, Pinewood Reservoir, Flatiron Reservoir, Ramsay-Shockey Open Space, and Lory State Park. Permits can be purchased at the entrance station, the self-service stations prior to entering the park, Lory State Park, and the Bison Visitor Center in Fort Collins.
Regulations	Camping is allowed in the backcountry with horses, but there are no designated sites. Campsite fires are prohibited. Bring water for rider and horse, since springs here are unreliable. Two permits are required: the standard daily entrance fee plus a backcountry camping permit (no charge). Fires, firearms, fireworks, firewood collection, and hunting are prohibited. See the Trail Savvy section (p. 12), website and posted regulations for additional information.
Special Notes	The prairie rattlesnake is the only poisonous snake in the foothills and is often spotted along the Horsetooth Falls Trail, the Soderberg Trail, and the service road. Garter snake, bull snake, and milk snake sightings are also frequent.

Directions to Trailhead

From Denver, take I-25 north to the Harmony Road/Timnath exit (Exit 265) and turn left (west) on Harmony Road. Continue 7 miles to the Taft Hill Rd. intersection, where the road becomes CR 38E. Head west on CR 38E approximately 4 more miles to the entrance at the south end of the reservoir. Another 2.3 miles past this is the trailhead and self-pay station on your right side. From Loveland, go north on Wilson Ave. until it becomes Taft Hill Rd. in Fort Collins. Turn left (west) onto County Road 38E and continue west to the reservoir.

Horsetooth Mountain Park, including Soderberg Open Space and Horsetooth Open Space, comprises a scenic, 2,700-plus-acre region to the west of Horsetooth Reservoir. Horsetooth Rock is one of the most outstanding features in the park and is a familiar landmark in Larimer County. The park is also known for waterfalls and tremendous views of the Front Range and the foothills of Larimer County. This park connects to Lory State Park via the Mill Creek Trail to the northwest and the Nomad Trail to the northeast. Most of the terrain in the park consists of natural-dirt and rocky trail surfaces. Vegetation is abundant, from prairie grasses, shrubs, and wildflowers to piñon pine, juniper, and even ponderosa pine.

There is something for everyone and every skill level at this park, with trails ranging from easy to difficult. Among the easier trails are Soderberg, Carey

Springs, Nomad, and the new Swan Johnson. For a little more challenge, try one of the moderate trails: Spring Creek, Westridge, Wathen, Herrington, Stout, Sawmill, Loggers, Horsetooth Rock, and Audra Culver. Only experienced riders and horses should test the difficult but breathtaking Horsetooth Falls or Mill Creek trails. The Horsetooth Falls Trail is narrow with steep drop-offs and gets much use from hikers. Segments may require hand-leading your mount.

The park has recently added a new trailhead at the historic Soderberg family homestead. This east entrance to the park is located just off of CR 25G, north of Inlet Bay Marina and the Inlet Bay North Campground. This new trail connects with Towers Road and the Nomad Trail and is also a great way to access the Stout and Loggers trails. Mule deer, black bears, and mountain lions reside in Horsetooth Mountain Park.

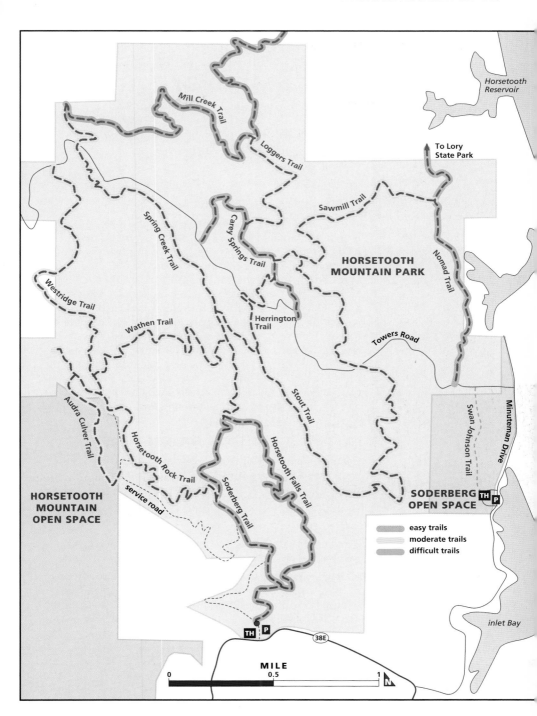

Horsetooth Reservoir

Mill Creek Trail

Loggers Trail

To Lory State Park

Sawmill Trail

Spring Creek Trail

Carey Springs Trail

Nomad Trail

HORSETOOTH MOUNTAIN PARK

Westridge Trail

Wathen Trail

Herrington Trail

Towers Road

Audra Culver Trail

Horsetooth Rock Trail

Stout Trail

Horsetooth Falls Trail

Swan Johnson Trail

Minuteman Drive

SODERBERG OPEN SPACE TH P

service road

Soderberg Trail

HORSETOOTH MOUNTAIN OPEN SPACE

easy trails
moderate trails
difficult trails

inlet Bay

TH P

38E

MILE

0   0.5   1

N

53 Lory State Park

Overall Ride Rating	✪✪✪✪✪
Trail Rating	Easy to difficult
Distance	12.6 miles of out-and-back and loop trails
Elevation	5,490–5,610 feet
Best Season	Year-round
Main Uses	Equestrian, hiking, mountain biking
Trailhead Amenities	The visitor center is near the entrance of the park and offers restrooms, park information, maps, and a water fountain. Bring water for riders and horses or use the water hydrant at the visitor center, as there is little water on the trails and none at the several parking areas. You can park at Soldier Canyon Parking at the Double Diamond Stables (rental horses available), which has restrooms, or the Eltuck parking area, with restrooms and picnic tables. Both lots can accommodate six to eight trailers (depending on parking). The South Valley lot is at the far south end of the park. The second to the last lot, just north of Arthur's Rock, is the best pull-through lot, with room for 6–10 rigs. This lot accesses all the trails but has no other amenities. Do not attempt to park at Arthur's Rock (the last lot), as there is no turnaround for trailers.
Dogs	On leash
Shoes	Required on the Mill Creek and Timber Trails
Maps	DeLorme *Colorado Atlas & Gazetteer*, p. 20; Colorado State Parks map, Lory State Park (http://parks.state.co.us)
Contact	Lory State Park
Fees	$5 entrance fee, also valid at Horsetooth Mountain Park (see Ride 52, p. 163)
Regulations	No camping with horses. See the Trail Savvy section (p. 12), website and posted regulations for additional information.
Special Notes	Watch for snakes. Call in advance for winter trail conditions. Hunting is allowed at certain times of year. Call ahead for information on where hunters may be in the park and outfit yourself and your mount in blaze orange. No backcounty camping with horses.

Directions to Trailhead

Take US 287 north from Fort Collins through Laporte and then turn left at the Bellvue exit onto CR 23N. Turn left again, go 1.4 miles, and then take a right on CR 25G. Drive another 1.6 miles to the park entrance. See trailhead amenities for parking locations.

This beautiful state park was formerly ranch land owned by Dr. Charles A. Lory, president of Colorado State University from 1909–1940. The park is bordered on the east by Horsetooth Reservoir and connects to the Horsetooth Mountain Park via the Mill Creek and South Valley trails on the southern end. Most of the terrain is comprised of natural-dirt paths with some rocky areas. The park offers unique rock outcroppings; sandstone hogbacks; open, grassy, wildflower-filled meadows; rolling hillsides trimmed in shrubby vegetation; and ponderosa pine forests. An equestrian cross-country jumping course is located at the south end of the park in the South Valley Trail loop area. Lory offers five equestrian trails that vary from easy, level dirt paths along the reservoir and roadside to more challenging mountainous rides.

The Shoreline Trail is a narrow, flat, easy, one-way natural-dirt path 1 mile in length. It begins at the Arthur's Rock parking area and leads down to Horsetooth Reservoir, offering striking views of the sandstone hogback. The East Valley Trail is an easy 2.2-mile, gently sloping natural-dirt path that begins at the rental stable and runs south along the main road to the junction of the South Valley Trail. The trail has several branches east taking you down to the reservoir. You may also want to try the West Valley Trail, another easy natural-dirt path trail that parallels the main road on the west side for 2.3 miles. You can begin at the stables or the Eltuck Picnic Area, crossing the road and following it south to connect with the Mill Creek or South Valley trails. The South Valley Trail provides a nice 2.7-mile loop around a cross-country jumping course at the south end of the park. At the southernmost point of the loop, the trail offers an easy transition into Horsetooth Mountain Park via the Nomad Trail. The Mill Creek link is accessible from the west side of the South Valley Trail. This 0.9-mile stretch is significantly more challenging and rocky than the other trails in the park and makes a transition to the upper elevations of Horsetooth Mountain Park.

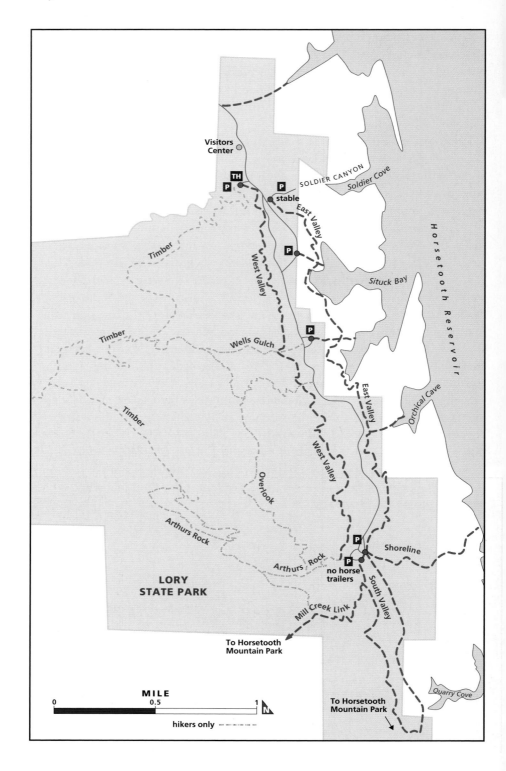

Visitors
Center

TH
P

stable

East Valley

SOLDIER CANYON

Soldier Cove

West Valley

Timber

P

Situck Bay

Horsetooth Reservoir

Timber

Wells Gulch

P

East Valley

Timber

West Valley

Orchical Cave

Overlook

Arthurs Rock

P

Shoreline

Arthurs Rock

P

no horse
trailers

South Valley

LORY
STATE PARK

Mill Creek Link

To Horsetooth
Mountain Park

MILE

0   0.5   1

N

hikers only

To Horsetooth
Mountain Park

Quarry Cove

54 Pineridge Natural Area

Overall Ride Rating	♦♦♦♦♦
Trail Rating	Easy
Distance	5.8 miles, plus miles of connecting loops
Elevation	5,150–5,300 feet
Best Season	Year-round
Main Uses	Equestrian, hiking, mountain biking
Trailhead Amenities	Parking easily accommodates large trailers along the north side of Horsetooth Rd. A portable toilet is located just prior to the trailhead entrance. Bring your own water for horses and humans. There's a drinking fountain at the dog park.
Dogs	Off leash in the fenced dog park area; on leash outside of the dog park
Shoes	Recommended
Maps	DeLorme *Colorado Atlas & Gazetteer,* p. 20; City of Fort Collins map, Pineridge Natural Area (http://fcgov.com/naturalareas/)
Contact	City of Fort Collins
Fees	None
Regulations	See the Trail Savvy section (p. 12), website and posted regulations for additional information.
Special Notes	Be watchful for rattlesnakes, prairie dog holes, waterfowl flying up from the brush around the reservoir, and bicyclists

Directions to Trailhead

From I-25 and the US 34 (Loveland exit), head west for approximately 6.5 miles to Wilson Ave. Turn right (north) on Wilson and travel approximately 8.9 miles to Horsetooth Rd., passing the trailhead for Coyote Ridge Natural Area/Rimrock Open Space and the Larimer County landfill. In Fort Collins, Wilson turns into S. Taft Hill Rd. Turn west (left) on Horsetooth and travel to a dead end at the trailhead. There is a second parking area available at the lot at CR 42C.

You will need to ride or lead your mount a short distance on Horsetooth Rd. to the trailhead entrance just past the dog park. There is little to no traffic, as this is a dead-end street, but you will most likely encounter numerous dogs.

Begin by riding west on the 0.6-mile Park Trail or due west on the 1-mile Ridge Trail, both gently sloping, wide, natural-dirt paths through short-grass prairie that gives way to hogbacks and the rolling foothills of Horsetooth Mountain. The Pineridge trails are well marked and well maintained. Each of these trails

intersects with others, allowing you to choose from a variety of different routes.

Among the most popular routes is the well-signed Foothills Trail, a 5.8-mile earthen trail that travels parallel to Horsetooth Reservoir from Dixon Reservoir to Campeau Open Space. Several small wooden bridges occur along narrow portions of this trail. The terrain becomes a little steeper, with a few rocky areas in places. Distant views of the peaks in Rocky Mountain National Park and the Horsetooth Dam can be enjoyed from atop the western ridge. The vegetation includes short-grass prairie decorated with wildflowers, mature cottonwood trees, various shrubs, and large areas of ponderosa pine. The park is home to a wide variety of wildlife, including deer, mountain lion, rabbits, foxes, coyotes, hawks, eagles, ospreys, pelicans, and a variety of songbirds. Combine one or more of the trails for shorter or longer loops connecting back to the trailhead and parking area, and enjoy the sights and sounds of this important transition area between the Eastern Plains and the Rockies.

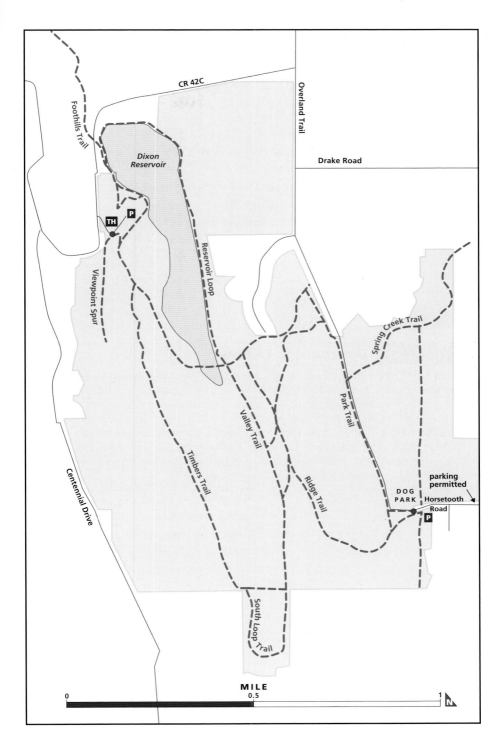

Dixon
Reservoir

CR 42C

Foothills Trail

Overland Trail

Drake Road

TH P

Viewpoint Spur

Reservoir Loop

Spring Creek Trail

Park Trail

Valley Trail

Timbers Trail

Ridge Trail

Centennial Drive

parking
permitted

DOG
PARK

Horsetooth
Road

P

South Loop Trail

MILE
0   0.5   1

N

55 Vespers Trail

Overall Ride Rating	♘♘♘♘♘
Trail Rating	Easy to moderate
Distance	1.5 miles one way, plus unlimited riding on 7,000 acres
Elevation	8,500–9,000 feet
Best Season	Open from May through October, call for availability.
Main Uses	Equestrian, hiking, hunting
Trailhead Amenities	This is a remote, historic working ranch with overnight accommodations for horses and riders. Water for horses is available at the office. See Accommodations (Tip Top Guest Ranch, p. 150) for information on camping, stabling, and amenities.
Dogs	Off leash, but must be kept away from ranch horses
Shoes	Recommended
Maps	DeLorme *Colorado Atlas & Gazetteer,* p. 20

Directions to Trailhead

From Fort Collins, take US 287 north. Do not take the 287 Bypass to Laramie. Continue 2 miles west to Laporte. Turn west on CR 52E (Rist Canyon Rd.). Go west through Bellvue and continue up the canyon approximately 12 miles. At the top of the switchback section of road, turn at the Tip Top Guest Ranch sign and continue to the brown metal gate. Please be sure to close the gate behind you. After going through the gate, continue about 1 mile down a steep, rough, dirt-and-gravel driveway. Do not attempt this road in bad weather or with an underpowered vehicle or oversized luxury rig.

The riding possibilities on this 7,000-acre private ranch are practically limitless. Because this is a working ranch, you experience typical ranch activities such as moving cattle from pasture to pasture and gathering the resident horses (about 30) in the early morning. Five riding trails offer unsurpassed scenery.

For the Vespers Trail, start at the ranch office and go west along a wagon track through an open gate. The land opens into a wide meadow with a pond on the left. Beautiful aspen trees border the area. Wildlife abounds here, and you may also encounter cattle on your ride. This path is rocky and has many tree roots, so watch the footing.

After a turn downhill and an ascent back up, the trail branches; stay left. At a prominent point, the trail ends with incredible views of Rocky Mountain National Park. Return to the ranch by the same route.

Jacks Gulch Campground and Trails at Pingree Park

Jacks Gulch Campground is an equestrian's dream come true: It includes a separate loop designed just for horses and mules and their humans. There are five sites in the trees (two back-in and three pull-through) with easy parking for large rigs. Each site includes a picnic table, fire grate, four pipe corrals, and a nearby dumpster for manure. The common area in the center of the loop includes restrooms with vault toilets, a water spigot (bring a hose if you need to connect to your camper), and a trash dumpster. There is no water or electrical hookups at individual sites. A day parking area for horse trailers is located on the main road just past the entrance and will accommodate four to five large rigs. Bring your own water, feed, and muck buckets. Availability is on a first-come, first-served basis for three of the five sites. Reservations are accepted at the group site, and individual sites 57 and 58 through www.ReserveAmerica.com or 1-800-678-2267. The campground is heavily used by equestrians during summer weekends. Plan to arrive early to ensure a spot. If the campground is full, there are several nice, large, level dispersed camping spots in the forest along Old Flowers Rd. Travel through the campground on the main road to its western side and pass through the gate. Here you can picket, hobble, or highline. Erecting electric fences in the lush meadows is a nice option as well. The campground host has a telephone available (credit card only) for emergencies only, and can be reached at 970-881-3530 ahead of time if you have other inquiries. No amenities are available at this location, but rigs could drive to the campground to access water and restrooms.

Best Season	Early summer to fall
Maps	DeLorme *Colorado Atlas & Gazetteer*, p. 19; National Geographic *Trails Illustrated Map 112, Poudre River/Cameron Pass*
Contact	Arapaho and Roosevelt National Forests, Canyon Lakes Ranger District
Dogs	On leash at campground and in the wilderness
Fees	There is no fee for day parking in order to ride the trails. However overnight camping at the equestrian sites at Jacks Gulch is $25.00 per night.
Regulations	Standard Forest Service and wilderness regulations apply. See the Trail Savvy section (p. 12), website and posted regulations for additional information.

Directions to Trailhead and Campground

From Fort Collins, drive 10 miles north on US 287. Turn left on CO 14 (at Ted's Place) and follow it 24 miles west through the Poudre Canyon to CR 63E (Pingree Park Rd.). Turn left (south) on CR 63E, cross the bridge, and drive 6.4 miles to Jacks Gulch on your right. Stop at the main kiosk sign on your right for information. The day-use parking is straight ahead at the end of the road. Overnight equestrian camping is at the first right.

56 Fish Creek Trail (No. 1009)

Overall Ride Rating	UUUUU
Trail Rating	Moderate
Distance	6.3 miles one way
Elevation	7,900–9,120 feet
Best Season	Late spring or early summer through fall
Main Uses	Equestrian, hiking, fishing, equestrian campground and backcountry camping,
Trailhead Amenities	See Jacks Gulch Campground information (p. 173).
Dogs	On leash at campground and in the wilderness
Shoes	Required
Maps	DeLorme *Colorado Atlas & Gazetteer,* p. 19; National Geographic *Trails Illustrated Map 112, Poudre River/Cameron Pass*
Contact	Arapaho and Roosevelt National Forests, Canyon Lakes Ranger District
Fees	There is no fee for day parking in order to ride the trails, however overnight camping at the equestrian sites at Jacks Gulch is $25.00 per night.
Regulations	Standard Forest Service and wilderness regulations apply. See the Trail Savvy section (p. 12), website and posted regulations for additional information.
Special Notes	Most of the trail is in the Comanche Peak Wilderness. Please observe wilderness regulations.

Directions to Trailhead

Follow directions to Jacks Gulch Campground (p.173) and park there. From the day parking area, take Old Flowers Rd. 1 mile west and head left (south) at the first fork onto the Little Beaver Creek Trail. At approximately 1 mile, the Fish Creek Trail intersects the trail and continues south. To start from the Fish Creek trailhead, travel 1.5 mile south of the Jacks Gulch Campground on CR 63E. Go past the Fish Creek trailhead sign on the right (west) and over the cattleguard. There is a nice parking area on the left (east) at the intersection with Monument Gulch Rd. Once you are tacked up and ready to ride, double back north a few feet through the gate (to avoid the cattleguard) and head up a steep incline on the hillside on the west side of the road to access the trail.

From the day parking area at Jacks Gulch Campground (see p. 173), take Old Flowers Rd. 1 mile west and head left (south) at the first fork onto the Little Beaver Creek Trail. You can ride side by side over and down the hill, crossing the stream and parklike meadow. Proceed through the gate and continue along this easy portion of trail, climbing only gentle hillsides for another mile until you reach the second Y, where the Fish Creek Trail intersects the Little Beaver Creek Trail and continues to the southwest and northeast.

You can also choose to start this trail a little farther south of Jacks Gulch (see Directions) at its actual trailhead. You begin here by riding up a hillside to the west just in front of the gate and cattleguard. The trailhead is 1 mile from the Comanche Peak Wilderness boundary. Continue in a west-southwest direction for 2 miles to reach the intersection with the Little Beaver Creek Trail.

From either access, the trail continues southwest, following the north side of Fish Creek. The narrow path winds through a forest of lodgepole pine and mountain mahogany intermixed with small flower-laden meadows. This area often receives its fair share of winter, and the trails bear evidence of Mother Nature's remnants come spring. You will likely need to cross fallen timber and duck below a few broken branches. In the last mile, the trail crosses the creek and descends southward to the Sky Ranch church camp. Here, the trail ends at its southernmost trailhead, which it shares with the Beaver Creek Trail. Beaver Creek lies just to the south.

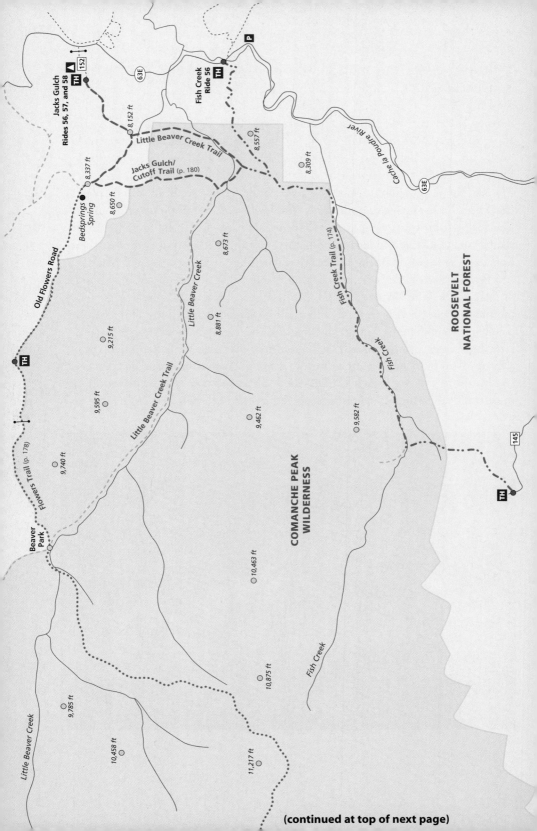

(continued at top of next page)

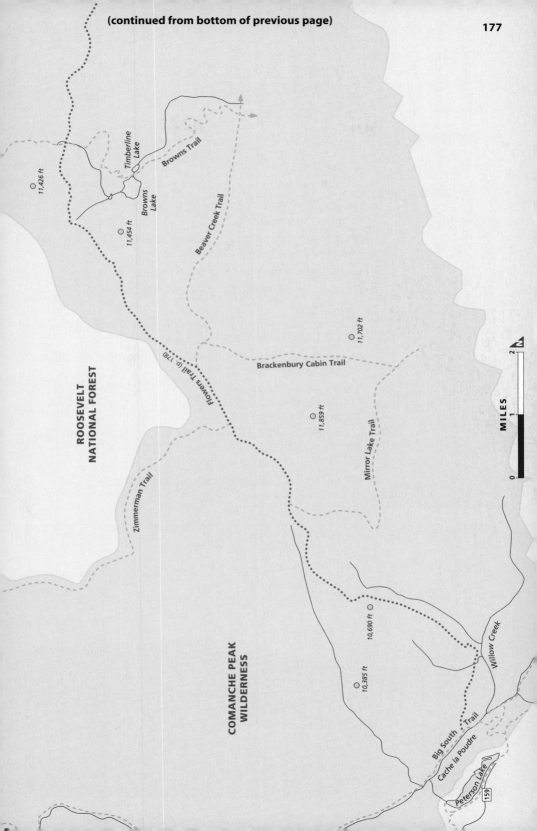

ROOSEVELT
NATIONAL FOREST

COMANCHE PEAK
WILDERNESS

Timberline
Lake

Browns
Lake

Browns Trail

Beaver Creek Trail

Brackenbury Cabin Trail

Mirror Lake Trail

Zimmerman Trail

Flowers Trail (p. 178)

11,426 ft

11,454 ft

11,702 ft

11,859 ft

10,690 ft

10,385 ft

Willow Creek

Big South Trail

Cache la Poudre

Peterson Lake

159

MILES

0   1   2

57 Flowers Trail
(No. 939) (For Trail Map see p. 176-177)

Overall Ride Rating	႘႘႘႘႘
Trail Rating	Moderate
Distance	18 miles one way; can loop with the Little Beaver Creek Trail
Elevation	9,000–11,350 feet
Best Season	Summer through fall
Main Uses	Equestrian, hiking, campground or (forest) dispersed camping. Motorized vehicles on Old Flowers Rd. only
Trailhead Amenities	See Jacks Gulch campground information (p. 173).
Dogs	On leash at campground and in the wilderness
Shoes	Recommended
Maps	DeLorme *Colorado Atlas & Gazetteer*, p. 19; National Geographic *Trails Illustrated Map 112, Poudre River/Cameron Pass*
Contact	Arapaho and Roosevelt National Forests, Canyon Lakes Ranger District
Fees	There is no fee for day parking in order to ride the trails. However overnight camping at the equestrian sites at Jacks Gulch is $25.00 per night.
Regulations	Standard Forest Service and wilderness regulations apply. See the Trail Savvy section (p. 12), website and posted regulations for additional information.
Special Notes	Most of the trail is in the Comanche Peak Wilderness. Please observe wilderness regulations.

| **Directions to Trailhead** |
See directions to Jacks Gulch Campground (p. 173)

Begin your ride heading west through the gate beyond the day parking area. Stay to the left on Old Flowers Rd. until you reach the well-signed junction with the Little Beaver Creek Trail. Here, stay right on the old road, formerly used as a wagon trail in the late 1800s. You ascend and descend slightly, making your way through giant meadows that are often painted with color by summer wildflowers, changing leaves, or layers of sediment from unique rock outcroppings. Soon you arrive at Bedsprings Spring, a seasonal spring and a nice watering spot for the horses when running. The actual trailhead lies another 2 miles ahead. Once at the trailhead, look for a commemorative plaque donated by the Colorado Mountain Club in honor of a World War II flight crew that crashed nearby in 1944.

The trail climbs gently uphill for about 1 mile from the trailhead until it drops into an area of beaver dams and ponds, appropriately named Beaver Park. Here, the trail meets Little Beaver Creek and the Little Beaver Creek Trail (No. 855). A wonderful loop is possible by taking the Little Beaver Creek Trail at this junction east back to Jacks Gulch Campground. If you decide to continue on the Old Flowers Trail, it begins a steep southward ascent for the next 4 miles, almost reaching timberline, then intersecting the Browns Trail (No. 941). It then continues its descent southwest 3.5 miles to intersect with the Beaver Creek Trail (No. 942), the Zimmerman Trail (No. 940), and the Mirror Lake Trail (No. 943). It finally culminates at the Big South Trail (No. 944) on the Cache la Poudre River, just east of pristine Peterson Lake. This is a wonderful backcountry journey with a multitude of excellent places to camp with stock along the way.

58 Jacks Gulch Trail/ Cutoff Trail (For Trail Map see p. 176)

Overall Ride Rating	UUUUU
Trail Rating	Easy to moderate
Distance	5-mile loop
Elevation	7,900–8,100 feet
Best Season	Early summer to fall
Main Uses	Equestrian, hiking, campground and dispersed camping, fishing
Trailhead Amenities	See Jacks Gulch Campground information (p. 173)
Dogs	On leash at campground and in the wilderness
Shoes	Required
Maps	DeLorme *Colorado Atlas & Gazetteer*, p. 19; National Geographic *Trails Illustrated Map 112, Poudre River/Cameron Pass*
Contact	Arapaho and Roosevelt National Forests, Canyon Lakes Ranger District
Fees	There is no fee for day parking in order to ride the trails. However overnight camping at the equestrian sites at Jacks Gulch is $25.00 per night.
Regulations	Standard Forest Service and wilderness regulations apply. See the Trail Savvy section (p. 12), website and posted regulations for additional information.

Directions to Trailhead

See directions to Jacks Gulch Campground (p. 173)

Jacks Gulch sits in a mixed forest of ponderosa pine and aspen interspersed with flower-laden meadows. The Comanche Peak Wilderness boundary lies just 0.5 mile to the south and 1 mile to the west and is home to numerous excellent equestrian trails. A short 1-mile equestrian trail around the campground called the Jacks Gulch Trail extends from the equestrian campsites on the northern edge of the property southwest to the

main trailhead on Old Flowers Rd., providing access to the Jacks Gulch Cutoff Trail, the Little Beaver Creek Trail, the Fish Creek Trail, and the Flowers Trail. You can also use Jacks Gulch as a base camp and drive a short distance to explore many additional miles of scenic trails.

For the Cutoff Trail, take the equestrian campground loop or ride west from the day parking area to Old Flowers Rd. After going through the gate, pass the first Y intersection with the Little Beaver Creek Trail and continue riding west to the second Y. The left fork takes you up a gently sloping hillside through a gate and into a lush meadow, painted with colorful wildflowers during the summer and luminous aspen during the fall. Descend a rocky hillside on your way down to the intersection with the Little Beaver Creek Trail. Once there, head left (east). Keep the creek on your right side as you navigate this single track and somewhat rocky terrain until you reach a T intersection. Head left (north) on the Little Beaver Creek Trail to make your way back to the trailhead and complete a fabulous loop.

59 Beaver Meadows Resort Ranch

Overall Ride Rating	ひひひひひ
Trail Rating	Easy, moderate, and difficult trails
Distance	25 miles of various loops
Elevation	8,400–9,030 feet
Best Season	Open year-round; equestrian activities best suited to late spring or early summer through fall
Main Uses	Equestrian, hiking, campground camping, mountain biking, fishing, hunting, cross-country skiing, ice skating, sleigh rides, snow tubing
Trailhead Amenities	See Accommodations (p. 149) for more information.
Dogs	On leash. Extra fee required for overnight accommodations
Shoes	Not required, but recommended on some trails
Maps	DeLorme *Colorado Atlas & Gazetteer*, p. 19; National Geographic *Trails Illustrated Map 111, Red Feather Lakes/Glendevey*
Contact	Beaver Meadows Resort Ranch (see Accommodations, p. 149)
Fees	No fees for using the trails. A wide variety of accommodations and activities are available. Call for pricing or visit the website (www.beavermeadows.com). Horse campsites are $35 per night. Overnight boarding at the barn in the stalls is $15 per night.
Regulations	Current health certificate or proof of vaccinations required. See the Trail Savvy section (p. 12), website and posted regulations for additional information.
Special Notes	Bring your own water bucket for horses if you are camping. Bring your own feed or you can purchase it at the ranch.

Directions to Trailhead

From Fort Collins, take US 287 (also known as College Ave.) northwest for 21 miles to Livermore. At Livermore, turn left (northwest) on CR 74E and travel 24.5 miles until you come to Red Feather Lakes. Continue until you see the Pot Belly Restaurant on the right side of the road and make a right (north) turn on CR 73C. It is 4.3 miles northwest to the ranch entrance. Continue past the log entryway to the main parking area.

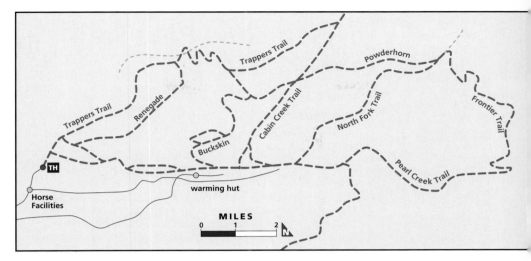

Beaver Meadows is a privately owned mountain resort and guest ranch that is open to the public for day use or overnight stays. The resort is located just north and west of the historic village of Red Feather Lakes, approximately one hour from Fort Collins and 100 miles from Denver. The resort lies in the picturesque North Fork of the Cache la Poudre River valley. The 840-acre ranch offers 25 miles of private trails that lead into 300,000 acres of the Roosevelt National Forest by special permit. This year-round destination presents guests with a variety of recreational opportunities, from cross-country skiing, snow tubing, and ice skating to trophy trout fishing. Equestrians can enjoy their own horses or indulge in the extensive horse program provided by the ranch, with options ranging from easy 1-hour rides to full-day excursions, private lessons, breakfast/dinner rides, and even sleigh rides through the winter wonderland. The trail system offers easy, wide, sandy/dirt roads through aspen and lodgepole pine forest; moderate, narrow, and gently sloping trails through lush green meadows and across streams; and more challenging mountain rides with spectacular vistas. The North Fork of the Cache la Poudre provides a natural source of water throughout the property. You'll enjoy a variety of vegetation, including forests of quaking aspen interspersed with lodgepole pine and, of course, numerous willow bordering the plentiful beaver ponds for which the resort was named. Along with the beaver, the ranch is home to deer, moose, and numerous bird species. Beaver Meadows Resort Ranch has something for everyone and is as horse-friendly as it gets.

60 North Lone Pine Trail (No. 953)

Overall Ride Rating	♘♘♘♘♘
Trail Rating	Easy to moderate
Distance	4.5 miles one way
Elevation	9,400–10,720 feet
Best Season	Summer to fall
Main Uses	Equestrian, hiking, dispersed and backcountry camping, mountain biking, cross-country skiing
Trailhead Amenities	This small trailhead will only accommodate two or three rigs depending on size. If possible, back in so that you can pull straight out. Three picnic tables and a kiosk information board are the only other amenities.
Dogs	Under voice and sight control
Shoes	Recommended
Maps	DeLorme *Colorado Atlas & Gazetteer*, p. 19; National Geographic *Trails Illustrated Map 111, Red Feather Lakes/Glendevey*
Contact	Arapaho and Roosevelt National Forests, Canyon Lakes Ranger District
Fees	None
Regulations	Standard Forest Service regulations apply. See the Trail Savvy section (p. 12), website and posted regulations for additional information.
Special Notes	Bring your own water, buckets, and feed for horses.

Directions to Trailhead

Travel 21 miles northwest of Fort Collins on US 287 (also College Ave.) to Livermore. At Livermore, turn left (northwest) on CR 74E (Red Feather Lakes Rd.) and travel for 22 miles, past the Red Feather Lakes community to CR 162. CR 162 also has a branch that turns to the south. Do not take this turn. When CR 162 becomes Deadman Gulch Rd., continue another 4 miles to the trailhead on your left. If there is no parking at the trailhead, use the nice, large pullout just before the trailhead on the right (north) or continue on to an excellent open area on the left (south) at the intersection of CR 162 and FR 300. Please note that ATV riders often use this parking area for access to nearby roads.

This lovely summer or fall ride travels southward from the trailhead along North Lone Pine Creek until the trail intersects FR 333 (an old logging road). You cross the creek several times, providing the horses with ample drinking opportunities. The third crossing can be a little more challenging than the first two, depending on how fast the water is flowing, so be sure to take your time and have a partner with reasonable water-crossing skills.

The terrain makes a gradual ascent, leaving the canopy of aspen and evergreen here and there. Several clearings in the forest expose incredible views of

Red Feather Lakes and South Bald Mountain. An unusual lime green, fernlike plant blankets the forest floor everywhere you look. The trail continues south past an abandoned Forest Service experimental station, North Bald Mountain, and Middle Bald Mountain before it ends at FR 517, a four-wheel-drive road. This is only 0.5 mile east of the 5.5-mile Killpecker Trail (No. 956), which would make an excellent loop if shuttle arrangements could be made between the Killpecker trailhead and the North Lone Pine trailhead just 3 miles east on CR 162. Please note that CR 162 would not be appropriate for riding back to your trailer due to the amount of vehicular traffic. For a shorter ride, travel south on the North Lone Pine Trail to the junction with FR 333 and go northwest, taking a hard right onto FR 333. Make another right onto FR 300 for 0.75 mile back to CR 162. Here, make yet another right and travel

another 0.75 mile back to the trailhead to complete the loop, keeping a careful watch on cars during this stretch on CR 162.

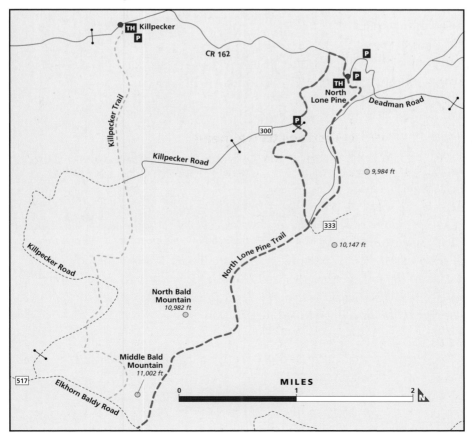

Chapter 4

Northwest Region

The northwest region of Colorado is an equestrian's paradise and should be at the top of every rider's list of places to travel with their equine partner. One could spend days, weeks, perhaps even months here and never set hoof on every trail that this beautiful land has to offer. As we can only devote one chapter to the northwest region in this statewide guide, we focus on the Flat Tops Wilderness, approximately 150 miles northwest of Denver. The area is defined by the Flat Tops Scenic and Historic Byway (CR 8) on the north, I-70 on the south, CO 13 on the west, and CO 131 on the east. CO 13, just east of the small town of Meeker, is the primary access to the trails and trailheads described on the following pages. See DeLorme *Colorado Atlas & Gazetteer* maps 22–26 and National Geographic *Trails Illustrated Map 122, Flat Tops NE/Trappers Lake* for trail and road information.

The Snell Creek trailhead offers a great scenic starting point.

The Flat Tops area is considered one of the birthplaces of the wilderness concept. In 1919, the U.S. Forest Service hired the landscape architect Arthur H. Carhart to survey the Trappers Lake area. Instead of development, Carhart recommended preservation of this unique and pristine area. Nearly 50 years later, in 1964, Congress passed the Wilderness Preservation Act, which would protect the innate character of the area for generations to come. Today, the Flat Tops Wilderness encompasses more than 267 square miles, two national forests, and hundreds of miles of superb trails. It offers excellent horse campgrounds, nearby RV parks, numerous dispersed camping spots, easily accessible trailheads, magnificent scenery, and plenty of wildlife viewing opportunities. Massive plateaus of rock and sediment, formed over hundreds of thousands of years of snow melt, erosion, and volcanic activity, dominate the landscape.

The area is home to Colorado's largest herd of elk and deer, in addition to coyotes, bear, beavers, mountain lions, many bird species, and the occasional bighorn sheep. Lush, grassy meadows grace numerous high lakes and willow-bordered ponds. The summer is a kaleidoscope of color, with a variety of wildflowers dotting the landscape. Fall presents vivid displays of yellows, oranges, and reds as quaking aspen stands contrast with the deep blues and greens of lodgepole pine, spruce, and fir. This area receives its fair share of precipitation. Daytime temperatures range from 40 degrees to 80 degrees in the summer months and below zero to 50 degrees in winter months. The wilderness is typically accessible between Memorial Day and Labor Day. Afternoon thunderstorms and lightning displays are common during the summer months and by November snowfall can be a daily occurrence.

Accommodations

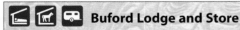 **Buford Lodge and Store**

20474 CR 8
Meeker, CO 81641 970-878-4745

The Buford Lodge and Store lies on the picturesque Flat Tops Scenic and Historic Byway, nestled on the banks of the White River in the White River National Forest, 22 miles east of Meeker. Ten rustic cabins are fully furnished with refrigerators, wood-burning cookstoves, electric coffeepots, eating and cooking utensils, and a screened porch or deck. Central modern restrooms and hot showers are just steps away. Two modern cabins also have full baths. Eight RV sites with electric and water are available.

Lodging is open from May 1 to mid-November. All cabins are nonsmoking units. Pets are allowed in cabin units for an additional fee or deposit. Corrals are available for horses. Owners must provide cleaning, feed, and buckets. Guided hunts for mule deer and elk are possible during rifle, archery, and black-powder big game hunting seasons.

River Camp RV Park, Campground, and Horse Hotel

38723 CO 13
Meeker, CO 81641

970-878-0805; 970-878-5677
www.whiterivercolorado.com • E-mail: info@whiterivercolorado.com

River Camp is a lovely, private, horse-friendly campground situated on 13 acres on CO 13. It offers 12 RV sites with electrical hookups and a potable water station on the property. A large fenced pasture for horses can be subdivided with your own portable panels or electric fencing. Your friendly hosts, Boots Campbell and her partner Walt, are very knowledgeable about the Flat Tops area and happy to share their wealth of trail knowledge. There are no trails on the property, but this is an excellent place to overnight on your way into or out of the Flat Tops.

Rides

**Horsethief Campground and
Trappers Lake Trails** 189
61 Carhart Trail (No. 1815) 190
62 Himes Peak Trail (No. 1877) ... 192
63 Stillwater Trail (No. 1814) 193
64 Trappers Lake Trail (No. 1816) 195
65 Wall Lake Trail (No. 1818) 197

**Marvine Campground and
Trailhead** 198
66 East Marvine Creek Trail
(No. 1822) 199
67 Marvine Creek Trail
(No. 1823) 201

Long Lost Trailhead 202
68 Long Park Trail (No. 1809) 203
69 Lost Creek Trail (No. 1808) and
Lost Park Trail (No. 1805) 205

Mirror Lake Trailhead 206
70 Big Ridge Trail (No. 1820) 207
71 Mirror Lake Trail (No. 1821) 209

Snell Creek Trailhead
72 Snell Creek Trail (No. 1810) 210

Horsethief Campground and Trappers Lake Trails

The Horsethief Campground, dedicated to equestrian use, is the best part of the Trappers Lake area. It sits near Trappers Lake at 9,900 feet elevation and accesses the Carhart, Himes Peak, Stillwater, Trappers Lake, and Wall Lake Trails. The Scotts Bay trailhead (for day use only) is best due to its excellent parking and turnaround space.

Horsethief Campground offers five pull-in/back-in sites with nice pipe corrals, as well as restrooms, picnic tables, grills, and trash service. Hookups are not available and the water is often not running, so bring your own. Trailer-parking skills are needed for this trip, especially for larger rigs. Campsites are on a first-come, first-served basis (no reservations).

Best Season	Summer to fall
Maps	DeLorme *Colorado Atlas & Gazetteer,* pp. 25 and 35; National Geographic *Trails Illustrated Map 122, Flat Tops NE/Trappers Lake*
Contact	Meeker Chamber of Commerce; White River National Forest, Blanco Ranger District
Dogs	On leash within 0.25 mile of Trappers Lake (except for dogs used as working stock, accompanying blind visitors, or used for legal hunting). Dogs should be on leash or under strict voice and sight control at all times.
Fees	Nightly camping fee is $15; a dump station is available at the Trappers Lake Campground for $5
Regulations	Locate campsites, campfires, and recreational stock 0.25 mile from lakeshores at Trappers, Hooper, Keener, and Smith Lakes. See the Trail Savvy section (p. 12), website and posted regulations for additional information.
Special Notes	Be cautious when riding and watch for standing dead timber. It can fall without warning. The area is also very popular with hunters beginning in October, so wear your blaze orange and be aware of hunters.

Directions to Trailhead and Campground

The Horsethief Campground is the equestrian section of the Trappers Lake camping area. It is best accessed by driving east from Meeker on CO 13 for 1 mile to the junction with CR 8. Turn right on CR 8 and continue for 39 miles, turning right (south) on FR 205 (North Fork Rd.). Go 10 miles to a fork in the road at the Trappers Lake Lodge on your left; take the right fork (a continuation of FR 205) over the bridge. The campground is 1 mile farther. **Do not take the left fork.** This dead-ends into the outlet trailhead (for car parking only), where it can be difficult if not impossible for a trailer to turn around.

61 Carhart Trail (No. 1815)

Overall Ride Rating	⋃⋃⋃⋃⋃
Trail Rating	Moderate
Distance	5 miles one way; can loop with connecting trails
Elevation	9,600–11,280 feet
Main Uses	Equestrian, hiking, campground and backcountry camping, fishing
Trailhead Amenities	See Horsethief Campground information (p. 189). A large gravel parking area at the Scotts Bay trailhead (day users only) also accommodates numerous large rigs and plenty of turnaround space. No water at Scotts Bay.
Shoes	Recommended

Directions to Trailhead

This trail can be accessed from the Scotts Bay trailhead near Trappers Lake and the Horsethief Campground (see directions, p. 189).

This trail circles one of the most beautiful natural lakes in Colorado and is restricted in many areas to foot and horse traffic only. A portion of the trail parallels the eastern shore of Trappers Lake, closely hugging the shoreline and offering a wonderful view of almost 300 acres of beautiful blue-green water. There is good fishing here, but you will need to familiarize yourself with the regulations. In addition to spectacular mountain views, you can also enjoy the alpine meadows surrounding the lake. As the trail reaches its farthest south-eastern point, it connects with the Trappers Lake Trail about 0.5 mile from the shore. Continuing west, then north and west again will allow you to connect with the Wall Lake Trail, adding additional mileage to your trip and completing a scenic loop back to the trailhead parking.

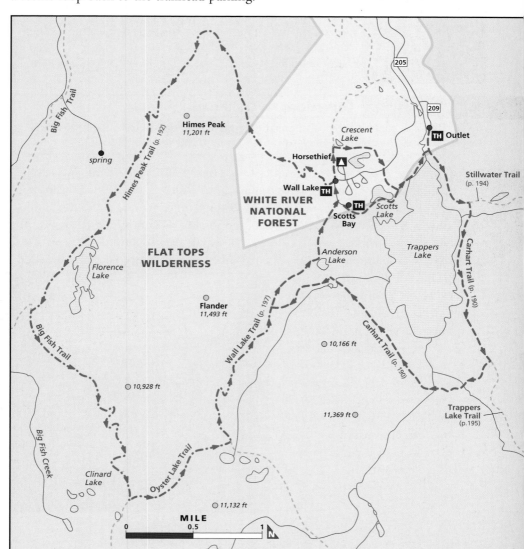

62

Himes Peak Trail
(No. 1877) (For Trail Map see p. 191)

Overall Ride Rating	♘♘♘♘♘
Trail Rating	Moderate
Distance	5 miles one way; can loop with connecting trails
Elevation	9,760–10,400 feet
Main Uses	Equestrian, hiking, campground and backcountry camping, fishing
Trailhead Amenities	See Horsethief Campground information (p. 189). A large gravel parking area at the Scotts Bay trailhead (day users only) also accommodates numerous large rigs and plenty of turnaround space. No water at Scotts Bay.
Shoes	Recommended

Directions to Trailhead

This trail can be accessed from the Scotts Bay and Wall Lake trailheads near Trappers Lake and the Horsethief Campground (see directions, p. 189).

This trail begins west and south of the Horsethief Campground and just a bit north of the Wall Lake trailhead (see Ride 65, p. 197) with a steep ascent to the meadow below Shepherds Rim. A more gradual climb for 2 miles then brings you around the northern point of 11,201-foot Himes Peak. At this point, the trail makes a sharp turn southward, descending nearly 600 feet through dense timber to Florence Lake almost 2 miles away. As you leave the lake, the trail meanders 0.5 mile west before reaching the junction with the Big Fish Trail. Continuing south along the Big Fish Trail for about 2 miles and then east on the Oyster Lake Trail makes a wonderful loop ride back to the trailhead via the Wall Lake Trail. You will encounter dense forest, beautiful mountain lakes, and rugged peaks before ending your journey.

63 Stillwater Trail (No. 1814)

Overall Ride Rating	UUUUU
Trail Rating	Moderate
Distance	5.5 miles one way; can loop with connecting trails or extend mileage
Elevation	9,720–11,230 feet
Main Uses	Equestrian, hiking, campground and backcountry camping, fishing
Trailhead Amenities	See Horsethief Campground information (p. 189). A large gravel parking area at the Scotts Bay trailhead (day use only) also accommodates numerous large rigs and plenty of turnaround space. No water at Scotts Bay.
Shoes	Recommended

Directions to Trailhead

This trail can be accessed from the Scotts Bay trailhead near Trappers Lake and the Horsethief Campground (see directions, p. 189).

Begin by going east out of the parking area, with Scotts Lake on your left and Trappers Lake on your right. After approximately 1 mile, this short trail around the southern part of the campgrounds and trailhead connects you to the Stillwater Trail. The actual trail begins at the northern tip of Trappers Lake heading south along the eastern shore of the lake for approximately 0.25 mile where it intersects the Carhart Trail and heads due east. This is where Cabin Creek begins its journey from Trappers Lake to Little Trappers Lake.

The trail offers a nice variety of scenery. At approximately 0.25 mile, you arrive at Coffin Lake, rumored to have good fishing. Another 0.5-mile ascent through a narrow canyon leads you to Little Trappers Lake, which is surrounded by lush, green meadows. From here, the massive Chinese Wall rises to an elevation of 11,225 feet. Shortly after leaving the lake, the trail begins to climb through stands of spruce and fir, victims of previous beetle infestation, until it emerges 2 miles later onto the plateau known as the Flat Tops. Continue east across the plateau for almost 1 mile to connect with the Chinese Wall Trail (an 18-mile trek north and south across the Flat Tops). You could also opt for a shorter route, taking the Bear River Trail for 3 miles to the lovely Stillwater Reservoir.

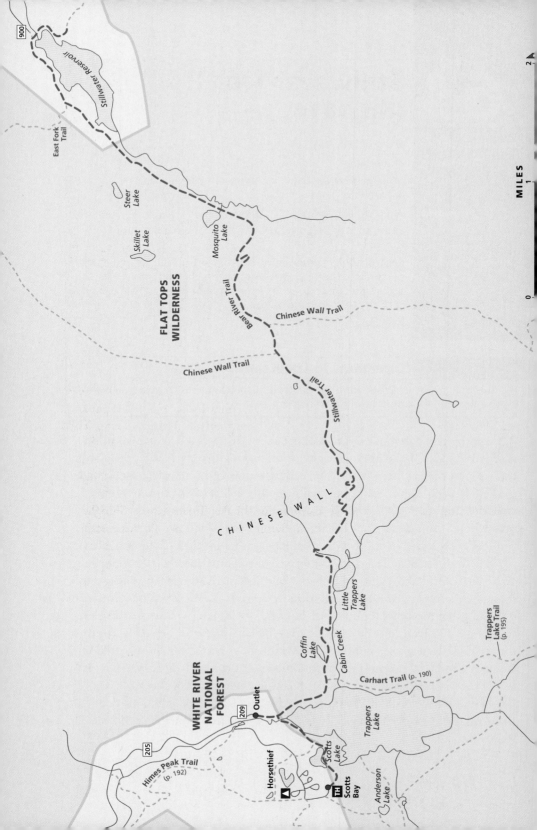

900

East Fork Trail

Stillwater Reservoir

FLAT TOPS
WILDERNESS

Steer
Lake

Skillet
Lake

Mosquito
Lake

Bear River Trail

Chinese Wall Trail

Chinese Wall Trail

Stillwater Trail

C H I N E S E   W A L L

Little
Trappers
Lake

Coffin
Lake

Cabin Creek

Carhart Trail (p. 190)

Trappers
Lake Trail
(p. 195)

WHITE RIVER
NATIONAL
FOREST

Outlet

209

205

Himes Peak Trail
(p. 192)

Horsethief

Scotts
Lake

Scotts Bay

Trappers
Lake

Anderson
Lake

MILES

0   1   2

64 Trappers Lake Trail (No. 1816)

Overall Ride Rating	♡♡♡♡♡
Trail Rating	Moderate
Distance	16 miles one way; can loop with connecting trails
Elevation	9,900–11,280 feet
Main Uses	Equestrian, campground and backcountry camping, fishing
Trailhead Amenities	See Horsethief Campground information (p. 189). A large gravel parking area at the Scotts Bay trailhead (day users only) also accommodates numerous large rigs and plenty of turnaround space. No water at Scotts Bay.
Shoes	Recommended

Directions to Trailhead

The Trappers Lake Trail is best accessed from the Carhart Trail at the southeastern edge of Trappers Lake, from the Scotts Bay trailhead, or from the Horsethief Campground (see directions on p. 189 and map on p. 196).

Trappers Lake is reputed to offer excellent summer fishing for cutthroat and brook trout, so don't forget to pack your fishing rod along with a picnic. The trail follows Fraser Creek southeast, crossing the stream several times and then passing Parvin Lake on its climb to the Flat Tops plateau at 11,275 feet. The trail is excellent for endurance riders, as a variety of loops are possible by connecting

with one or more of the following trails: Carhart, Wall Lake, Turret Creek, Shingle Peak, Sweetwater, Rim Lake, W Mountain, Deer Lake, Chinese Wall, Island Lake, and the list goes on. One can ride for days!

The trail migrates from one ecosystem to another, beginning in montane areas of lush mountain parks and grassy meadows, flanked by lodgepole pine and aspen groves. It climbs through subalpine zones of spruce and fir, where its edges are dotted with wildflowers, and finally tops out close to timberline. Here, the forest gives way to the tundra of the Flat Tops, where cooler temperatures and harsh winds weather the open expanses of massive rock beneath you. Along the way, you'll find plenty of water from sources like Fraser Creek, the South Fork of the White River, and Shepherd Lake. The trail heads southwest to its final ending point a little past Indian Camp Pass, following Dry Sweetwater Creek for only 0.25–0.5 mile and culminating its long and beautiful journey at the Triangle Mountain four-wheel-drive road.

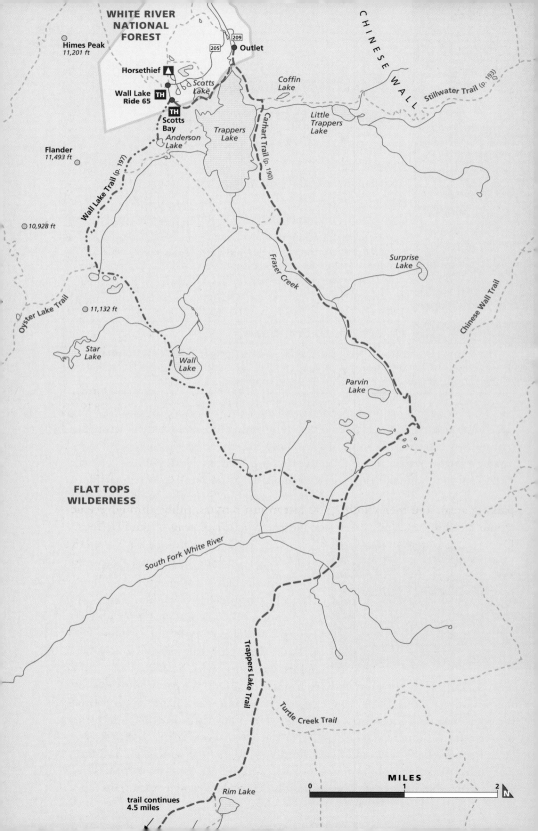

WHITE RIVER
NATIONAL
FOREST

CHINESE WALL

◉ Himes Peak
11,201 ft

205 209
● Outlet

Horsethief △

◇ Scotts
Lake

Coffin
Lake

Stillwater Trail (p. 193)

Wall Lake
Ride 65 TH

TH

Scotts
Bay

Little
Trappers
Lake

Garhart Trail (p. 190)

Anderson
Lake

Trappers
Lake

Flander
11,493 ft ◉

Wall Lake Trail (p. 197)

◉ *10,928 ft*

Fraser Creek

Surprise
Lake

Oyster Lake Trail

◉ *11,132 ft*

Chinese Wall Trail

Star
Lake

Wall
Lake

Parvin
Lake

FLAT TOPS
WILDERNESS

South Fork White River

Trappers Lake Trail

Turtle Creek Trail

MILES
0   1   2

N

trail continues
4.5 miles   *Rim Lake*

65 Wall Lake Trail
(No. 1818) (For Trail Map see p. 196)

Overall Ride Rating	♡♡♡♡♡
Trail Rating	Moderate
Distance	7 miles one way; can loop with connecting trails
Elevation	9,700–12,000 feet
Main Uses	Equestrian, hiking, campground and backcountry camping, fishing
Trailhead Amenities	See Horsethief Campground information (p. 189). A large gravel parking area at the Scotts Bay trailhead (day users only) also accommodates numerous large rigs and plenty of turnaround space. No water at Scotts Bay. A smaller but adequate lot is available for a few rigs at the Wall Lake Trailhead.
Shoes	Recommended

Directions to Trailhead

The Wall Lake trailhead is just south of the Horsethief Campground and just north of the Scotts Bay trailhead, near the end of FR 205. See the directions to Horsethief Campground (p. 189).

As you leave the Wall Lake trailhead traveling south-southwest, you enter an area of downed dead spruce and lodgepole pine on your way to the lovely meadow surrounding Anderson Lake (approximately 0.5 mile from the parking area). You then climb 2,300 feet in just 3 miles, riding through scenic alpine meadows and lush forest prior to reaching the plateau of the Flat Tops. Once on the plateau, you have access to the 25-mile Oyster Lake Trail. Wonderful views of Flanders Park and the Chinese Wall at the base of Trappers Peak greet

you as you make your way to Wall Lake, 2 miles away. Leaving the lake, the trail swings to the south and east for about 2 miles, crossing the North and South Forks of the White River before intersecting the Trappers Lake Trail. Sections of the trail are nice, level dirt paths, but there are also a number of very rocky areas.

Marvine Campground and Trailhead

Marvine is heaven for passionate equestrians who like to camp with their equine partners. This terrific, horse-friendly area has three main sections—two campgrounds and one day-use area—with excellent parking for large rigs. The East Marvine camping area is the first you come to as you drive into the area. It offers two large wooden corrals and a large, grassy dispersed camping area to the left of the road to the trailhead. Several horses can be accommodated in each corral or you can erect portable pens. The main Marvine campground is another 0.1 mile farther on your right. It offers five more large wooden corrals, plus one pipe corral at sites 19–25. Approximately 0.2 mile farther on the left is a third large parking area primarily used for day parking that provides access to the Marvine Creek Trail and the East Marvine Creek Trail. The two additional corrals here are available for public use only when they are not in use by area outfitters. The main trailhead offers public vault bathrooms, horse unloading docks, and hitching posts. Hand-pumped water is available at both campgrounds, though the pump at the main Marvine campground is the better of the two. Trash service is also provided. The trailhead is popular with hunters in the fall, so be sure to outfit yourself and your horse in blaze orange during hunting season and be prepared for a crowd.

Best Season	Summer to fall
Maps	DeLorme *Colorado Atlas & Gazetteer,* pp. 25 and 35; National Geographic *Trails Illustrated Map 122, Flat Tops NE/Trappers Lake*
Contact	Meeker Chamber of Commerce; White River National Forest, Blanco Ranger District
Dogs	On leash or under strict voice and sight control at all times
Fees	Camping is $13 per night without corrals and $15 per night with corrals
Regulations	See the Trail Savvy section (p. 12), website and posted regulations for additional information.

Directions to Trailhead

The best access to the Marvine trailhead is by driving east from Meeker on CO 13 for 1 mile to the junction of CR 8. Turn right at CR 8 and continue east for 28 miles. Look for the signs to Marvine and Ute Creek. Turn right (south) onto CR 12 (Marvine Creek Rd.) for 1 mile and then left at the fork in the road for 6 miles to the trailhead.

66 East Marvine Creek Trail (No. 1822)

Overall Ride Rating	☼☼☼☼
Trail Rating	Moderate to difficult
Distance	10.5 miles one way; can loop with connecting trails
Elevation	8,100–11,150 feet
Main Uses	Equestrian, hiking, campground and backcountry camping , fishing
Trailhead Amenities	See Marvine Campground and trailhead information (p. 198)
Shoes	Recommended

Directions to Trailhead

The trail begins just left of the corrals at the main trailhead (see directions to Marvine Campground and trailhead, p. 198).

The trail makes a significant climb of 3,900 feet toward the top of Big Marvine Peak, presenting breathtaking panoramic views of the Flat Tops. Horses should be well conditioned and given frequent rest stops to make this climb. Initially, the trail crosses East Marvine Creek and then follows it on its way

to several small mountain lakes. After approximately 0.5 mile, you reach the wilderness. The next mile toward Johnson Lake climbs 500 feet. The intersection for the Wild Cow Park Trail and the Big Ridge Trail lies another 0.5 mile ahead, followed by Guthrie Lake just 1.5 miles later. Within the next few miles, you pass three beautiful little lakes: Rainbow Lake, Shallow Lake,

and Mary Loch Lake. The trail ascends through a forest of aspen and lodgepole pine at lower elevations and gives way to large spruce and fir at higher elevations until reaching its highest elevation at the junction with the Marvine Peak Trail (a 4-mile round-trip spur to the summit of Big Marvine Peak at

12,000 feet). The East Marvine Creek drainages and lakes provide ample opportunities for trout fishing along the trail. Continue for approximately 2 miles past the lakes to emerge onto the Flat Tops plateau. Once on the plateau, you are rewarded with fabulous views of the Little Marvine Peaks, Big Marvine Peak, and Rat Mountain. The trail dead-ends at the 25-mile Oyster Lake Trail. For some good endurance riding, use this trail to connect to the north with the Big Fish Trail or to the south with the Marvine Creek Trail.

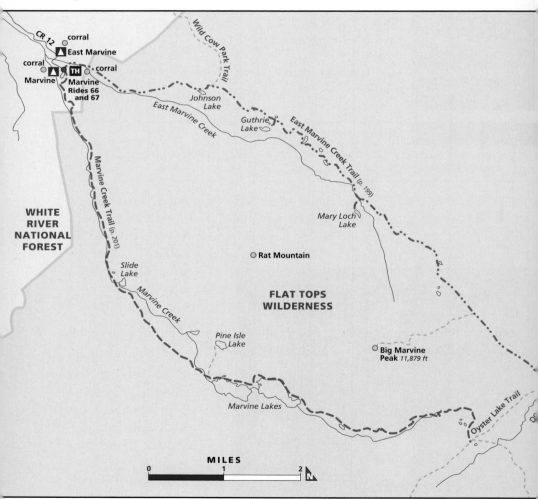

67 Marvine Creek Trail
(No. 1823) (For Trail Map see p. 200)

Overall Ride Rating	UUUU
Trail Rating	Moderate
Distance	11.5 miles one way; can loop with connecting trails
Elevation	8,100–10,950 feet
Main Uses	Equestrian, hiking, campground and backcountry camping, fishing
Trailhead Amenities	See Marvine Campground and trailhead information (p. 198)
Shoes	Recommended

Directions to Trailhead

See directions to Marvine Campground and trailhead (p. 198)

The Marvine Creek Trail begins to the right of the corrals and horse-loading area, heading south out of the parking lot at the main trailhead. You'll have plenty of opportunities to water your horse as well as fish in creek bottoms, trout streams, and beaver ponds. Anglers are also sure to enjoy one of the several beautiful lakes along the trail—Marvine, Slide, and Pine Isle. The panoramic views of the lush, green valley surrounding the Flat Tops are a feast for the eyes.

The first 0.5 mile before reaching the wilderness is a gradual climb over a couple of small ridges. The next 0.5 mile meanders along the Marvine Creek bed until opening into a lovely, grassy meadow surrounded by evergreen and aspen. Another 3 miles puts you at Slide Lake, which can be difficult to negotiate in the spring due to wet and often boggy conditions from snowmelt. Slide Lake is known for its beautiful, clear water as well as plentiful brook trout. The trail later travels past the 65-acre lower Marvine Lake followed by the 88-acre upper Marvine Lake. From here, it climbs much more aggressively through spruce and fir forest toward the plateau of the Flat Tops nearly 2,000 feet above. Approximately 11.5 miles from the trailhead, the route reaches the plateau, where you can connect with the 25-mile Oyster Lake Trail. By taking the Oyster Lake Trail north and east for approximately 1.5 miles, riders can intersect the East Marvine Creek Trail (see Ride 66, p. 199). This makes an excellent loop totaling 23.5 miles.

Long Lost Trailhead

The Long Lost trailhead is excellent for day use and provides access to the Long Park Trail (No. 1809), the Lost Creek Trail (No. 1808), the Lost Park Trail (No. 1805), and the Salt Park Trail (No. 1114). The main attraction for equestrians at this trailhead is a nice, large, level, grassy parking area with plenty of room for a number of large rigs. The only other amenity is a hitching post. Bring your own water for riders and horses and tank up before leaving the parking area, as the water supply may be limited on the trails. There is no camping at this site, but you can use the established equestrian campgrounds at Marvine (p. 198) or Horsethief (p. 189) in addition to dispersed camping at the Mirror Lake trailhead just a few miles to the east . Backcountry camping is also an option.

Best Season	Summer to fall
Maps	DeLorme *Colorado Atlas & Gazetteer,* p. 25; National Geographic *Trails Illustrated Map 122, Flat Tops NE/Trappers Lake*
Contact	Meeker Chamber of Commerce; White River National Forest, Blanco Ranger District
Dogs	On leash or under strict voice and sight control at all times
Fees	None
Regulations	Locate campsites, campfires, and recreational stock at least 100 feet from streams, lakes, and trails. Largest party size is 25 heartbeats. See the Trail Savvy section (p. 12), website and posted regulations for additional information.

Directions to Trailhead

This trailhead is easily accessed from Meeker by driving east on CO 13 for 1 mile to the junction of CR 8. Turn right at CR 8 (Flat Tops Scenic and Historic Byway).

68 Long Park Trail (No. 1809)

Overall Ride Rating	◡◡◡◡◡
Trail Rating	Difficult
Distance	2.8 miles one way; can loop with connecting trails
Elevation	7,540–8,900 feet
Main Uses	Equestrian, hiking, campground, dispersed, and backcountry camping, mountain biking, snowmobiling
Trailhead Amenities	See the Long Lost trailhead information (p. 202)
Shoes	Recommended

Directions to Trailhead

See directions to Long Lost trailhead (p. 202)

The trail heads northeast out of the parking area, making a steep climb for the first 0.5 mile, then begins to level as you reach the ridge. At about 1.5 miles, the route picks up the lower end of Long Park Creek. The trail travels through some oak brush along the lower elevations and culminates at Long Park, a very large, grassy meadow bordered by aspen groves and lodgepole pine. The meadow is filled with wildflowers during the summer months, making it a perfect spot for a nice picnic. Along the trail are incredible views of the White River Valley hundreds of feet below.

You near the end of the trail at the Long Park Creek crossing and shortly thereafter connect to the Long Park Loop four-wheel-drive road. You can extend the ride by following the road north for approximately 2 miles to pick up the Lost Park Trail. At this point, you have three more options: (1) make a nice loop with the Lost Creek Trail by heading south for approximately 3 miles back to the trailhead; (2) continue north on the west fork of the Lost Creek Trail for another 4 miles to the Salt Park Trail; or (3) take the east fork of Lost Creek Trail for 2 miles to the Williams Fork Trail (No. 1113). All are nice choices.

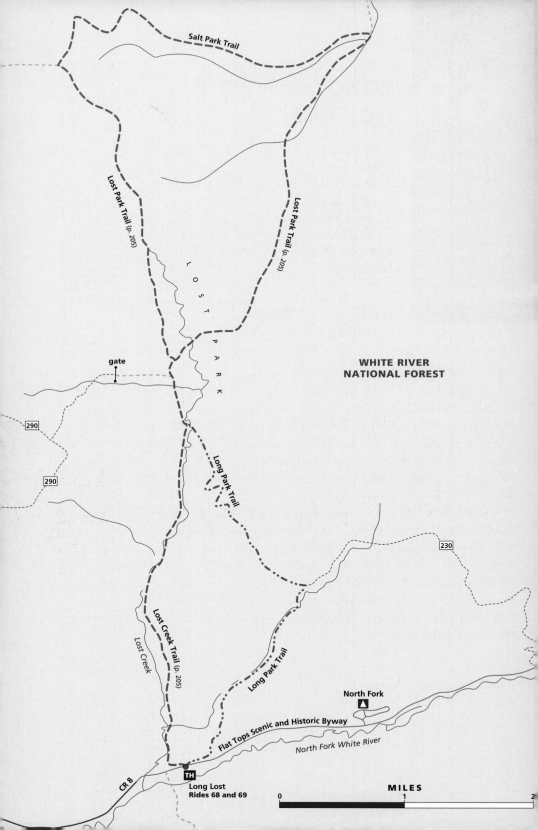

Salt Park Trail

Lost Park Trail (p. 205)

Lost Park Trail (p. 205)

L O S T   P A R K

WHITE RIVER
NATIONAL FOREST

gate

290

290

Long Park Trail

230

Lost Creek Trail (p. 205)

Lost Creek

Long Park Trail

North Fork

Flat Tops Scenic and Historic Byway

North Fork White River

CR 8

TH

Long Lost
Rides 68 and 69

MILES

0   1   2

69 Lost Creek Trail (No. 1808)
Lost Park Trail (No. 1805)

(For Trail Map see p. 204)

Overall Ride Rating	UUUUU
Trail Rating	Easy
Distance	15-mile loop
Elevation	7,500–9,550 feet
Main Uses	Equestrian, hiking, campground, dispersed and backcountry camping, mountain biking, fishing
Trailhead Amenities	See Long Lost trailhead information (p. 202)
Shoes	Recommended

Directions to Trailhead

See directions to Long Lost trailhead (p. 202)

The Lost Creek Trail heads north out of the parking area and parallels Lost Creek for approximately 4 miles up to Lost Park. In the late spring, Lost Park becomes a preferred place for calving elk, while Lost Creek is reported to be good fishing for native rainbow and brook trout. Shortly after reaching the park, the trail divides. Both the left and right forks lead to the Salt Park Trail (No. 1114), which runs east and west, connecting the two forks at their northernmost points to create a scenic loop in either direction. The area is often used for cattle grazing and there are several fences, so be sure to close

gates behind you. The trail climbs a bit over 2,000 feet and features several water crossings, a forested mix of ponderosa pine and quaking aspen, and nearly every wildflower imaginable.

Mirror Lake Trailhead

Best Season	Summer to fall
Maps	DeLorme *Colorado Atlas & Gazetteer*, p. 25; National Geographic *Trails Illustrated Map 122, Flat Tops NE/Trappers Lake*
Contact	Meeker Chamber of Commerce; White River National Forest, Blanco Ranger District
Dogs	On leash or under strict voice and sight control at all times
Fees	None
Regulations	Locate campsites, campfires, and recreational stock at least 100 feet from streams, lakes, and trails. Largest party size is 25 heartbeats. See the Trail Savvy section (p. 12), website and posted regulations for additional information.

Directions to Trailhead

From Meeker, take CO 13 east for 1 mile; turn right on CR 8 and continue east for approximately 39 miles. Take another right onto FR 205 (North Fork Rd.) and travel south for approximately 3.5 miles to the trailhead access road. Look for the Mirror Lake signs. We recommend setting up camp or day parking within the first 0.1 mile from the road in the large, open, grassy meadow, as the actual trailhead is far too small for trailer parking. It would be difficult, even impossible, for a rig to turn around at the trailhead, so parking in the meadow prior to the trailhead will keep you out of trouble. The Mirror Lake trailhead is immediately on your right after turning south on FR 205.

70 Big Ridge Trail (No. 1820)

Overall Ride Rating	UUUU
Trail Rating	Difficult
Distance	12.5 miles one way, plus 2 miles access
Elevation	7,500–10,160 feet
Main Uses	Equestrian, hiking, trailhead and backcountry camping
Trailhead Amenities	See Mirror Lake trailhead information (p. 206). The nearest campground facilities and water are at Horsethief and Marvine Campgrounds (pp. 189 and 198).
Shoes	Recommended

Directions to Trailhead

See map and directions to the Mirror Lake trailhead (p. 206)

Travel south from the Mirror Lake trailhead on the Mirror Lake Trail for approximately 2 miles to the intersection with the Big Ridge Trail and head west. Riders are soon presented with incredible views of the Marvine drainages, the Little Marvine Peaks, and Rat Mountain. As the trail moves to higher elevations, it leaves the aspen and lodgepole pine for spruce and fir. Lovely Sable Lake lies 3 miles west of Mirror Lake. Later, be sure to stop and enjoy the grassy meadows and beautiful wildflowers at Big Park 9.5 miles into your ride. Here, the Wild Cow Park Trail heads south toward the East Marvine Creek Trail. From Big Park, it is about 5 more miles to the Big Ridge trailhead on CR 12. Except for Sable Lake and Mirror Lake (farther south on the Mirror Lake Trail), there is no water on this lengthy trail, so tank up before leaving the trailhead and make sure your mounts have ample time to drink at these lakes. This trail travels through scattered standing and downed timber, open grassy meadows blanketed in wildflowers, and a variety of coniferous vegetation as you make your 2,661-foot climb up the Big Ridge. Make sure your horses are in good condition and stop occasionally for breaks. This would make an excellent shuttle ride if you can have a truck/trailer (and water) waiting at the end of the trail for you.

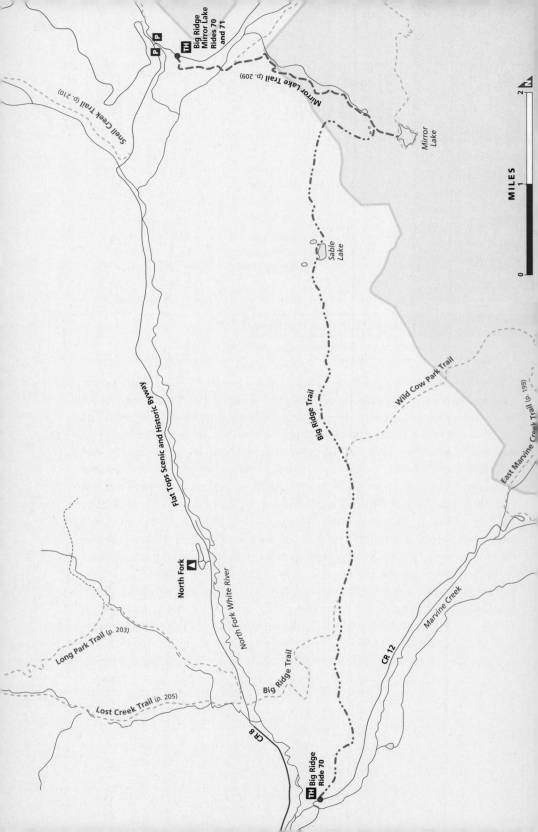

Big Ridge
Mirror Lake
Rides 70
and 71

P P

Snell Creek Trail (p. 210)

Mirror Lake Trail (p. 209)

Mirror
Lake

Sable
Lake

Big Ridge Trail

Wild Cow Park Trail

East Marvine Creek Trail (p. 199)

Flat Tops Scenic and Historic Byway

North Fork

North Fork White River

Long Park Trail (p. 203)

Big Ridge Trail

Lost Creek Trail (p. 205)

Big Ridge Trail

Marvine Creek

CR 12

CR 8

Big Ridge
Ride 70

N

MILES

0   1   2

71 Mirror Lake Trail
(No. 1821) (For Trail Map see p. 208)

Overall Ride Rating	UUU
Trail Rating	Difficult
Distance	2.5 miles one way; can loop with connecting trails
Elevation	8,590–10,100 feet
Main Uses	Equestrian, hiking, trailhead, dispersed and backcountry camping, fishing
Trailhead Amenities	See Mirror Lake trailhead information (p. 206)
Shoes	Recommended

Directions to Trailhead

See directions to Mirror Lake trailhead (p. 206)

The trail travels south from the parking lot through roughly 0.75 mile of private property, crossing the North Fork of the White River. It then follows Mirror Creek to Shamrock Lake 2 miles away. Just after the lake, the route intersects the picturesque 12.5-mile Big Ridge Trail, finally culminating at Mirror Lake. Mirror Lake lies hundreds of feet below the plateau of the Flat Tops just 3 miles south of the trailhead; its beautiful blue-green waters are said to shelter many brook trout, so pack your fishing rod and a picnic to enjoy once you reach the lake. The ride takes you from a montane zone of lodgepole pine and aspen to a subalpine zone of Engelmann spruce and alpine fir. This is a lovely short ride, but if you are in the mood to add some mileage, you can venture off on the Big Ridge Trail (see Ride 70, p. 207) as you head back north on the trail.

72 Snell Creek Trail (No. 1810)

Overall Ride Rating	☺☺☺☺☺
Trail Rating	Moderate
Distance	5.5 miles one way; can loop with connecting trails
Elevation	8,400–10,000 feet
Main Uses	Equestrian, hiking, backcountry camping, mountain biking, fishing, snowmobiling
Trailhead Amenities	Nice large pipe corrals are available to the public for day use only when not in use by the owners (the Watson Ranch) during the last two weeks of June and first two weeks of October. Please be respectful of this privilege and clean up after your horses. The corrals are fenced and cross-fenced and can easily accommodate 20–30 horses (will require pairing of friendly horses). The parking area can accommodate four to six rigs depending on size. There is no camping at this trailhead, but dispersed camping is available at the nearby Mirror Lake trailhead (p. 206) or at the established Horsethief and Marvine Campgrounds (pp. 189 and 198). No water or other amenities are available.
Shoes	Recommended

Note: Information on Best Season, Maps, Contact, Dogs, Fees, and Regulations is found on p. 206 (Mirror Lake trailhead).

Directions to Trailhead

Take CO 13 east from Meeker for 1 mile; turn right on CR 8 and continue east for 38 miles to the Snell Creek trailhead. Parking is on the right (south) side of the road at a large pull-off area.

The trail begins 0.25 mile above Snell Creek on CR 8 to the north of the road. The sign is a little confusing, as it does not reference the Snell Creek Trail but rather Pagoda Lake and Pagoda Peak. The Snell Creek Trail connects CR 8 to the Pagoda Lake Trail 5.5 miles to the north. It follows Snell Creek north through Snell Canyon for roughly 1.5 miles until the creek splits into the east and west forks, following the east fork for about 0.6 mile northeast and then switching back to the northwest and picking up the west fork. There are opportunities for brook, rainbow, and native trout fishing in Snell Creek, so bring your fishing rod along and toss some flies. The terrain and vegetation varies from timbered areas of lodgepole pine, spruce, and fir to groves of aspen and large, lush meadows. Snell Mountain dominates the landscape, along with evidence of a 19th-century fire. The trail crosses the creek several times, providing ample water for your horses and excellent water-crossing practice. It then dead-ends at the 6.5-mile Pagoda Lake Trail. You might consider extending your ride for at least 1 mile to Pagoda Lake, which lies at the base of 11,120-foot Pagoda Peak, named for its unusual shape.

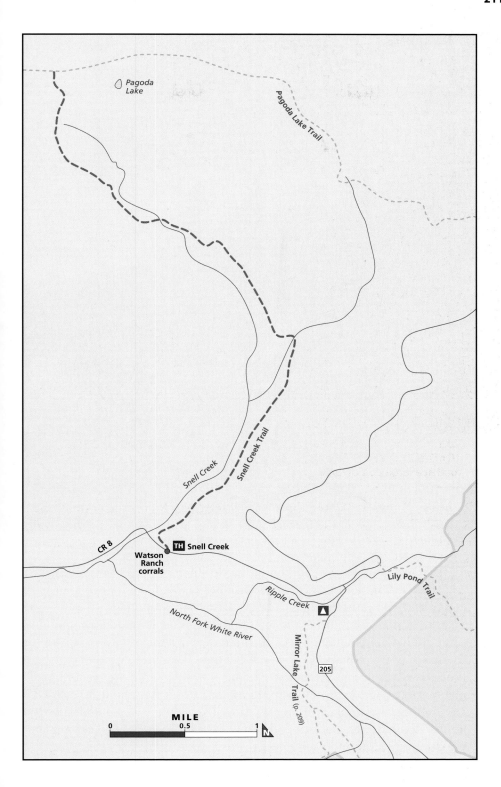

Pagoda Lake

Pagoda Lake Trail

Snell Creek Trail

Snell Creek

CR 8

TH Snell Creek

Watson Ranch corrals

Ripple Creek

Lily Pond Trail

North Fork White River

Mirror Lake Trail (p. 209)

205

MILE

0   0.5   1

N

Chapter 5

West-Central Region

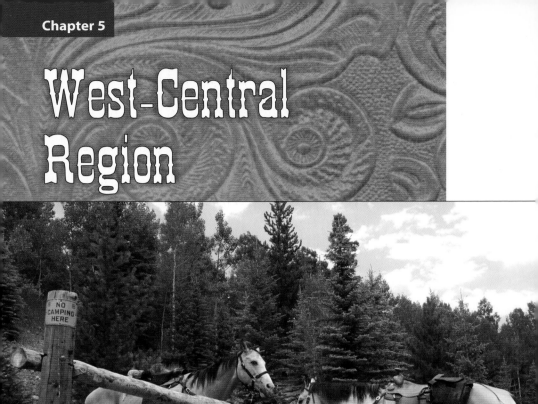

The Maroon Creek Trails offer great rides and mountain views.

The west-central region lies approximately 200 miles west of the Denver metro area high in the beautiful Colorado Rockies. We focus on two areas in this gorgeous region (see DeLorme *Colorado Atlas & Gazetteer* maps 46 and 57–58). First we explore the charming mountain towns of Aspen and Snowmass, once silver mining camps and now a cultural mecca and world-renowned ski area near the famed Maroon Bells–Snowmass Wilderness. This area promises equestrians unsurpassed scenery and memorable riding opportunities. However, advanced trip planning is crucial here and reservations are a must. Restrictions are numerous and overnight camping with horses, as well as stabling accommodations, are limited. Fortunately, many opportunities exist for backcountry packing and camping via saddle and pack stock.

Our second focus is on the wildflower capitol of Colorado, Crested Butte, which provides equestrians an open door to a vast portion of the 1.7 million acres of public lands in the Gunnison National Forest. The Crested Butte area offers excellent horse/trailer camping and trails galore. If you haven't camped at Horse Ranch Park, it will become one of your new favorite places. But showing up on Friday afternoon will probably not get you a spot, as it has become a tremendously popular equestrian camping area. The Gunnison Valley is also famous for its incredible fishing. Be aware that the trails outside of the wilderness are also very popular with mountain bikers. Expect warm summer days with cool to freezing temperatures at night and frequent afternoon thunderstorms often accompanied by lightning.

Accommodations

 7-11 Ranch and Fossil Ridge Guide Service

5291 CR 76
Parlin, CO 81239

970-641-0666
www.coloradodirectory.com/711ranch/

Since 1958, Rudy and Deb Rudibaugh have hosted outdoor experiences in heart of the West Elk Wilderness from their old-style working cattle and horse ranch on Quartz Creek. They offer pack trips, fishing in a private stocked lake, riding in adjacent BLM and national forest lands, RV hookups, campsites, rustic hunting cabins, and overnight stabling. Deb and Rudy are intimately familiar with the West Elk Wilderness and are happy to assist guests in any way possible.

Cozy Point Ranch

210 Juniper Hill Road   970-925-4446; 970-922-6754
Aspen, CO 81611   www.cozypointranch.com

One of the few overnight accommodations in the area, Cozy Point Ranch is a full-care 170-acre horse and cattle ranch located midway between the communities of Aspen and Snowmass Village. The ranch has 29 indoor heated stalls and 19 small outdoor uncovered paddocks available for guest horses. Be sure to make reservations as far in advance as possible, as accommodations are often booked long in advance (particularly during the very busy summer months). Guests enjoy amenities such as a large indoor heated arena, large- and medium-sized outdoor arenas, and an outdoor round pen. The ranch is located within a few minutes drive of some of the most spectacular high-country trail riding in the Rocky Mountains. Cozy Point hosts a number of events, clinics, summer camps, and shows. Room is also available to leave your rig parked at Cozy Point and go into Aspen or Snowmass for people accommodations. For guests who are interested in particularly long rides or pack trips that begin at one point and end at another, the ranch will assist with pick-up and drop-off arrangements for you and your horses. Please call for pricing and availability.

 Gunnison County Fairgrounds

275 S. Spruce Street
Gunnison, CO 81230   970-641-8561

The Gunnison Fairgrounds are open from June through the end of September (except for the second and third weeks of July). The fairgrounds offers 10-by-10-foot covered stalls and RV hookups for only $5 per night (30 sites have electric only and 15 have water and electric). This is a self-care facility. Horse owners are required to provide their own feed, buckets, and clean up. The facility is conveniently located near shopping, restaurants, and lodging at the west end of town just off of US 50 (near the Safeway). Call for availability, reservations, and arrangements.

Rides

Aspen/Snowmass
73 Capitol Creek Trail (No. 1961).. 215
74 Hay Park Trail (No. 1957) 218
75 Maroon Creek Trail (No. 1982)/
East Maroon Creek Trail (No. 1983)/
West Maroon Creek Trail
(No. 1970) 220

Crested Butte
76 Cliff Creek Trail (No. 840)/
Beckwith Pass Trail (No. 842)/
Three Lakes Trail (No. 843)..... 223
77 Dark Canyon Trail (No. 830) ... 226
78 Dyke Trail (No. 838)/Lake Irwin
Trail (No. 837)..................... 229
79 Mill Castle Trail (No. 450)....... 231

73 Capitol Creek Trail (No. 1961)

Overall Ride Rating	ʊʊʊʊʊ
Trail Rating	Moderate
Distance	10 miles one way, including 2-mile access road to trailhead; can loop with other trails
Elevation	9,400–12,070 feet
Best Season	Summer to fall
Main Uses	Equestrian, hiking, trailhead camping, mountain climbing
Trailhead Amenities	Kiosk at the trailhead. Horses and riders will park and camp at the Hay Park trailhead parking area (see directions below and on p. 218) and ride the 2-mile four-wheel-drive dirt road south to the Capitol Creek trailhead. There is no water or amenities at either trailhead, so bring your own drinking water. Water for horses can be found on trail.
Dogs	On leash
Shoes	Required
Maps	DeLorme *Colorado Atlas & Gazetteer*, p. 46; National Geographic *Trails Illustrated Map 128, Maroon Bells/Redstone/Marble*
Contact	White River National Forest, Aspen Ranger District
Fees	None
Regulations	See the Trail Savvy section (p. 12), website and posted regulations for additional information.
Special Notes	Do not attempt to drive a horse trailer beyond this parking lot. Neither the roads nor the parking conditions are appropriate for horse trailers.

Directions to Trailhead

From Aspen, drive 14 miles northwest on CO 82 to Snowmass. Turn left (south) at the gas station and drive 2 miles to the T intersection. Take a right onto CR 9 (Capitol Creek Rd.). The road is paved for the first 4.5 miles. Just before the pavement ends, park in the BLM meadow on the right approximately 2 miles below the trailhead, where there is signed public parking. The rest of the road is a very rough, steep four-wheel-drive route that is impassable for horse trailers. There is no parking for trailers beyond this point. This is also the parking for the Hay Park Trail (see Ride 74, p. 218). Equestrians will have to ride from here 2 miles down the dirt access road for the Capitol Creek trailhead.

This is a popular equestrian and hiking trail with to-die-for views and access to several other excellent wilderness trails. The trail descends steeply southward from the trailhead, losing 500 feet in elevation in the first 0.5 mile as it passes through sagebrush and gambel oak. After a short trot through lovely aspen groves, the trail emerges into an open, grassy clearing before crossing Capitol Creek. This is a lovely spot for a cool drink of water and some grass for the horses, as the next 5 miles are uphill from here. After the crossing, the path climbs a wooded and swampy beaver-dammed area to reach open meadows with views of Mount Daly and Capitol Peak. Shortly after, at about 4 miles, is the signed West Snowmass Trail on the left. This is a wonderful ride around Haystack Mountain and can be taken as a loop back to the trailhead or as an extension of your ride if you want more incredible scenery. The Capitol Creek Trail continues south, paralleling the creek most of the way up the drainage. Note that camping is not allowed in the meadows or within 200 feet of the gorgeous little Capitol Lake at 5.6 miles, where the 14,130-foot Capitol Peak looms overhead. Don't count on

the lake for watering the horses, as this little gem is guarded by slabs of granite and steep talus slopes. Just below the lake is a junction with the Capitol Peak climbers' trail. At 6 miles, the trail switchbacks lead to a double log crossing and, at mile 6.5, crosses the creek once more. In the timber on the right at 7 miles are the last campsites along the trail. The Capitol Creek Trail ends at the junction with the Avalanche–Silver Creek Trail (No. 1959). Riders who want additional mileage can continue northwest or southeast along the Avalanche–Silver Creek Trail, and those who don't can simply return to the trailhead via the fabulous Capitol Creek Trail heading north.

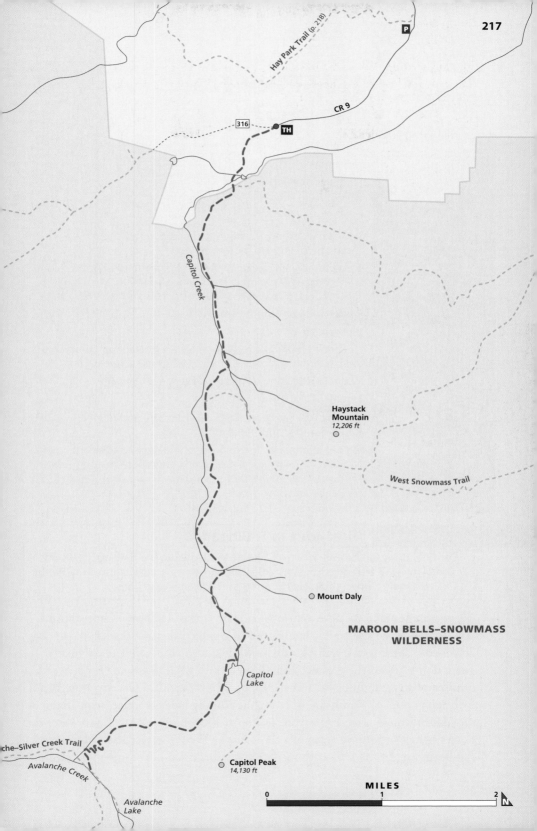

Hay Park Trail (p. 218)

P

CR 9

316

TH

Capitol Creek

Haystack
Mountain
12,206 ft

West Snowmass Trail

Mount Daly

MAROON BELLS–SNOWMASS
WILDERNESS

Capitol
Lake

che–Silver Creek Trail

Avalanche Creek

Capitol Peak
14,130 ft

Avalanche
Lake

MILES

0   1   2

N

74 Hay Park Trail (No. 1957)

Overall Ride Rating	♡♡♡♡♡
Trail Rating	Moderate
Distance	4.4 miles one way
Elevation	8,400–9,680 feet
Best Season	Summer to fall
Main Uses	Equestrian, hiking, trailhead and backcountry camping, mountain biking. No motorized vehicles.
Trailhead Amenities	Large, level grassy lot on BLM land. No restrictions for overnight trailer or tent camping at the trailhead parking area. No other facilities. Bring your own water for horses and people.
Dogs	Under voice and sight command
Shoes	Barefoot okay
Maps	DeLorme *Colorado Atlas & Gazetteer*, p. 46; National Geographic *Trails Illustrated Map 128, Maroon Bells/Redstone/Marble*
Contact	White River National Forest, Sopris Ranger District
Fees	None
Regulations	See the Trail Savvy section (p. 12), website and posted regulations for additional information.
Special Notes	Do not attempt to drive a horse trailer beyond this parking lot. Neither the roads nor the parking conditions are appropriate for horse trailers. This trail is popular with mountain bikers, so please be watchful.

Directions to Trailhead

See directions for the Capitol Creek Trail (Ride 73, p. 215). The parking area is not signed by any trail or trailhead names but provides access to the Hay Park, Capitol Creek, Hardscrabble, Hell Roaring, and Williams Lake trails.

If you are looking for an exceptional ride on one of Colorado's hot summer days, the Hay Park Trail is it. A forest of gigantic, dense aspen trees stretches above you, shading the trail like a veil, while a lush and varied assortment of vegetation blankets the ground, including colorful wildflowers and bold, broad, fernlike plants standing 3–4 feet in height. It is a beautiful place to ride. Begin by heading due west from the BLM public parking area on a nice, wide, natural-dirt path through a large grassy area. Stop at a small creek crossing to water the horses before beginning an uphill climb to the Forest Service kiosk that marks the beginning of the trail at about 0.5 mile. You encounter three more creek

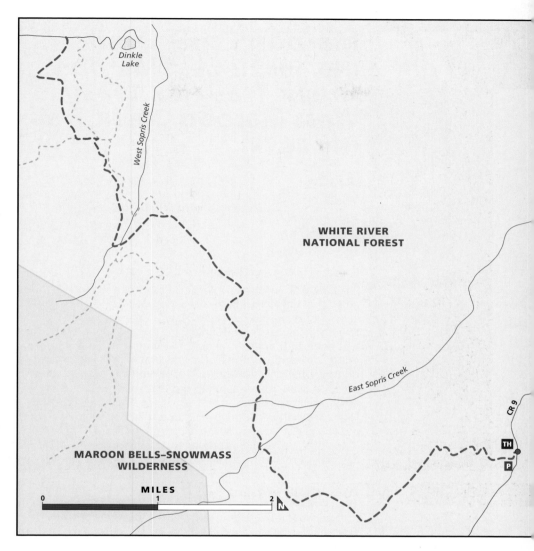

crossings in the next 3 miles of climbing, including at East Sopris Creek. In addition to a cool drink, be sure to give your mounts a little breather here and there. Turn right for just a few feet when you meet the road and you will pick up the trail again on your left.

Occasionally, the trail clears just enough to expose incredible views. Look to the northeast to see McCartney Mesa, and don't miss captivating Capitol Peak (14,130 feet) and Haystack Mountain (12,206 feet) on your return to the trailhead. You may encounter a few downed trees, but nothing that a trail-savvy horse can't negotiate. The Hay Park Trail connects to the more rugged 6-mile Mount Sopris Trail at its ending point if you would like to extend your ride.

75 Maroon Creek Trail (No. 1982)/ *East Maroon Creek Trail* (No. 1983)/ West Maroon Creek Trail (No. 1970)

Overall Ride Rating	∪∪∪∪∪
Trail Rating	Moderate
Distance	10.5 miles one way
Elevation	8,710–11,800 feet
Best Season	Summer to fall
Main Uses	Equestrian, hiking, backcountry camping, fishing
Trailhead Amenities	The East Maroon Portal parking area receives a significant amount of traffic from both cars and truck/trailer rigs. Arrive early to ensure a place to park. The area includes restrooms, two hitching posts, a stock-unloading dock (do not block), barbeque grills, and two picnic tables on the parking lot side of the trailhead. Additional picnic tables and grills are located on the far side of the trailhead across the bridge. You can water horses at both the water pump and the creek, but it's recommended you bring your own drinking water. There is no camping for horses in the developed recreation area; however, backcountry packing and camping are permitted.
	The West Maroon Portal parking area is less crowded than the East Maroon and can accommodate three to four rigs depending on size and car parking. Please note that riders are not allowed on the trail around the lake itself. The Maroon Creek Trail provides access to the West Maroon Creek Trail, which in turn provides riders with a lovely view of Maroon Lake and East Maroon Pass.
Dogs	On leash
Shoes	Recommended
Maps	DeLorme *Colorado Atlas & Gazetteer*, p. 46; National Geographic *Trails Illustrated Map 128, Maroon Bells/Redstone/Marble*
Contact	White River National Forest, Aspen Ranger District
Fees	None
Regulations	See the Trail Savvy section (p. 12), website and posted regulations for additional information.
Special Notes	Parking is limited at this very popular trailhead. Consider arriving early and position your trailer for an easy way out. Bug spray for you and your horses is highly recommended. Horses are not allowed on the path around Maroon Lake due to extremely high foot traffic.

Directions to Trailhead

From Aspen, go 0.5 mile west on CO 82 and turn left (south) onto Maroon Creek Rd. at the stoplight. Keep right and continue 6.5 miles to the East Maroon Portal or 9 miles to the West Maroon Portal (with access to the Maroon Creek Trail via the West Maroon Creek Trail). From mid-June through September, Maroon Creek Rd. is closed from 8:30 a.m. to 5:00 p.m. except to horse trailers. However, if you want to get a parking spot, it is recommended to get there before the cars do, which means before 8:30 a.m.

This description primarily details the route from the East Maroon Portal to East Maroon Pass via the Maroon Creek and East Maroon Creek trails. Riders may also get to the East Maroon Pass from the West Portal via the West Maroon Creek Trail.

This glorious wilderness ride begins by crossing a significant, horse-safe bridge over West Maroon Creek and veering right on a natural-dirt path through colorful displays of wildflowers, aspen trees, and evergreen. Depending on weather conditions, the path may be wet through this area, so please be careful. Once out of the trees, look for the multicolored layers of sedimentary rock piled one upon the other to form the 14,018-foot Pyramid Peak to the southwest. At 1.5 miles, the trail forks. The West Maroon Creek Trail continues on the right branch to the West Portal parking area and Maroon Lake.

Continuing on the East Maroon Creek Trail, which is the left branch of the above fork, offers spectacular views of the snow-capped Bells as the path approaches the mouth of the glacial valley. Beautiful meadows grace what was once the East Maroon Toll Road of 1887. Now a two-track trail replaces the old roadbed above the beaver ponds and aspen. At 5.5 miles, the remnants of an old mine and miners' cabins are evident. Continue on for cool water as you cross East Maroon Creek twice. At 9.4 miles, take the right junction to East Maroon Pass. The left branch leads to Copper Pass, Triangle Pass, and Conundrum Pass. At the top of East Maroon Pass is access to Copper Lake and the town of Gothic. Awe-inspiring, 360-degree views await you, with 15 peaks in the immediate vicinity over 12,000 feet, six over 13,000 feet, and two over 14,000 feet, in addition to four high-mountain lakes. This is wilderness at its finest and the best way to experience it is undoubtedly from the saddle. When you are ready, return to the trailhead the way you came, or take the Copper Creek Trail (No. 983) to the Conundrum Creek Trail and back to the East Maroon to complete a triangular loop as a grand finale.

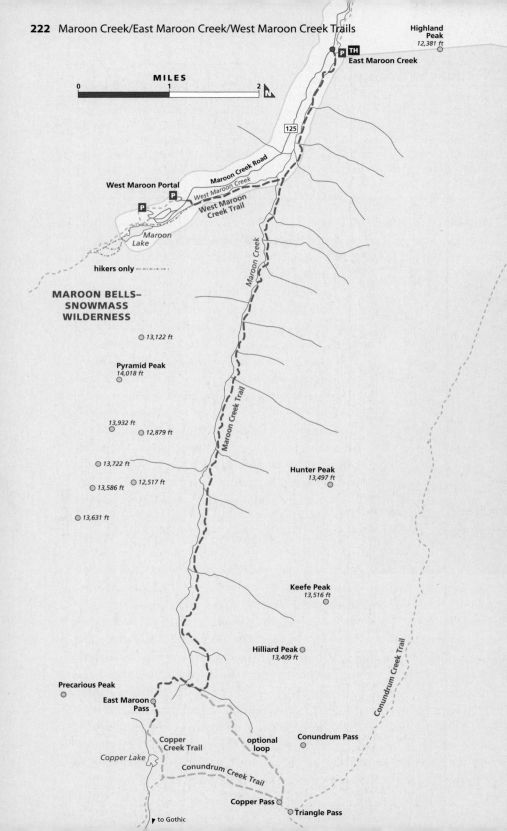

Highland
Peak
12,381 ft

East Maroon Creek

MILES

0   1   2

N

125

Maroon Creek Road

West Maroon Portal

West Maroon Creek

West Maroon
Creek Trail

Maroon
Lake

hikers only

**MAROON BELLS–
SNOWMASS
WILDERNESS**

Maroon Creek

13,122 ft

Pyramid Peak
14,018 ft

13,932 ft

12,879 ft

Maroon Creek Trail

13,722 ft

Hunter Peak
13,497 ft

13,586 ft   *12,517 ft*

13,631 ft

Keefe Peak
13,516 ft

Conundrum Creek Trail

Hilliard Peak
13,409 ft

Precarious Peak

East Maroon
Pass

Copper
Creek Trail

**optional
loop**

Conundrum Pass

Copper Lake

Conundrum Creek Trail

▶ to Gothic

Copper Pass

Triangle Pass

76 Cliff Creek Trail (No. 840)/ Beckwith Pass Trail (No. 842)/Three Lakes Trail (No. 843)

Overall Ride Rating	♘♘♘♘♘
Trail Rating	Moderately difficult (especially in wet conditions)
Distance	15 miles total (6 miles one way, plus a 3-mile loop)
Elevation	9,000–9,970 feet
Best Season	Summer to fall
Main Uses	Equestrian, hiking, trailhead and back country camping, fishing
Trailhead Amenities	Horse Ranch Park, just down the road from the Cliff Creek trailhead, is an excellent place for equestrian camping and can easily accommodate 20–30 rigs depending on size and arrangement. A restroom is located at the end of FR 795. The Forest Service has installed numerous large, four-sided permanent feeders to which four horses at a time can be tied for feeding and/or overnight restraint. Electric fences, portable panels, highlines, and hobbles can also be used for overnight camping. Bring your own water. There are no other amenities.
Dogs	Under voice and sight command on trails, at Horse Ranch Park, and at trailheads. Must be on leash at the Lost Lake Campground. Since Lost Lake is a tent campground, riders should avoid the camping area except to use the facilities. If you are using the area, you must have your dog on a 6-foot leash and make sure to clean up after your horses.
Shoes	Recommended
Maps	DeLorme *Colorado Atlas & Gazetteer*, pp. 57–58; National Geographic *Trails Illustrated Map 133, Kebler Pass/Paonia Reservoir*
Contact	Gunnison National Forest, Paonia Ranger District
Fees	None
Regulations	See the Trail Savvy section (p. 12), website and posted regulations for additional information.

Directions to Trailhead

ACCESS 1: From the southwest corner of the town of Crested Butte, take CR 12 (Kebler Pass Rd.) west about 12 miles to FR 795 and turn right (north) into Horse Ranch Park. Park at the parking/camping area. To access the trail, ride across Kebler Pass Rd. to the south and then go west to the Cliff Creek trailhead 0.1 mile ahead. The trail is through the gate and uphill on the left.

ACCESS 2: Follow CR 12 from Crested Butte to the Cliff Creek trailhead 0.1 mile past Horse Ranch Park. Turn left at the gravel road past the gate and travel a short distance uphill to the trailhead. There is room for 2-3 rigs, with a Forest Service kiosk sign and two feeders. Bring your own water; no other amenities.

This high-altitude jewel begins in a forest of old-growth aspen at the Cliff Creek trailhead, perched upon a wildflower-laden hillside overlooking Anthracite Creek. From the Forest Service sign, head south and then west for 2.5 miles through conifer interspersed with alpine parks and lush meadows embellished with wildflowers. The flowers are at their best in July and early August; you are likely to see as many as 70 different species as you meander through the spruce and fir. **A note of caution**: This section of trail may be wet, muddy, and slippery due to the combination of shade, snowmelt, and summer thunderstorms.

At 2.5 miles, riders meet the junction with the Beckwith Pass Trail. We recommend taking a short 0.5-mile ride to the left (south) through open meadows for unobstructed, stunning views of East Beckwith Mountain. A grand perspective on the 17,600-acre, tree-studded West Elk Wilderness awaits your climb toward Beckwith Pass, which tops out at almost 10,000 feet. Once you've had your fill of the spectacular vistas, turn around and ride north, back toward the junction with the Cliff Creek Trail. Once at the junction, continue north/northwest for 3 miles. The jagged edges of the Ruby Range in the Raggeds Wilderness form the backdrop to parklike meadows. The trail meanders in and out of the trees until it finally arrives at the junction with the Three Lakes Trail, which encircles Lost Lake Slough. Be sure to bring the fishing rod along and wet a line. Reportedly, the fishing is fairly good and occasionally restocked.

Just to the northwest of the junction lies the Lost Lake tent campground. Continue following the trail from the campground west and then southwest along Lost Lake Rd. for a short distance to pick up the trail again. Take the trail 1 mile south to arrive at a once-in-a-lifetime setting for a picnic lunch, with Lost Lake to the immediate west, Dollar Lake to the immediate east, Lost Lake Slough just to the north, and East Beckwith Mountain just to the south. Savor the moment, for it is a marvel of nature. After fishing and lunch, a short 1.5-mile ride north through the forest rejoins the Three Lakes Trail. You can trace the Beckwith Pass Trail and your hoofprints back to your trailer in time for dinner and maybe even a campfire at Horse Ranch Park.

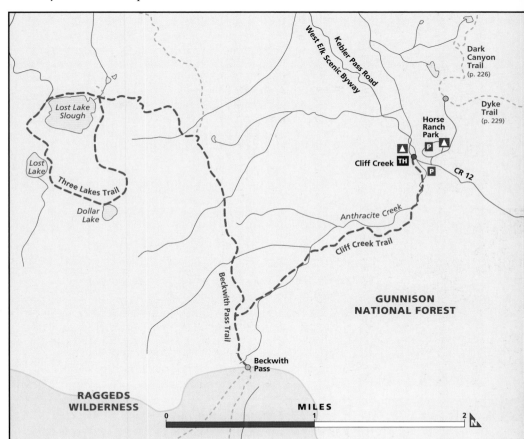

77 Dark Canyon Trail (No. 830)

Overall Ride Rating	♥♥♥♥
Trail Rating	Moderate to difficult
Distance	13 miles one way
Elevation	7,000–9,200 feet
Best Season	Late spring to fall
Main Uses	Equestrian, hiking, campground camping, fishing. No motorized vehicles or bicycles
Trailhead Amenities	At the north end of Erickson Springs Campground is a large parking area with trail access across the creek. This is a nice loop for horse trailers and can accommodate 8–10 rigs depending on size. There are five campsites. The Forest Service has installed nice, large, permanent feeders where four horses at a time can be fed and tied overnight. Highlines, portable panels, hobbles, and electric fences are also possible. A water spigot and a vault toilet are found in the center of the campground, and a Forest Service kiosk is located at the trailhead.
Dogs	On leash
Shoes	Required
Maps	DeLorme *Colorado Atlas & Gazetteer*, pp. 57–58; National Geographic *Trails Illustrated Map 133, Kebler Pass/Paonia Reservoir*
Contact	Gunnison National Forest, Paonia Ranger District
Fees	None
Regulations	See the Trail Savvy section (p. 12), website and posted regulations for additional information.
Special Notes	This is a very rocky canyon but well worth it! Equestrians using the Erickson Springs camping area have not done a good job of cleaning up after themselves. Please practice the Leave No Trace principles described in the Trail Savvy section (p. 12) and leave your campsites clean for the next users to enjoy.

Directions to Trailhead

ACCESS 1: From the southwest corner of Crested Butte, take CR 12 (Kebler Pass Rd.) west about 18 miles (past Horse Ranch Park on the right, and Lost Lake Rd. on the left). Continue west. At about 18 miles, after the road turns north, you come to the Anthracite Creek/Erickson Springs Campground. Turn right onto the campground road. The road is long and narrow. Pass several camping areas as you travel to the end into a large, level loop with equestrian camping.

ACCESS 2: From Crested Butte, take CR 12 west about 12 miles to FR 795 and turn right (north) into Horse Ranch Park. Travel to end of the dirt road, where the trailhead is marked for the Dark Canyon Trail (No. 830).

This description begins at Erickson Springs Campground and trailhead and ends at the Horse Ranch Park Campground and trailhead, but the trail could also be ridden in reverse by starting at Horse Ranch Park and heading north. For additional details about Horse Ranch Park or its surrounding trails, see Ride 78, the Dyke Trail and the Lake Irwin Trail (p. 229), or Ride 76, the Cliff Creek/Beckwith Pass/Three Lakes Trails (p. 223).

Begin by riding a short distance northeast at the Forest Service trailhead marker to reach a large, horse-safe bridge. Depending on your comfort level, as well as that of your mount, you may want to dismount and hand-lead your friend across. The sturdy wooden planks and the sound of the rushing water can be a bit intimidating. Once on the north side of the bridge, the route travels along Anthracite Creek and the steep, rugged walls of Dark Canyon, entering the Raggeds Wilderness at 0.5 mile. Early in the season, waterfalls cascade in the background as you follow the forested path of lush plantings along the creek, which is studded with rock outcroppings and gigantic boulders. Camping is limited for the first 6 miles, but the fishing can be good. Striking and colorful

Marcellina Mountain lies to the south as the path crosses two bridges along the way.

At about 7 miles, the path forks. The left fork goes north to the Munsey-Ruby Stock Driveway (No. 831) and the North Anthracite Trail (No. 832). Trail No. 831 makes a loop back to the trailhead but is very difficult and not well maintained. The right fork of the Dark Canyon Trail continues south. Just after passing an old, unmaintained trail heading straight up Middle Anthracite Creek, the path begins an ascent up the Devils Stairway, a succession of switchbacks that gain 1,200 feet in 0.75 mile. From here, this wonderful trail intersects the Ruby Anthracite Trail (No. 836) to the west, then the Silver Basin Trail (No. 834) to the east, passes several nice streams for watering the horses, and climbs through aspen and evergreen onto a ridge to finally arrive at Horse Ranch Park.

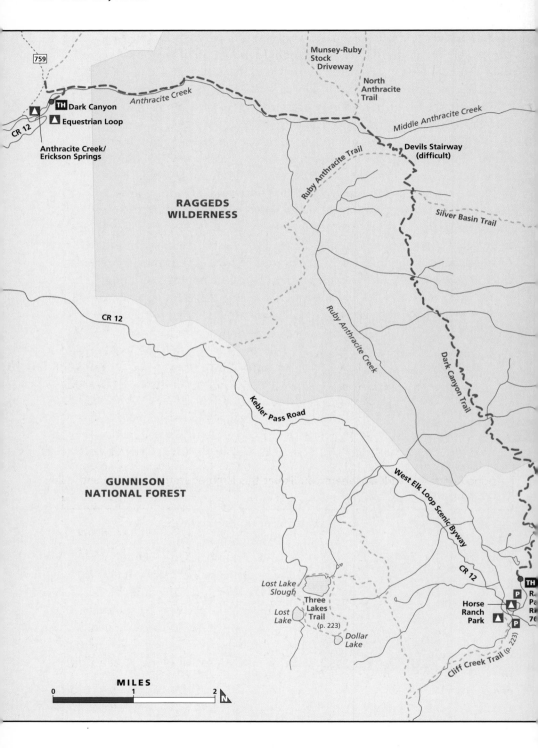

759

Dark Canyon
Equestrian Loop

Anthracite Creek/
Erickson Springs

CR 12

Anthracite Creek

Munsey-Ruby
Stock
Driveway

North
Anthracite
Trail

Middle Anthracite Creek

Devils Stairway
(difficult)

Ruby Anthracite Trail

Silver Basin Trail

RAGGEDS
WILDERNESS

CR 12

Ruby Anthracite Creek

Dark Canyon Trail

Kebler Pass Road

GUNNISON
NATIONAL FOREST

West Elk Loop Scenic Byway

CR 12

Horse
Ranch
Park

TH

R
Pa
Ri
7(

Lost Lake
Slough

Three
Lakes
Trail
(p. 223)

Lost
Lake

Dollar
Lake

Cliff Creek Trail (p. 223)

MILES

0   1   2

78 Dyke Trail (No. 838)/ Lake Irwin Trail (No. 837)

Overall Ride Rating	UUUUU
Trail Rating	Easy
Distance	6.5 miles one way
Elevation	9,000–10,323 feet
Best Season	Summer to fall
Main Uses	Equestrian, hiking, campground camping, mountain biking, fishing
Trailhead Amenities	See amenities for Horse Ranch Park (p. 223)
Dogs	Under voice and sight command
Shoes	Recommended
Maps	DeLorme *Colorado Atlas & Gazetteer*, pp. 57–58; National Geographic *Trails Illustrated Map 133, Kebler Pass/Paonia Reservoir*
Contact	Gunnison National Forest, Paonia Ranger District
Fees	None
Regulations	See the Trail Savvy section (p. 12), website and posted regulations for additional information.

Directions to Trailhead

From the southwest corner of Crested Butte, take CR 12 (Kebler Pass Rd.) west approximately 12 miles and turn right (north) into Horse Ranch Park at the signed entrance. Park anywhere you like at this large equestrian parking and camping area.

This is the kind of stuff that trail riding is really made of! If you haven't been here, put it on the priority list and treat yourself to that once-a-year big reward that every horse and horse owner needs and deserves. To access the trail, follow the road to the north end of the Horse Ranch Park campground. The Dark Canyon Trail heads north from the road, but instead take the Dyke Trail (No. 838) east uphill through a cool canopy of aspen for approximately 1.5 miles. The natural-dirt single track is bordered by lush vegetation and teems with wildflowers during July and August. The horses will have no problem picking their way around the occasional rocks. A sharp turn to the north reveals the grandeur of Ruby Peak (12,644 feet), Mount Owen (13,058 feet), and Purple Peak (12,810 feet) lying at the edge of the 65,019-acre Raggeds Wilderness. The Lake Irwin Trail (No. 837) comes in from the east as you reach the 1.5-mile mark. As you follow the rocky slope uphill to the east, impressive igneous rock formations known as The Dyke come into view. They resulted from the cooled remains of liquid magma forced through thin perpendicular openings in the ridge. From The Dyke, continue east through wildflower-sprinkled meadows intermixed with spruce and aspen forest to arrive at the road to the Lake

Irwin Lodge, which rests peacefully upon a hillside to the north. The lodge is closed for remodeling through late 2007. Continue east over and down the hillside for a sip of the cool blue waters of Lake Irwin, a gorgeous 30-acre alpine lake completely surrounded by a thick forest of evergreen and home to rainbow and brook trout. Pause for a while to enjoy the dramatic setting, hobble the horses, and have a picnic. The Lake Irwin campground has water and restrooms. Every step of elevation gained is worth the magic and beauty of this breathtaking place.

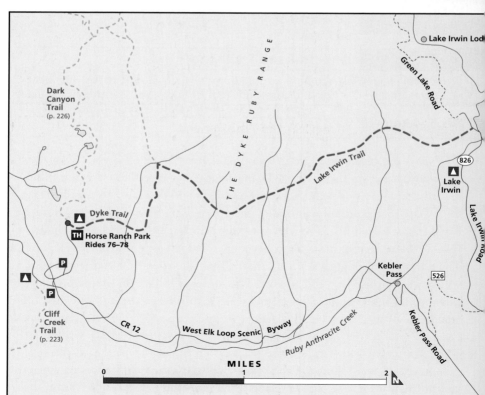

79 Mill Castle Trail (No. 450)

Overall Ride Rating	UUUUU
Trail Rating	Easy to Mill Creek; difficult thereafter
Distance	14.3 miles one way
Elevation	9,160–12,460 feet
Best Season	Summer to fall
Main Uses	Equestrian, hiking, backcountry camping, fishing
Trailhead Amenities	An outhouse and level parking area for two to three rigs is available at the first parking area, with no other amenities. Bring water for horses and humans and park for an easy way out at the end of your ride. The second parking area is 0.5 mile farther west on Mill Creek Rd., but is generally full with vehicles. The trailhead kiosk can be found another 0.5 mile farther west on Mill Creek Rd.
Dogs	On leash
Shoes	Recommended up to Mill Creek and required thereafter
Maps	DeLorme *Colorado Atlas & Gazetteer*, p. 58; National Geographic *Trails Illustrated Map 133, Kebler Pass/Paonia Reservoir* and *Map 134, Black Mesa/Curecanti Pass*
Contact	Gunnison National Forest, Gunnison Ranger District
Fees	None
Regulations	See the Trail Savvy section (p. 12), website and posted regulations for additional information.

Directions to Trailhead

ACCESS 1: From Crested Butte, travel 6 miles west on CR 12 (Kebler Pass Rd.). Where the road divides, take the left fork, CR 730 (Ohio Creek Rd.), and travel south for approximately 9.5 miles to FR 727 (Mill Creek Rd./BLM 3118). Turn right (west) and travel 3.5 miles to the first parking area, 4 miles to the second parking area, or 4.5 miles to the trailhead. The Ohio Creek Rd. is difficult between CR 12 and FR 727 and is not recommended for horse trailers that exceed a small two-horse in length. If your trailer is large, approach the trailhead from the Gunnison access instead (access 2).

ACCESS 2: From the center of Gunnison, travel 3 miles north on CO 135 to CR 730 (Ohio Creek Rd.). Drive 9 miles north on CR 730 to FR 727 and turn left (west) for the trailhead.

Note: There is a lower parking area with no trailhead signs and only an outhouse for amenities. The Lowline Trail begins approximately 0.5 mile west of the lower parking area on the right (north) side of FR 727. Continue another 0.5 mile or so to find a second parking area. The Mill Castle trailhead sign is just 0.5 mile beyond the second parking area. It's nice to park in the first lot if there is room, but neither lot is large, and both the Lowline and the Mill Castle trails are popular. Wherever you choose to park, position yourself so that you have an easy way out.

To begin one of the most scenic horseback tours in Colorado, head west into the magnificent West Elk Wilderness from FR 727 and the Mill Castle trailhead. The first 1.25 miles make a nice warm-up, riding in and out of the trees and up and down gently sloping and mildly rocky terrain. At 1.25 miles, enjoy the "Kodak moment" before you cross Mill Creek. The views here are

absolutely stunning. Wildflowers and lush grasses lie like a fine wool blanket across the ground. A forest of deep green spruce and fir surround the base of giant rock formations that jut above the trees like castle spires, earning the apt name, "The Castles." The trail becomes faint and almost fades away among the willow and salt cedar in the sandy creek bottom where the trail crosses Mill Creek. A little exploration should soon reveal the way. If nothing else is visible, ford the stream; once on the north side, the trail becomes apparent again as it begins to climb the hillside.

Continue a slow, steady climb to the west, paralleling Mill Creek for 5.5 miles. At 11,800 feet, the trail forks. The left fork is a 1.5-mile trek to the summit of North Baldy Mountain. Take the right fork, continuing on the Mill Castle Trail, which climbs steeply to Storm Pass (12,460 feet). The route passes through a previously burned area scarred by interesting snags and populated by huge boulders and new growth. Keep a watchful eye on the mountaintops for little alpine meadows sitting in basins and trees that grow straight out of slits in sheer vertical rock faces. A second awe-inspiring view of The Castles can be enjoyed from Storm Pass.

The descent from Storm Pass is as steep as the ascent. The trail continues north into the Castle Creek drainage and then turns east, following South Castle Creek after crossing over it to the north side. The trail stays close to the creek for approximately 1.5 miles before heading north out of the drainage toward The Castles for an up-close view. In the next 2 miles, you encounter two lovely unnamed alpine lakes sitting peacefully at 10,000 feet. This is a nice place for a cool drink of water and a snack before you begin the significant trek back to the trailhead. The horses might enjoy some of the sweet mountain grass as well. In 2 more miles lies the intersection with the Lowline Trail (No. 438). For people interested in a long pack trip, this is fabulous area with numerous options, including links to the Beckwith Pass Trail, the Pass Creek Trail, and the Dark Canyon Trail for days of wonderful riding.

This unique and scenic journey is well worth the steep climb in the last half. It is critical for horses to be conditioned prior to this ride, which is best undertaken by experienced riders and horses in small groups.

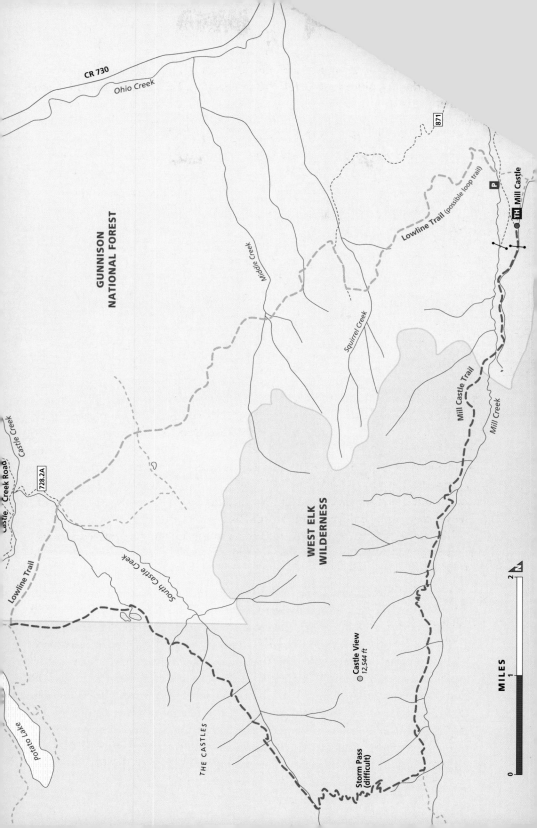

CR 730

Ohio Creek

GUNNISON
NATIONAL FOREST

Middle Creek

Squirrel Creek

871

Lowline Trail (possible loop trail)

P

TH

Mill Castle

Mill Castle Trail

Mill Creek

WEST ELK
WILDERNESS

Castle Creek

Castle Creek Road

728.2A

Lowline Trail

South Castle Creek

Castle View
12,544 ft

THE CASTLES

Storm Pass
(difficult)

Potato Lake

MILES

0   1   2

Preparing for a pack trip at the Burnt Timber trailhead

Lying on the western slope of the Continental Divide, the 1,869,931-acre San Juan National Forest is the foundation of the diverse southwest region of Colorado (see DeLorme *Colorado Atlas & Gazetteer* maps 64–68, 74–78, and 84–88). Broad elevation ranges (8,000 to 14,309 feet), beautiful alpine lakes, deep glacial valleys, cascading waterfalls, giant alpine meadows bound by aspen and evergreen and laced with wildflowers characterize the landscape. Huge expanses of land and views that seem to extend forever are punctuated by brilliant layers of color laid one upon another in numerous stunning rock outcroppings. The incredible San Juan Mountain Range is known for its numerous rugged peaks with elevations that range in excess of 12,000 and 13,000 feet; at 14,309 feet, the Uncompaghre Peak tops the list.

The Weminuche, Colorado's largest and most visited wilderness, is the heart and soul of this breathtaking region. Boasting some of the best hunting, fishing, hiking, and horseback riding Colorado has to offer. The Weminuche is also home to a vast array of wildlife, including mule deer, elk, bears, bighorn sheep, mountain lions, grouse, turkeys, and ducks.

Short, cool summers and long, severe winters are the norm. The elevations range from 8,000–14,000 feet, with the average around 10,000 feet. Most trails are open for both horse and foot travel by July and possibly earlier at lower elevations. Expect cool to freezing temperatures at night and nice, warm days between 60 and 80 degrees during the summer months. The trails are as unique and wonderful as the landscape itself, beckoning the weary urban trail warrior away from the city to enjoy a little slice of heaven with their equine partner.

Accommodations

  Fireside Inn Cabins

1600 E. Hwy. 160
Pagosa Springs, CO 81147

970-264-9204; 888-264-9204
www.firesidecabins.com

This is an absolute must-visit! Guy and Dianne Ludwig have created the ideal accommodations for people who want to experience the San Juans with their horses without having to camp. They offer 15 excellent one- and two-bedroom cabins with newer wood interiors and exteriors, and conveniences such as phones, TVs, and microwaves. Each cabin is beautifully decorated to reflect the western culture and horsey heritage we all love, and comes complete with linens, cooking utensils, and other kitchen amenities. Guests have access to a washer and dryer, ice machine, and the hot tub—perfect for a nice soak after a long, hard ride. If you're lucky, you might have the pleasure of riding alongside Guy or Dianne, who know nearly every mile of trail near and far. Guests traveling with their horses and mules will enjoy the complimentary 16-by-16-foot outdoor stalls and 40-foot round pen. Electricity for late arrivals is available at the barn. Alfalfa and grass hay can be purchased on site. Trailer parking is plentiful, with easy access in and out. Horse owners are responsible for their own feeding, watering, and daily stall cleaning, with pitchfork, shovel, and wheelbarrows provided by the ranch. There are no hookups, but plenty of room to park self-contained units. Health certificates and Coggins tests (for out-of-state travelers) are required. Fireside Inn is located on 10 pristine acres along the San Juan River on US 160 just 0.25 mile east of US 84. Their convenient location is within minutes of Pagosa Springs as well as some of the best trail riding Colorado has to offer. This is the kind of place that riders can only hope to discover when traveling with horses.

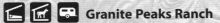

Granite Peaks Ranch

25080 CR 501
Bayfield, CO 81122

970-884-2626 (Colorado); 405-275-9988 (Off-season)
www.granitepeaksranch.net

The Granite Peaks Ranch is a horse-friendly ranch bordering the Weminuche Wilderness, open seasonally from May to October. The Pine River Trail (see Ride 82, p. 244) lies on their property. The ranch offers accommodations for horses and riders, as well as lessons, rental horses, living-quarter trailer accommodations, and parking. Pets are always welcome. The ranch has three historic cabins, built in 1936 and completely furnished with everything you need to spend the night or week. Guests are free to enjoy social hour around the Granite Peaks campfire or a long soak in one of the hot tubs.

If you want to reach the owners for reservations or questions during the off-season (November to April), please call their off-season number. (See contact info above.)

The Jolly Rancher

12751 CR 25
Cortez, CO 81321

970-564-9101; 888-564-9101
www.thejollyrancher.com • E-mail: ellenr@thejollyrancher.com

Ellen Ragsdale welcomes you to her lovely bed-and-breakfast just 3 miles from downtown Cortez. Sitting on a 15-acre hilltop surrounded by farmland, this gorgeous country home is bright, open, and spacious. Distinctive furnishings and fine linens appoint each room, with nonsmoking guest rooms adjacent to the private reading/TV area. Downstairs offers a large great room, while a relaxing outdoor hot tub promises incredible views of the La Plata Mountains, Mesa Verde

National Park, and Ute Mountain. The Jolly Rancher offers four guest rooms in the main home as well as a separate guesthouse. It also offers a nice bed for the horses at the barn, with enclosed stalls and runs, exercise turn out, and wash rack. They provide feed or you can supply your own. Out-of-state horses must have a negative Coggins test and all horses must have health certificates verifying E & W tetanus, Flu/Rhino, West Nile and distemper vaccinations. A home-cooked breakfast is available to all guests, and other meals may be had upon special request. Guest will enjoy the multitude of nearby trails that can be trailered to and from Ellen's beautiful home.

 **Sauls Creek Stables**

3113 CR 527 970-884-0218
Bayfield, CO 81122 www.saulscreekstables.com • E-mail: Tim@saulscreekstables.com

Laurie Alexander and Tim Wiegert are the friendly owners of this excellent horse hotel and RV facility. They offer four sites with complete RV hookups and four covered stalls with 25-by-50-foot runs, plenty large enough for sharing by friendly horses. The ranch is located 25 miles east of Durango, 35 miles west of Pagosa Springs, 3 miles from US 160, and has access to 35,000 acres of the San Juan National Forest right out of the arena gate. They also offer a wash rack, round pen, and hay. Health certificates, negative Coggins, and West Nile vaccinations are required in addition to routine vaccinations. Laurie and Tim host social hour at their western-style Sauls Creek Cowboy Bar, a fun way to meet fellow equestrians and talk trails after a long day in the saddle. You are certain to enjoy the care, attention, and good times here.

Rides

Cortez/Mancos
80 Transfer Corral and Area Trails.. 238
  • Aspen Loop Trail
  • Box Canyon Trail (No. 617)
  • Chicken Creek Trail (No. 615)
  • Gold Run Trail (No. 618)
  • Morrison Trail (No. 610)
  • Rim Trail (No. 613)
  • Sharkstooth Trail (No. 620)
  • Transfer Trail
  • West Mancos Trail (No. 621)

Durango/Bayfield
81 Burnt Timber Trail (No. 667)... 242
82 Pine River Trail (No. 523) 244
83 Vallecito Trail (No. 529) 247

Pagosa Springs
84 Piedra River Trail (No. 596)..... 250
85 Weminuche Trail (No. 592) 253
86 Williams Creek Trail (No. 587).. 255

80 Transfer Corral and Area Trails

Overall Ride Rating	ՍՍՍՍՍ
Trail Rating	Easy to moderately difficult
Distance	86.65 total miles; individual trail distances vary (see Description for specific mileages)
Elevation	8,910–11,000 feet
Best Season	Summer to fall
Main Uses	Equestrian, hiking, mountain biking, trailhead and backcountry camping, fishing, hunting; ATVs on the Aspen Loop Trail
Trailhead Amenities	The area called the Transfer Corral is separate from the Transfer Campground and is specifically designed for equestrians. It offers four very large wooden paddocks that each accommodate multiple friendly horses. Your own electric fences or portable panels could be used to further subdivide the paddocks if necessary. Five campsites (somewhat close quarters) are located on a small loop next to the paddocks for riders and their rigs. Fire pits and grates are available in each site. Water, picnic tables, and restrooms are on the east side (across FR 561) at the main Transfer Campground.
Dogs	On leash in the campgrounds; under voice control at your side or on leash while in the Transfer area of the national forest
Shoes	Not necessary on all trails but recommended so as not to limit your choice of trails. The Rim Trail is the rockiest of the area trails, and many can be muddy depending on precipitation.
Maps	DeLorme *Colorado Atlas & Gazetteer,* p. 85; Latitude 40° *Durango, Colorado Recreation Topo Map*
Contact	San Juan National Forest, Dolores Ranger District
Fees	$4 horse camping fee at the Transfer Corral
Regulations	See the Trail Savvy section (p. 12), website and posted regulations for additional information.
Special Notes	This is one of our favorite areas to ride in the state. The excellent trails, quality horse-camping area, seclusion, and sheer beauty are tough to beat. Note that there are many trails in this area not covered in the below descriptions. Research thoroughly before you explore the additional trails.

Directions to Trailhead

From Mancos, take CO 184 north for 0.25 mile then turn right (east) on FR 561 (W. Mancos Rd., or CR 42 in DeLorme *Colorado Atlas & Gazetteer*). Travel about 7 miles on the gravel road and look for signage for the Transfer Campground. The Transfer Corral is just past the entrance to the campground on the left (west) side of FR 561.

The setting couldn't be better. Large, safe, wooden horse corrals, of evergreen and aspen with mountains as the backdrop, and a v̄ trails will keep you interested and exploring for several days. Also, the amenities are quite convenient. Following are descriptions of some of the ṃany equestrian options in the Transfer Recreation Area.

Aspen Loop Trail: This trailhead is 0.5 mile past the campground on FR 565 at an elevation of 9,000 feet. This is a 39-mile system of easy-to-moderate trails designed specifically for off-road vehicles, but used by many others as well. The terrain includes single-track and double-track trails, old logging roads through spruce forests, and aspen stands at the highest elevation of 11,000 feet at Windy Gap. Be aware of ATVs.

Box Canyon Trail (No. 617): The easy 5.8-mile Box Canyon Trail intersects the Rim Trail (No. 613) 1 mile south of the campground on W. Mancos Rd. (FR 561), descending approximately 0.75 mile to the river. After crossing the river the trail heads downstream to Box Canyon Creek and continues to Bay Seal Springs. It then turns into an old jeep trail that crosses the mesa, passes Slate Reservoir and drops into Deer Lick Creek. Continue following the jeep trail down to the West Mancos river, cross it and then head upstream to the right, paralleling a fence until you reach a gate. After passing through the gate you will arrive at Golconda, the site of a late 1800s through early 1900s post office and general store that supplied the local miners.

Chicken Creek Trail (No. 615): This easy-to-moderate trail begins approximately 0.25 mile north of the Transfer Corral in a beautiful stand of quaking aspen, merging with the Morrison Trail for the first 0.5 mile. At the junction of the Chicken Creek and Morrison trails is a sign for the Rim Trail (1.5 miles), the Lost Canyon Trail (4 miles), and the Bear Creek Trail (8 miles). The trail drops into the Chicken Creek drainage to travel south, arriving in approximately 7.8 miles at Mancos State Park and Jackson Gulch Reservoir.

Gold Run Trail (No. 618): The well-established Gold Run Trailhead can be accessed via the West Mancos Road (FR 561) 8 miles north of the campground. The trailhead offers parking, pit toilets and a corral. This is one of the shortest (2.5 miles) and most difficult of the area trails. It drops steeply into Bear Creek Basin via several switchbacks but is designed to handle saddle stock. The trail merges with the Bear Creek Trail at mile 6. If you travel upstream, you connect with the Highline Loop National Recreation Trail (No. 622).

Morrison Trail (No. 610): The trail begins approximately 0.25 mile north of the Transfer Corral and combines with the Chicken Creek Trail for the first 0.5 mile. It then splits from the Chicken Creek Trail and heads north out of the Chicken Creek drainage and across the creek, crossing Haycamp Mesa Rd. at approximately 4.75 miles. The trail then climbs the ridge to Haycamp Mesa at 9,785 feet, approximately 7 miles into the trail. Lost Canyon is next on the trail as you descend and then ascend the other side. The route descends into the Dolores River valley to merge with the Bear Creek Trail and then terminates at the Morrison trailhead at the Wallace Ranch. The trail is 9.25 miles long and is moderately difficult.

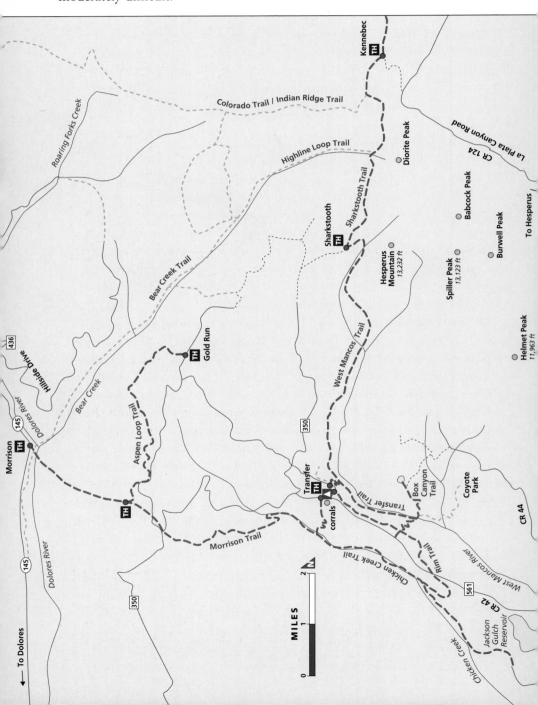

Rim Trail (No. 613): The Rim trailhead is east and south of the campground at the West Mancos Overlook on the right side of the road, prior to the entrance of the Transfer Campground. The trail travels south along the rim of Box Canyon to join the Box Canyon Trail access road. Be cautious and watch for the signs marking the trail—some are missing and the trail is poorly defined in areas. This 3-mile (one-way) trail can be very rocky and narrow, making it a bit more difficult than some of the other nearby routes. The trail continues to Doc Lowell Flats. Follow a two track road across the West Mancos Road to pick up the Rim Trail on the other side and down into Chicken Creek.

Sharkstooth Trail (No. 620): This is a moderately difficult trail of approximately 6.8 miles one way. The trail can be accessed by riding east on the West Mancos Trail or from the Sharkstooth trailhead. To reach the trailhead, take the West Mancos Rd. (FR 561) to Spruce Mill Rd. Continue for 6 miles to FR 346 then another 1 mile to the trailhead. The Sharkstooth Trail begins 0.5 mile northeast of Twin Lakes on FR 346 (Twin Lakes Rd.) at approximately 10,900 feet elevation. This trail climbs between Sharkstooth Peak and Centennial Peak and offers the opportunity to explore Windy Williams Mine approximately 1.4 miles from the trailhead. The trail descends into the Bear Creek drainage over the next 2.8 miles, then drops into the La Plata River Canyon and connects with the Colorado Trail on the Indian Ridge Trail, terminating after 1 mile at Kennebec trailhead at the end of CR 124.

Transfer Trail is a moderate 1.5-mile ride that begins just east of the corrals, FR 561 and the campground. It heads downstream to the West Mancos River connecting with the Box Canyon Trail. Riders can add several additional miles to their trip by taking the Box Canyon Trail east to end at the Box Canyon Reservoir. Or a nice 3.5-mile loop can be made by heading west on the Box Canyon and then north on the Rim Trail.

West Mancos Trail (No. 621): Located east of the campground, this moderate, 10-mile trail merges with the Big Al Trail for the first 0.5 mile, then drops steeply via a series of switchbacks into the canyon toward the South Fork of the West Mancos River. The Transfer Trail heads south downriver and the West Mancos Trail heads north, following the river through the canyon for approximately 1 mile before the canyon walls narrow; for the next 2 miles, sheer cliffs rise above the trail. The aspen trees in this section of the canyon are reportedly some of the largest specimens in the world. As you leave the canyon and cliffs, cross Aspen Creek and head southeast toward the historic mining town of Golconda. The trail reenters the canyon for another 0.5 mile, prior to the steep 1-mile climb to the Hesperus Mountain base, which sits at approximately 10,000 feet. The trail circles the north side of Hesperus Mountain and after approximately 2 miles crosses the North Fork of the West Mancos. It then climbs out of the canyon and terminates at Sharkstooth trailhead at the base of the spectacular Hesperus Mountain and FR 346 (Twin Lakes Rd.).

81 Burnt Timber Trail (No. 667)

Overall Ride Rating	∪∪∪∪∪
Trail Rating	Moderate
Distance	7 miles one way
Elevation	8,410–11,600 feet
Best Season	Summer to fall
Main Uses	Equestrian, backcountry camping, hiking, fishing, hunting
Trailhead Amenities	Large parking area for 10 or more horse trailers if others have not blocked any spots. Hitching posts and loading platforms are available. There is water at the Transfer Park Campground.
Dogs	On leash
Shoes	Recommended
Maps	DeLorme *Colorado Atlas and Gazetteer*, p. 86; National Geographic *Trails Illustrated Map 140, Weminuche Wilderness*
Contact	San Juan National Forest, Columbine Ranger District
Fees	Fees are required for the Transfer Park Campground and the campground at Florida Recreation Area. However, camping is not allowed with horses at either campground.
Regulations	Horses are not allowed in the campground. If you plan to fish, check regulations regarding limits and lure/bait restrictions. See the Trail Savvy section (p. 12), website and posted regulations for additional information.
Special Notes	We did not continue riding beyond the intersection of the Burnt Timber Trail and the City Reservoir Trail (No. 542), but there are additional trails to explore in the area.

Directions to Trailhead

From Bayfield, travel 9 miles north on CR 501 to its intersection with CR 240 and turn left (northwest). Continue 3 miles to CR 243, turn right (north), and head 7 miles to the Transfer Park Campground and Burnt Timber trailhead 1 mile past the Florida Recreation Area.

The rocky trail begins as a single track at the northern end of the trailhead parking lot. Shortly after you enter the wilderness 0.4 mile north of the trailhead, the trail climbs a steep grade for 3 miles (gaining almost 1,000 feet in elevation in the first mile). Riders cross two drainages and three creeks on the way. Depending on the yearly precipitation, the creeks should provide ample water for the horses. Among the lodgepole pine and fir at the 4-mile point, merge with a double-track trail to the right; do not take the double-track trail to the left. (Note that this intersection does not appear on the map.) At 5.5 miles, the trail curves to the northeast for roughly 1 mile before turning due north again. The trail terminates at 7 miles, where it junctions with the City Reservoir Trail. The trail was named for a significant fire that swept through the area a number of years ago. In its wake are left dramatic views of alpine meadows blooming with wildflowers during the summer months and intense exhibits of varietal color during the fall.

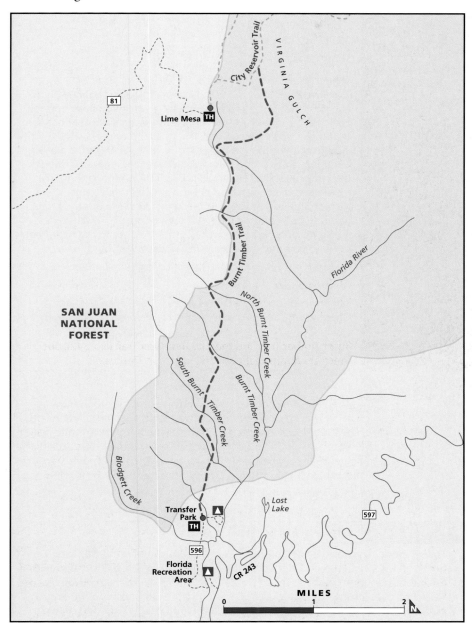

82 Pine River Trail (No. 523)

Overall Ride Rating	∪∪∪∪∪
Trail Rating	Moderate
Distance	24.5 miles one way
Elevation	8,000–11,100, feet
Best Season	Summer to fall
Main Uses	Equestrian, hiking, backcountry camping, fishing, hunting
Trailhead Amenities	The Pine River trailhead is very popular. Plan to arrive early and position your rig to pull out easily when you have finished your ride. The parking area will accommodate approximately 6–10 rigs depending on size. The trailhead offers several hitching posts, an outhouse, picnic tables, fire pits, and trash service. Camping is permitted but is not ideal at the trailhead due to the congestion; the trailhead is best utilized for parking (the 6 sites at the campground are too small for many rigs). It is recommended to camp with stock in the backcountry 3 miles down the trail after reaching the wilderness boundary. There is also no potable water and no public access to the river. Plan to bring your own water as well as water for your horse.
Dogs	On leash or under voice and sight control at all times
Shoes	Recommended
Maps	DeLorme *Colorado Atlas & Gazetteer,* pp. 77 and 87; National Geographic *Trails Illustrated Map 140, Weminuche Wilderness*
Contact	San Juan National Forest, Columbine Ranger District
Fees	$10 per night for camping
Regulations	See the Trail Savvy section (p. 12), website and posted regulations for additional information.
Special Notes	The Pine River Trail begins on private property at the Granite Peaks Ranch (for stabling and overnight accommodations, see p. 236). Please respect the no trespassing regulations and leave gates as you find them, open or closed. The trail offers excellent fly-fishing opportunities for rainbows, brookies, browns, and cutthroats after the first 3 miles. Be sure to check the fishing regulations and pack your gear in the saddlebags.

Directions to Trailhead

Travel about 18 miles east of Durango via US 160 to the town of Bayfield. Turn north on CR 501 (Vallecito Lake Rd.). After 9 miles, you reach the junction with CR 240. Continue straight (north) on CR 501 for another 4.5 miles until you reach Vallecito Lake. Turn right (east) on FR 603 to cross the dam and continue north, crossing Pine River (or Los Pinos River) via a covered bridge. Turn left (west) in 0.4 mile and stay east through the residential area, merging with FR 602. The Pine River trailhead is 3.8 miles north on FR 602, just past the campground.

Access at the trailhead is through a gate on the Granite Peaks Ranch. This is private property, so please respect the landowners' rights and stay on the trail. This popular single-track trail is bordered by aspen, ponderosa pine, spruce, and fir for most of its length. The Pine River is to your right (east) as you travel northeast and away from the trailhead and ranch. Cross Indian Creek at approximately 1.2 miles and pass through a gate. The boundary of the Weminuche Wilderness lies 2.7 miles into the trail. The Emerald Lake Trail (No. 528) intersects the Pine River Trail at approximately 6.3 miles and provides a nice opportunity for a shorter ride to the cool, blue-green waters of its namesake lake. This is a lovely spot for a picnic lunch.

Remain on the Pine River Trail through several more creek crossings to enjoy the waterfalls at approximately 13.2 miles. The well-traveled route offers a colorful wildflower display during the mid- to late-summer months. The fall is equally captivating, with thousands of aspen trees radiating beautiful reds, oranges, and yellows. After crossing Flint Creek and ascending moderately for approximately 1.4 miles, you encounter Pope Creek, an excellent area for beaver-pond trout. Farther up the trail lies the intersection with the Pine-Piedra Trail (No. 524). At approximately 17.5 miles, you reach the Forest Service Granite Peak Guard Station, a manned guard station not open to the public.

Continue northeast on the Pine River Trail, paralleling the river and alternating between trees and grassy meadows. After traveling approximately 1.8 miles, you cross the Continental Divide Trail (CDT). The CDT travels east to west and provides an outstanding view of Weminuche Pass. The trail continues on to the Continental Divide at Weminuche Pass, where it becomes the Weminuche Trail (No. 818) at 24.5 miles and continues to a trailhead approximately 4 miles farther. Given the significant length of this ride, you may turn around at any point or take advantage of one of many excellent backcountry camp spots along the way to enjoy an overnight in the Weminuche Wilderness.

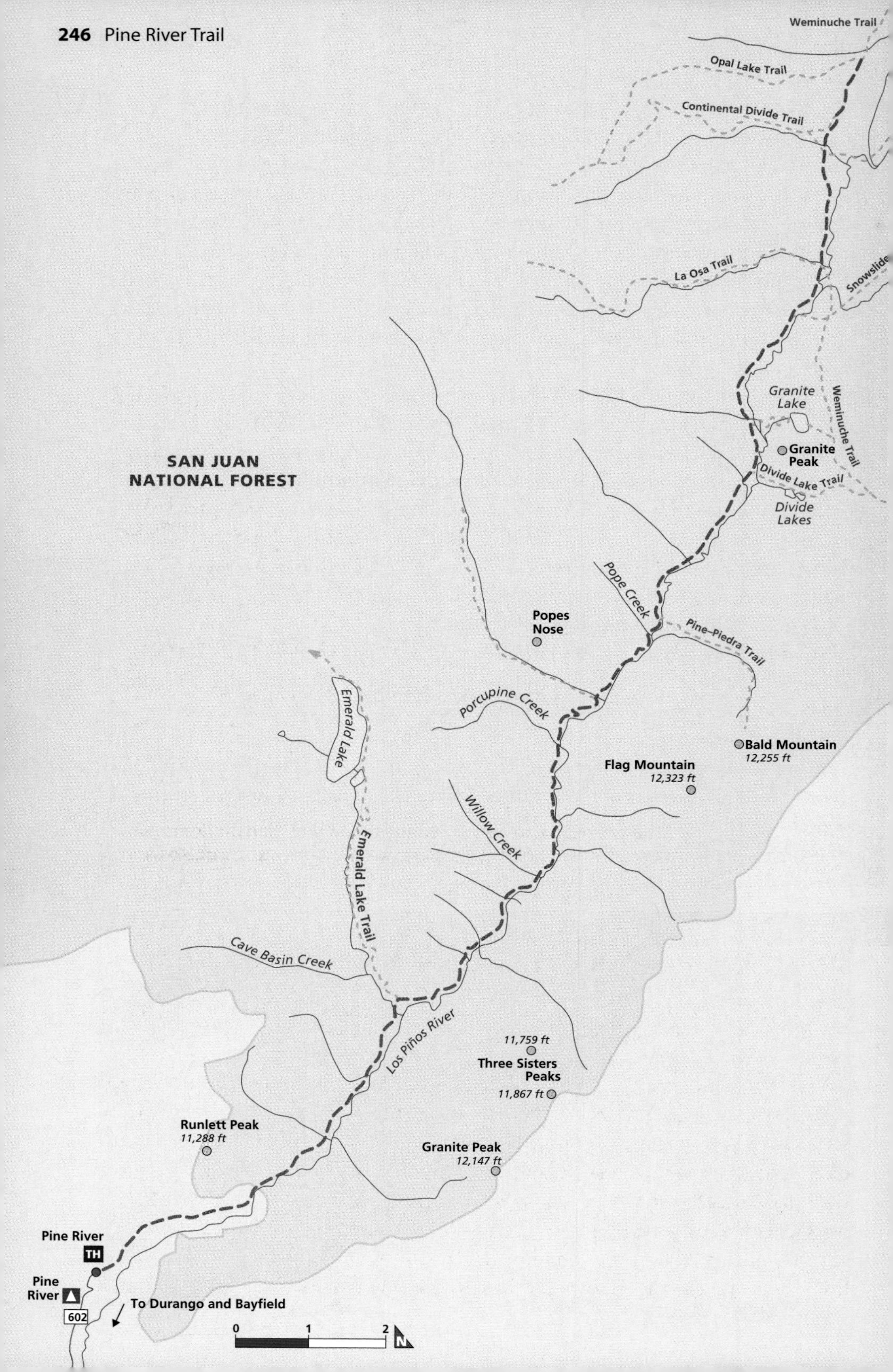

Weminuche Trail

Opal Lake Trail

Continental Divide Trail

La Osa Trail

Snowslide

**SAN JUAN
NATIONAL FOREST**

*Granite
Lake*

Weminuche Trail

Granite
Peak

Divide Lake Trail

*Divide
Lakes*

Pope Creek

**Popes
Nose**

Pine–Piedra Trail

Emerald Lake

Porcupine Creek

Bald Mountain
12,255 ft

Flag Mountain
12,323 ft

Willow Creek

Emerald Lake Trail

Cave Basin Creek

Los Piños River

11,759 ft

**Three Sisters
Peaks**

11,867 ft

Runlett Peak
11,288 ft

Granite Peak
12,147 ft

Pine River
TH

**Pine
River**
602

To Durango and Bayfield

0   1   2

N

83 Vallecito Creek Trail (No. 529)

Overall Ride Rating	೮೮೮೮೮
Trail Rating	Moderate to difficult
Distance	19.5 miles one way
Elevation	8,000–12,500 feet
Best Season	Spring to fall
Main Uses	Equestrian, hiking, backcountry camping, fishing, hunting,
Trailhead Amenities	Hitching post, unloading docks, and vault toilets are available at the trailhead. The lot can accommodate 10 trailers, but be aware that this can be a very busy, crowded parking area and is often full. Water and picnic tables are available at the main campground. Backcountry camping with livestock is permitted, but camping with horses is not permitted at the trailhead or in the campground.
Dogs	On leash or under voice and sight control at all times
Shoes	Recommended
Maps	DeLorme *Colorado Atlas & Gazetteer,* pp. 77 and 87; National Geographic *Trails Illustrated Map 140, Weminuche Wilderness*
Contact	San Juan National Forest, Columbine Ranger District
Fees	None
Regulations	If you plan to fish, check regulations regarding limits and lure/bait restrictions. See the Trail Savvy section (p. 12), website and posted regulations for additional information.
Special Notes	The trailhead can be very congested. If you plan on riding on a weekend or holiday, get an early start to secure a parking spot.

Directions to Trailhead

From Durango, travel east on US 160 approximately 18 miles to Bayfield. Turn north on CR 501 (Vallecito Lake Rd.) and continue 18.8 miles past Vallecito Lake. At the intersection north of the lake, turn left on CR 500. Follow CR 500 for approximately 2.8 miles to the trailhead and campground.

A vertical canyon wall of muti-colored granite forms an impressive backdrop at the beginning of this popular and scenic trail. The Vallecito trailhead is set in a stand of giant old-growth ponderosa pine. Begin at the western end of the parking lot, traveling only a couple hundred yards, and then follow the trail north paralleling the campground. At approximately 0.5 mile, Fall Creek marks the first of numerous stream crossings. The trail begins a gradual ascent at this point and enters the Weminuche Wilderness at approximately 0.6 mile from the trailhead. It then splits for the next 0.6 mile; horses take the left fork and hikers continue straight. The trail parallels the bubbling creek for the next 1.7 miles and splits again briefly. Again, horses bear left and hikers right. Navigate the Taylor Creek at approximately mile 3.5 followed by trail namesake Vallecito Creek.

Over the next few miles, you'll cross the creek several more times. The surrounding flora changes from ponderosa pine to fir, spruce, and aspen, interspersed with wildflower-filled meadows during the summer months. The trail crosses Rock Creek at approximately 14.8 miles, intersecting the Rock Creek Trail (No. 655) as it heads southeast and terminates at Rock Lake in about 5 miles. The junction of the Vallecito Trail and the Rock Creek Trail is as far as we rode, but farther up the Vallecito Trail you can find waterfalls in the creek as the trail begins a more significant ascent. Enjoy the breathtaking views of mountain peaks soaring above 13,000 feet and the fresh water pools left by waterfalls spilling down the granite rock faces. At approximately 17.6 miles, the unsigned Continental Divide Trail (CDT) branches off on the east side of the trail. Backcountry campers can find numerous excellent spots along the way, or can check out other trails; many extend to lovely high-mountain lakes just waiting to be explored. Don't forget to pack the fishing gear and be sure to take your time along this wonderful trail.

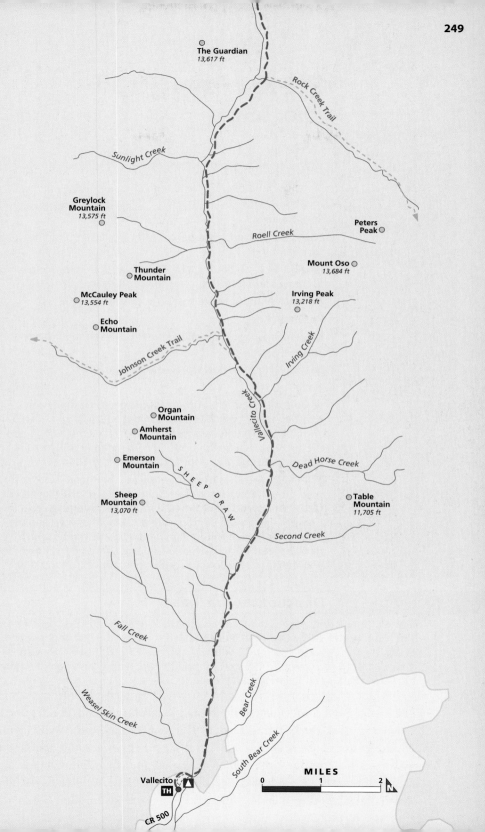

The Guardian
13,617 ft

Rock Creek Trail

Sunlight Creek

Greylock
Mountain
13,575 ft

Peters
Peak

Roell Creek

Thunder
Mountain

Mount Oso
13,684 ft

McCauley Peak
13,554 ft

Irving Peak
13,218 ft

Echo
Mountain

Irving Creek

Johnson Creek Trail

Organ
Mountain

Amherst
Mountain

Vallecito Creek

Emerson
Mountain

Dead Horse Creek

S H E E P   D R A W

Sheep
Mountain
13,070 ft

Table
Mountain
11,705 ft

Second Creek

Fall Creek

Bear Creek

Weasel Skin Creek

South Bear Creek

Vallecito
TH

CR 500

MILES

0   1   2   N

84 Piedra River Trail (No. 596)

Overall Ride Rating	♘♘♘♘♘
Trail Rating	Easy, moderate, and difficult sections
Distance	12 miles one way
Elevation	7,700–8,330 feet
Best Season	Summer to fall
Main Uses	Equestrian, hiking, backcountry camping, fishing, hunting, rock climbing
Trailhead Amenities	Parking for 6–10 horse trailers; no other amenities. Bring water for horses and humans.
Dogs	On leash or under voice and sight control
Shoes	Recommended
Maps	Delorme *Colorado Atlas & Gazetteer*, p. 87; San Juan National Forest map
Contact	San Juan National Forest, Pagosa Ranger District
Fees	None
Regulations	If you plan to fish, check regulations regarding limits and lure/bait restrictions. Group size in the South San Juan and Weminuche Wildernesses is limited to a maximum of 15 people and 10 stock. See the Trail Savvy section (p. 12), website and posted regulations for additional information.
Special Notes	The Piedra Area has been set aside as a protected habitat for river otters. Be sure to look for these reclusive and playful but rare animals. The Piedra Area is under consideration as a possible wilderness pending the settlement of water rights issues. This region is popular with big game hunters from mid-September through mid-January. Outfit yourself and your horse in blaze orange during these months for safety.

Directions to Trailhead

From Pagosa Springs, drive 2.5 miles west on US 160 to CR 600 (Piedra Rd.) and turn right (north). (Note that the Piedra Road starts out as CR 600 and is shown as this on the DeLorme map.) CR 600 will become FR 631. Travel 16 miles on Piedra Rd. until you cross the Piedra River bridge. The trailhead is approximately 300 yards farther on the left side of the road.

The Piedra River Trail is one of the most spectacular trails in all of Colorado, traveling along the beautiful Piedra River and through the canyon formed by its watercourse. Start off heading south from the trailhead on a double track along a western ridge above the river. The terrain and surrounding landscape is magnificent, with the resident peaks of the Weminuche Wilderness visible to the north. After less than 1 mile, you arrive in a gorgeous meadow where the trail becomes a single track. Ride in July and August for a promise of meadows teeming with a multitude of wildflower color or in the fall just in time for the unparalleled aspen displays that are mixed amongst old-growth ponderosa pine, Douglas fir, and Colorado spruce.

Soon you enter the canyon, a massive vertical rise of rock forming one side and tree-covered slopes forming the opposite. Here the trail climbs steadily up the ridge on the northwest side of the Piedra River. At approximately 2 miles, the trail leaves the river to negotiate the Williams Creek drainage at Ice Cave Ridge. As you ride west, you intersect a number of trails heading north from the Piedra, including the Piedra Stock Trail (No. 583), the Lower Weminuche Trail (No. 595), and the Sand Creek Trail (No. 593).

The trail continues along the ridge above the Piedra River until climbing above the Sand Creek drainage on the northeast side and then down again on the southwest side. The trail narrows and the side slopes drop dramatically to the river hundreds of feet below the ridge. In a few places you can feel the edges of the trail falling away and down the steep side slopes underneath you. This particular segment moves from easy to very difficult and is definitely not for the faint of heart, the scared of heights, the inexperienced rider, or the inexperienced horse. If you do not want to challenge yourself, or your horse, it is probably best to turn around at Sand Creek or explore one of the previously mentioned trails.

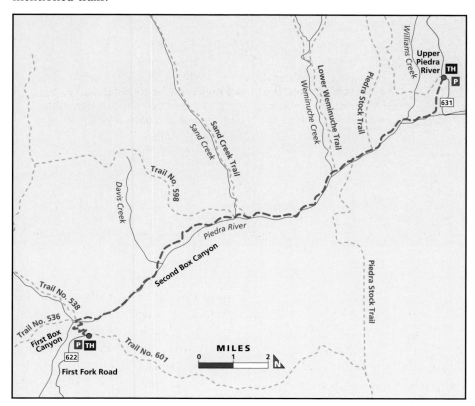

Provided you have dry trail conditions and a surefooted, calm mount, this is definitely an exhilarating and wonderfully scenic journey. Upon leaving the dramatic second box canyon, vast and colorful rangelands of the Piedra stretch to the south while snow-capped peaks jut to the north. The trail then descends to the river's edge, offering a cool drink of water for the horses, a nice place to test some of the state's finest fly-fishing waters, or a level, grassy, shady spot for a picnic. Continue from here to the trail termination at the First Fork trailhead on FR 622 (First Fork Rd.) where there are restrooms and picnic tables.

85 Weminuche Trail (No. 592)

Overall Ride Rating	◡◡◡◡◡
Trail Rating	Moderate
Distance	11 miles one way
Elevation	9,210–10,700 feet
Best Season	Summer to fall
Main Uses	Equestrian, backcountry camping, hiking, fishing, hunting
Trailhead Amenities	A kiosk, two hitching posts, and one loading platform are located here, but no water or restrooms. The trailhead has a spacious parking area with diagonal and fringe parking that easily accommodates 15 large rigs.
Dogs	On leash or under voice and sight control
Shoes	Recommended
Maps	DeLorme *Colorado Atlas & Gazetteer*, p. 77; National Geographic *Trails Illustrated Map 140, Weminuche Wilderness*
Contact	San Juan National Forest, Pagosa Ranger District
Fees	None
Regulations	Group size in the South San Juan and Weminuche Wildernesses is limited to a maximum of 15 people and 10 stock. See the Trail Savvy section (p. 12), website and posted regulations for additional information.

Directions to Trailhead

From Pagosa Springs, travel west on US 160 2.8 miles to FR 631 (Piedra Rd.). (Note that the road starts out as CR 600 and is shown as this on the DeLorme map; however, it eventually becomes FR 631.) Bear right (north) onto FR 631 and travel about 26 miles to FR 640 (Williams Creek Rd.), passing two campgrounds and staying left at two forks in the road. Turn right north and continue for another 3.5 miles to FR 644 (Poison Park Rd.). Turn left on FR 644 and travel about 3 miles to the end of the road to reach the trailhead at Poison Park.

The trail begins to the northwest as a single track through a lovely wildflower meadow. The level terrain begins its descent along a mild grade, with long switchbacks and stream crossings for the first 2 miles. The trail crosses a drainage and meanders through the trees at a private property fence line.

At approximately 2.4 miles, you reach the wilderness boundary at Hossick Creek and the junction with the Hossick Creek Trail (No. 585), which heads northeast. Use caution at this creek crossing, especially in the spring and early summer when water levels might be high. Just ahead lies the junction with the Shaw Creek Trail (No. 584), which branches into the Falls Creek Trail (No. 673). Continue north through an open meadow to cross Milk Creek at about 3 miles, a nice spot for a cool drink before the next mile or so of steep uphill grade.

At 4.6 miles, your mount will be ready for another rest as the trail returns to level ground at Elk Park. This is also a nice picnic spot for you and the horses.

The trail meanders in and out of the trees and fords several creek drainages prior to reaching the East Fork Weminuche Creek at 7 miles. Avoid an old, unsafe bridge and ford the creek only if water levels are low enough to do so safely. The trail intersects with the East Fork Weminuche Trail (No. 659) heading to the right (northeast) as you enter a meadow. Continue straight on the Weminuche Trail past the junction with the Divide Lake Trail (No. 539), which travels to the west at around mile 7.8. Granite Peak and Granite Lake lie just ahead to the west, offering some nice backcountry campsites. The Weminuche Trail terminates at approximately 11 miles, where it intersects the Snowslide Trail (No. 653), the Pine River Trail (No. 523), and the La Osa Trail (No. 525).

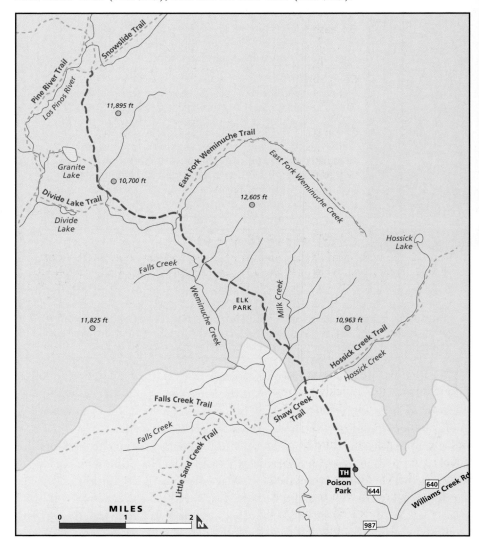

86 Williams Creek Trail (No. 587)

Overall Ride Rating	♡♡♡♡♡
Trail Rating	Moderate
Distance	14 miles one way
Elevation	8,360–11,760 feet
Best Season	Summer to fall
Main Uses	Equestrian, hiking, backcountry camping, fishing, hunting
Trailhead Amenities	Spacious parking area for numerous large rigs. Vault toilets are available but no water.
Dogs	On leash or under voice and sight control
Shoes	Recommended
Maps	DeLorme *Colorado Atlas & Gazetteer,* pp. 77–78; National Geographic *Trails Illustrated Map 140, Weminuche Wilderness*
Contact	San Juan National Forest, Pagosa Ranger District
Fees	None
Regulations	Group size in the South San Juan and Weminuche Wildernesses is limited to a maximum of 15 people and 10 stock. See the Trail Savvy section (p. 12), website and posted regulations for additional information.
Special Notes	Use caution crossing Williams Creek when spring runoff is high.

Directions to Trailhead

Take US 160 west from Pagosa Springs 2.8 miles and turn right (north) onto CR 600 (Piedra Rd.), which becomes FR 631. Continue on FR 631 for about 26 miles, turning right (east) onto FR 640 (Williams Creek Rd.). Pass the Williams Creek Reservoir and the Cimarrona Campground. FR 640 terminates at the Williams Creek trailhead.

The Williams Creek Trail leaves the trailhead to the northeast as a double track that quickly becomes a single track, traveling through stands of aspen and limber pine. Gambel oak and Douglas and white fir are interspersed with meadows of magnificent wildflowers during the summer. If you watch closely, you might see deer, elk, numerous bird species, wild turkeys, marmots, and picas. The trail

is flat through a boulder-filled drainage that is normally dry and begins to narrow as it ascends through switchbacks climbing the ridge.

At approximately 2.1 miles, you reach the junction with the Indian Creek Trail (No. 588); stay to the left to continue on the Williams Creek Trail. A fabulous view of the fluted volcanic cliffs emerges as you enter a meadow at 2.6 miles. The trail crosses a ridge and then descends to Williams Creek at approximately 3 miles. After about 7.5 miles, and several more creek crossings, you'll spot the cool, blue water of Williams Lake, accessed by the Williams Fork Lake Trail (No. 664), which treks east past the lake to intersect the Continental Divide Trail (No. 813). Continue left (northwest) past the junction and on to the intersection with the Continental Divide Trail. This is the turnaround point unless you are ready to spend the night and explore additional trails in the area.

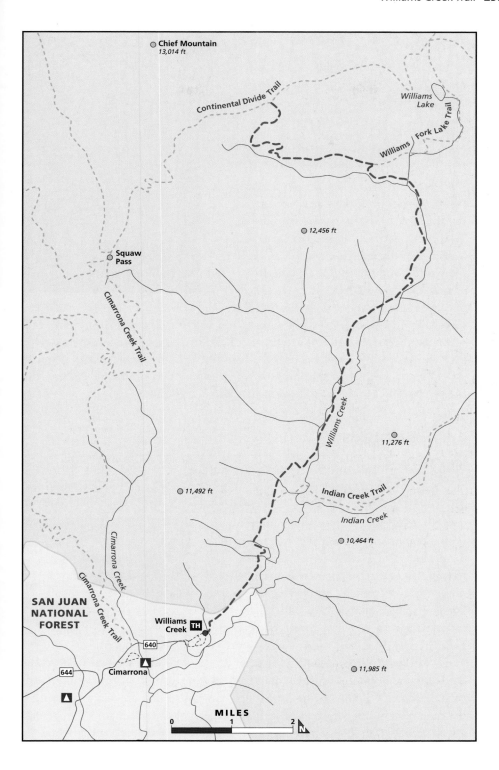

Chief Mountain
13,014 ft

Continental Divide Trail

Williams
Lake

Williams / Fork Lake Trail

12,456 ft

Squaw
Pass

Cimarrona Creek Trail

Williams Creek

11,276 ft

11,492 ft

Indian Creek Trail

Indian Creek

10,464 ft

Cimarrona Creek

SAN JUAN
NATIONAL
FOREST

Cimarrona Creek Trail

Williams
Creek TH

640

644

Cimarrona

11,985 ft

MILES

0   1   2

N

Chapter 7

South-Central Region

The south-central region of Colorado stretches from the Eastern Plains at the southern end of the state west to the Greenhorn Mountains and the San Luis Valley, the largest high-elevation valley in the world (see DeLorme *Colorado Atlas & Gazetteer* maps 69–73 and 79–83). It encompasses city and state parks, the San

Aspen on the Comanche Lake Trail

Isabel and Rio Grande National Forests and several wilderness areas. The landscape is a diverse mix of mountainous terrain, lofty peaks, numerous reservoirs and lakes, deep river canyons, pancake-flat mesas, rolling hillsides, and dense forest. This is a vast playground for the equestrian, with a multitude of excellent trails, camping locations, and accommodations to explore.

Accommodations

The Double Spur Lodge & Ranch

P.O. Box 190 • 17228 Hwy. 160   719-657-2920 (lodge); 719-657-3139 (ranch)
Del Norte, CO 81132   www.doublespurlodge.com • E-mail: info@doublespurlodge.com

The Double Spur is a beautifully appointed luxury lodge and horse hotel located just 3 miles west of Del Norte on US 160. The lodge features three separate wings, each accommodating 6–12 people. Every wing has its own living area, kitchen, bedrooms, baths, and individual design theme, and connects to the grand Rocky Mountain Great Room, where guests can meet other cowboys and cowgirls,

enjoy a game of pool, or just sip on a glass of wine in front of the floor-to-ceiling rock fireplace. While you enjoy the lodge, your horse can enjoy the amenities at the ranch, including an enclosed stall at the barn or a covered run. Also available are an arena, an indoor round pen, a heated indoor washroom and 300 acres of pasture to ride. The Double Spur is a real treat: well priced, beautifully appointed, safe, clean, friendly, and convenient to excellent trails.

The Historic Pines Ranch

P.O. Box 311
Westcliffe, CO 81252
719-783-9261; 1-800-446-9462
www.historicpines.com

The Historic Pines Ranch has four cabins, each housing two units with one to four bedrooms, a bathroom, and a living room. The cabins have been recently been redecorated. The ranch also offers a remodeled, four-bedroom, Victorian-era home built in 1893 after being purchased from a Montgomery Ward catalog for less than $900. Amenities include daily maid service, televisions and VCRs, and an indoor heated pool, hot tub, and sauna. Rental horses are available from the ranch or you can bring your own. Horseback riding, fishing instruction, guest and staff shows, overnight pack trips, white-water rafting, cookouts, wedding hosting and guest rodeos are just a few of the activities offered at the ranch. Guests can also participate in cattle moving, fence mending, and roping, or take advantage of guided hunting packages for elk, deer, and bear. An excellent children's program and babysitting make this a family-friendly place. Three buffet-style home-cooked ranch meals can be provided. The ranch accommodates a maximum of 40 people from May through October and is an excellent place for groups. The Historic Pines Ranch is more of a typical guest ranch for people without their own horses, but the friendly owners, Dean and Jodi, will also make arrangements for visitors traveling with their own stock. Call for pricing, availability, special arrangements, and reservations.

Lodge Motel

825 Hwy. 160
Fort Garland, CO 81133
719-379-2880
www.coloradodirectory.com/lodgemotel/

Open year-round, the Lodge Motel is ideally located: Situated in the center of the San Luis Valley, it enjoys an annual average of 300 days of sunshine and is surrounded by the majestic Sangre de Cristo and San Juan Mountains. The views of Blanca Peak are gorgeous. The motel has a rustic feel, with modern amenities like air-conditioning, cable television, internet data ports, and daily maid service. Horseback riding, fishing, and hiking are as close as the nearby Great Sand Dunes National Park and Preserve. Available for equestrians are a large paddock for friendly horses to share or two 12-by-12-foot box stalls with 12-by-24-foot runs. These cost $15 per night with fresh, clean water from troughs and stall cleaning included. Alfalfa hay is available for purchase. Contact Richard Gabe (owner) at the above number for motel and paddock availability and reservations.

Pueblo West Campground, Cabins & Arena

480 E. McCulloch Boulevard
Pueblo West, CO 81007

719-547-9887; 877-547-7070
www.pueblowestcampground.org

The Pueblo West Campground and National Horsemen's Arena offer 48 living-quarter trailer/RV sites, with water, 50-amp electrical, and sewer hookup on pull-throughs, or 14 camper cabins with refrigerators, microwaves, heat, air-conditioning, and television. Large partially covered runs are available for the horses. Horse owners are required to provide their own feed, buckets, and clean up. Amenities include an indoor swimming pool with hot tub, small general store, laundry, game arcade, barbeque grills, meeting rooms, and public phones. The campground is located within minutes of Lake Pueblo State Park, just west of I-25 and 1.5 miles north of US 50 on McCulloch Blvd. Fees are $25 per night for camper cabins, $20 per night for RVs, and $10 per night for horse stalls.

Rides

Beulah
87 Pueblo Mountain Park.......... 261

Del Norte
88 Middle Frisco Trail (No. 801)... 263
89 West Frisco Trail (No. 850) 265

Mosca
90 Great Sand Dunes National
   Park and Preserve................ 267
   • Little Medano Creek Trail
   • Mosca Pass Trail
   • Medano Pass Trail
   • Sand Ramp Trail

Pueblo
91 Arkansas Point Trail System/
   Lake Pueblo State Park 270
92 Dam Trail/Lake Pueblo
   State Park 273

Westcliffe
93 Comanche Lake Trail (No.1345)/
   Venable Lake Trail (No1347).. 276

87 Pueblo Mountain Park

Overall Ride Rating	UUUUU
Trail Rating	Easy to moderate
Distance	6-mile trail network within the park, plus two connecting Forest Service trails
Elevation	6,690–7,410 feet
Best Season	Summer to fall
Main Uses	Equestrian, hiking, mountain biking
Trailhead Amenities	The large main parking area has room for 4 to 8 rigs, depending on size and pedestrian parking. Southwest of the main parking area is the Tower Trail trailhead. We recommend parking at the main parking area and riding to the Tower Trail via park roads. On the north end of the park are two additional trailheads, Circle Trip and Mace Trail. Recommended parking for all trails and trailheads is at the main parking area near the Pavilion Horseshoe Lodge. Plan to bring water for yourself and your mount.
Dogs	On leash at all times
Shoes	Required
Maps	DeLorme *Colorado Atlas & Gazetteer,* p. 72; Mountain Park Environmental Center map (www.hikeandlearn.org/MPEC_MAP.html)
Contact	City of Pueblo Parks and Recreation
Fees	No fees or special permits required. Reservations required for the lodge and ramadas
Regulations	See the Trail Savvy section (p. 12), website and posted regulations for additional information.
Special Notes	The Mountain Park Environmental Center (MPEC) at Pueblo Mountain Park is a nonprofit educational organization dedicated to the promotion of ecological literacy. MPEC offers environmental education programs for all ages.

This park is a 611-acre hidden jewel, tucked into the Greenhorn Mountains on the border of the San Isabel National Forest. It has a diverse array of flora and fauna. The exhibits and handouts at the Mountain Park Environmental Center are recommended to learn more about the local plants and animals that reside in the park. Several trails make up a small but interesting trail system, consisting of an out-and-back trail, two small spurs, and one loop.

From the main parking area, follow the signs heading left (southwest) to connect with the Tower Trail, a lovely single-track route set in a shady forest of pine and aspen. The trail travels primarily southwest until it connects to the South Creek Trail (FS 1321). From this intersection, the Tower Trail turns north

Directions to Trailhead

From Pueblo, travel southwest on CO 78 approximately 23 miles to a fork in the road. Go left at the fork and head 2.7 miles to the main entrance on the right. Take the first left uphill and continue 0.1 mile. The main parking is near the Pavilion Horseshoe Lodge on the east end of the trail system.

to reach the rocky loop of the park. Although the trails actually form two smaller loops, equestrians should keep to the outer loop, consisting of the Mace and Northridge trails, to avoid the sheer rock conditions on the Devil's Canyon Trail. The terrain is partially forested, with occasional views of the surrounding area, and a nice mix of ascents and descents. Seasonal stream crossings provide opportunities for horses to drink when water is flowing. Take the Squirrel Creek Trail (FS 1384) and South Creek Trail if you want to extend your ride. The Squirrel Creek Trail, which is also open to motorbikes, is a moderate 5-mile ride that begins at Pueblo Mountain Park and ends at Davenport Campground. The South Creek Trail (FS 1321) is a moderate to difficult ride of 7.39 miles (also open to motorized traffic).

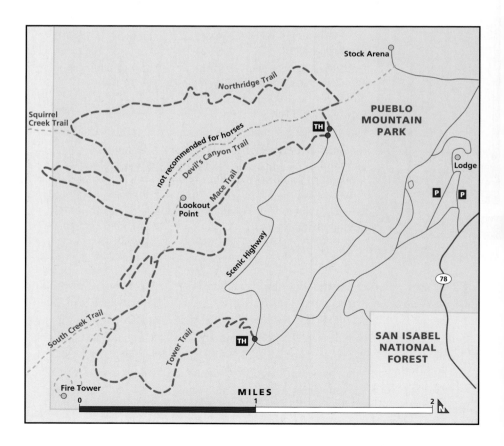

88 Middle Frisco Trail
(No. 801) (For Trail Map see p. 266)

Overall Ride Rating	☺☺☺☺☺
Trail Rating	Moderate
Distance	6.2 miles one way
Elevation	9,000—11,610 feet
Best Season	Early summer to fall
Main Uses	Equestrian, hiking, fishing, mountain biking, trailhead and backcountry camping, hunting
Trailhead Amenities	This excellent trailhead offers two large hitching posts, several tether lines that accommodate three horses each, and three pipe corrals (made possible by the Trailwise Back Country Horsemen, the Rio Grande National Forest, and funding from Colorado State Trails grants). Parking is available for as many as 30 large rigs. This is an ideal area for group rides or group camping trips. No other facilities. Plan to bring water for humans and horses, although horses can also often be watered from the creek.
Dogs	Under voice and sight control or on leash
Shoes	Recommended
Maps	DeLorme *Colorado Atlas & Gazetteer*, p. 79; National Geographic *Trails Illustrated Map 142, South San Juan/Del Norte*
Contact	Rio Grande National Forest, Divide Ranger District
Fees	None
Regulations	See the Trail Savvy section (p. 12), website and posted regulations for additional information.
Special Notes	This is a very popular area with hunters. Be careful during hunting season; outfit yourself and your horse in blaze orange.

Directions to Trailhead

From the east end of Del Norte, turn south on CR 13 (French St.) at the sign stating "National Forest Access San Francisco Creek." The trailhead is approximately 9.8 miles down a dirt road. The trail is on the left (east) at the end of FR 320.

The locals as well as the signage refer to this area, the trailhead, and the trails by the abbreviated name "Frisco"—not to be confused with San Francisco. The Frisco trailhead supports the Middle Frisco Trail as well as the West Frisco Trail, just a bit down the road past the corrals. There are two parking areas right next to each other and you can park at either one to access the trails. The parking area closest to the Middle Frisco Trail is best for horse trailers as it is the larger of the two.

From the lower (or first) parking area nearest to the pipe corrals, proceed toward the creek bed, cross the creek (you'll see a Carsonite sign), and begin your journey amongst the aspen and evergreen which eventually give way to limber pine, ponderosa pine, and Douglas fir.

The clearly marked single-track path climbs to the southwest up the creek drainage on an earthen base scattered with occasional rocks. Incredible views of the 12,840 Pintada Mountain to the east present themselves in the last few miles of trail before a significant climb past the San Francisco Lakes. A series of 12 switchbacks lead even higher to an ancient stand of bristlecone pine standing watch over the upper lake. The trail intersects the West Frisco Trail on the ridge just below the summit of Bennett Peak (13,203 feet). At this point, you can return the way you came or make a loop using the West Frisco Trail to return to the trailhead (see Ride 89, p. 265). A number of good campsites can be found in the meadows along the trail with creeks and lakes for plenty of water.

89 West Frisco Trail (No. 850)

Overall Ride Rating	○○○○○
Trail Rating	Easy
Distance	6.5 miles one way
Elevation	9,600–13,200 feet
Best Season	Early summer to fall
Main Uses	Equestrian, hiking, trailhead and backcountry camping, fishing, mountain biking, hunting, ATVs
Trailhead Amenities	In addition to the Middle Frisco trailhead described in Ride 88 (see p. 263) which also services the West Frisco Trail, there is a circular pull-through lot with room for five to six rigs at this trailhead. There are no restrooms, drinking water or other amenities.
Dogs	Under voice control or on leash
Shoes	Recommended
Maps	DeLorme *Colorado Atlas & Gazetteer*, p. 79; National Geographic *Trails Illustrated Map 142, South San Juan/Del Norte*
Contact	Rio Grande National Forest, Divide Ranger District
Fees	None
Regulations	See the Trail Savvy section (p. 12), website and posted regulations for additional information.
Special Notes	This is a very popular area with hunters. Be cautious during hunting season; outfit yourself and your horse in blaze orange.

Directions to Trailhead

Follow the directions from Del Norte to the Middle Frisco trailhead (see Ride 88, p. 263). The West Fork trailhead is approximately 0.25 mile southwest of the Middle Frisco trailhead beyond the three pipe corrals.

The West Frisco Trail begins southwest out of the parking area. Aspen groves soon give way to forests of pine and fir. The easy-to-follow route makes a gradual climb up the West Fork of the San Francisco Creek drainage on an occasionally rocky trail surface. Pack the fishing rod and try for some Frisco Creek trout (flies and lures only).

The trail joins the Middle Frisco Trail below the ridge of the lofty 13,203-foot Bennett Peak. At this point, return the way you came or make a loop ride with the Middle Frisco Trail (see Ride 88, p. 263) and enjoy the San Francisco Lakes and the gorgeous views of Pintada Mountain. The West Frisco Trail terminates at Bennett Peak, but can be looped back to the trailhead with the Middle Frisco Trail.

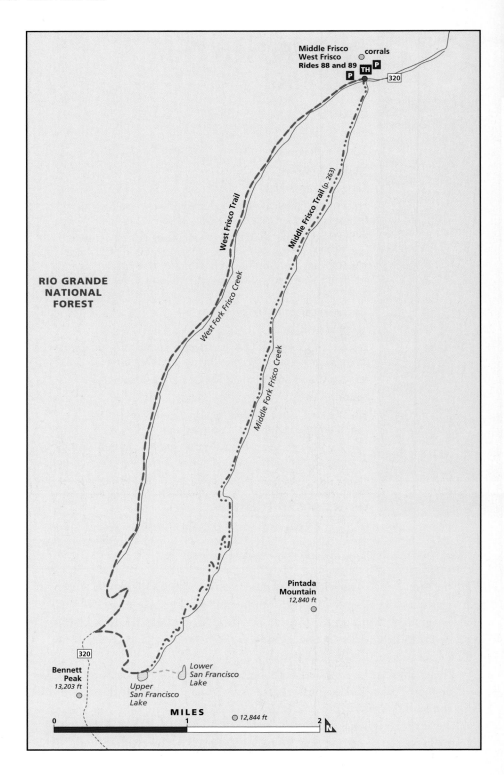

Middle Frisco
West Frisco
Rides 88 and 89

corrals

320

West Frisco Trail

Middle Frisco Trail (p. 263)

West Fork Frisco Creek

**RIO GRANDE
NATIONAL
FOREST**

Middle Fork Frisco Creek

**Pintada
Mountain**
12,840 ft

320

**Bennett
Peak**
13,203 ft

*Upper
San Francisco
Lake*

*Lower
San Francisco
Lake*

MILES

0   1   2

12,844 ft

N

90 Great Sand Dunes National Park & Preserve

Overall Ride Rating	❂❂❂❂❂
Trail Rating	Easy to moderate
Distance	See Description for individual trail mileages
Elevation	8,250–10,198 feet (Medano Pass); 8,250–9,720 feet (Mosca Pass Trail); 8,200–8,600 feet (Little Medano Creek Trail); 8,250–9,308 (Sand Ramp Trail)
Best Season	Year-round depending on weather
Main Uses	Equestrian, hiking, backcountry camping, fishing, mountain biking, hunting
Trailhead Amenities	Horse parking is available at three locations. The amphitheater parking area is the best for horse trailers. It is paved and has room for six to ten rigs depending on size. There is an RV dump station (please do not block it), trash receptacles, and an aluminum can recycling center (which can be loud and possibly spook horses). The parking lot at the Montville Nature Trail/Mosca Pass trailhead could accommodate one or possibly two small rigs depending on car parking. The Point of No Return area is for day use only if space permits. Plan to bring water for yourself and your horses at all trailheads.
Dogs	On leash at all times
Shoes	Recommended
Maps	DeLorme *Colorado Atlas & Gazetteer,* p. 81; National Geographic *Trails Illustrated Map 138, Sangre de Cristo Mountains;* National Park Service www.nps.gov/grsa/maps/grsa_map.jpg
Contact	Great Sand Dunes National Park and Preserve
Fees	$3 per day for adults. A free backcountry permit is required for camping
Regulations	Please ride away from the main use areas. The Wellington Ditch Trail is closed to horses, as is the Montville Nature Trail (except the portion required to access the Mosca Pass Trail, which requires hand-leading horses). Also closed to horses are the Pinyon Flats Campground; visitor center parking lot area and nature trail; Dunes parking lot; the Mosca Creek picnic area; the dunes and Medano Creek directly west of the Dunes parking lot as far as the High Dune; any paved roads, except when crossing; and the Sand Ramp Trail between the Pinyon Flats Campground and Point of No Return trailhead. The park strictly enforces these regulations. All other areas are open to horseback riding.

Please clean up after your horse when you leave. Overnight stock use is permitted only in the backcountry. Camping with horses is permitted at the Little Medano, Aspen, Cold Creek, and Sand Creek backcountry camps. A free permit is required, which you may obtain from the visitor center. You may also camp in the wilderness areas (except those closed to horses as specified above) and anywhere in the national preserve except the Medano Rd. designated campsites. Do not set up camp within 300 feet of lakes and 200 feet of streams. In the national park, groups camping with horses or pack animals are limited to 6 humans and 6 animals. In the national preserve, group size is limited to 25 total people and stock.

See the Trail Savvy section (p. 12), website and posted regulations for additional information.

Directions to Trailhead

From Alamosa, take US 160 14.4 miles to CO 150. Turn left (north) and continue 16 miles to the park entrance.

Great Sand Dunes National Park and Preserve is home to North America's tallest sand dunes, which rise over 750 feet across 30 square miles against the backdrop of the magnificent Sangre de Cristo Mountain Range. The Sand Dunes were designated as a national monument and preserve in 1932 and were re-classified in 2004 as our 58th (and newest) national park. The Great Sand Dunes National Park and Preserve now encompasses a wide variety of terrain and habitats, including tundra, grasslands, spruce and pine forests, aspen stands, cottonwood groves, and wetlands. We describe four wonderful trails within the national park and preserve, all offering unique opportunities for the equestrian.

The Little Medano Creek Trail/Sand Ramp Trail begins just to the northwest of the Pinyon Flats Campground near site 62 at approximately 8,200 feet elevation. It is 5.5 miles one way and ends at Little Medano Creek backcountry camping area and Sand Creek/Ramp trailhead. This trail is closed to horses between the Pinyon Flats Campground and the Point of No Return trailhead. Riders should begin on the Medano Pass Primitive Rd., which parallels the trail just to the west. The park's intention is to provide a path for riders that avoids the heavily used and developed Pinyon Flats Campground. Once past the campground, riders can jog east of the road and pick up the trail heading north.

The Medano Pass Trail can be accessed from within the park. Follow the Medano Pass Primitive Rd. from the amphitheater parking area to the Sand Creek/Ramp trailhead. Follow the right fork to the northeast. Creek crossings can be challenging during times of high volume. The trail forks a second time at 5.75 miles from the Sand Ramp trailhead; here the right fork leads to Medano Pass and terminates at a campground near the intersection of FS Rd. 559 and FS 412. The left fork leads to Medano Lake via the 3.5-mile Medano Lake Trail (No. 887) beginning at 10,000 feet and climbing to an elevation of 12,000 feet.

The Mosca Pass Trail (No. 883) is an easy 3.5-mile trail one way, beginning at 8,250 feet at the Montville parking area (0.25 mile north of the visitor center) and climbing to 9,720 feet at Mosca Pass in the Sangre de Cristo Mountains. The trail starts in a steep-walled canyon, leaving the National Park and entering the National Preserve almost immediately. It follows the route of an old wagon road along Mosca Creek in the company of aspen, spruce, and fir for approximately 2 miles. The trail begins to level at a series of open meadows for the last 1.5 miles before ending at Mosca Pass where it meets Forest Rd. No. 583. The views of the dunes, San Luis Valley, and Wet Mountain Valley are impressive and singularly worth the beautiful ride.

The Sand Ramp Trail may also be labeled as the Sand Creek Trail on some maps. From the Sand Creek trailhead it continues northwest for an additional

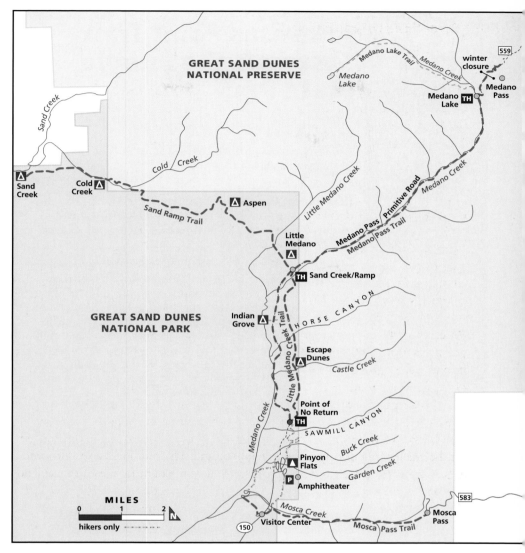

6 miles. This trail follows the base of the foothills, where sand encounters the mountains on the northeastern edge of the dunes. Located along the trail are eight backcountry sites where horse camping is allowed. A free backcountry permit is required and may be obtained from the visitor center. The trail provides a striking overlook of most of the park as well as the dunes complex south and west of the trail.

We have only discussed the trail possibilities in the lower portion of the park and preserve. It is possible to research and ride a variety of additional excellent nearby trails in the Sangre de Cristo Wilderness, the Rio Grande National Forest, and the San Isabel National Forest.

91 Arkansas Point Trail System/Lake Pueblo State Park

Overall Ride Rating	♘♘♘♘♘
Trail Rating	Easy to moderate
Distance	2.1 miles on a double loop, plus a vast network of social trails for extended mileage
Elevation	4,380–5,150 feet
Best Season	The state park facilities are closed during the winter months, but access to the reservoir exists year-round. The summer months can be hot, so we advise riding early or late or avoiding hot summer days entirely.
Main Uses	Equestrian, hiking, fishing, mountain biking, hunting, boating
Trailhead Amenities	The Arkansas Point Campground lot just south of the main visitor center and entrance station has ample room for horse trailers. Also open to horses is the Arkansas Point Campground overflow parking area, a paved lot to the north of the campground at the Southshore Marina and boat dock on the southern edge of the reservoir; it has room for 30 or more trailers. Drinking water and restrooms are available at the visitor center. However, the park hopes to add amenities—possibly even equestrian amenities—in the future.
Dogs	On a leash at all times
Shoes	Barefoot okay
Maps	DeLorme *Colorado Atlas & Gazetteer*, p. 73; Lake Pueblo State Park map (http://parks.state.co.us)
Contact	Lake Pueblo State Park
Fees	$5 daily entrance fee or annual $55 state parks pass required
Regulations	Horses are not allowed at swim beaches. No overnight camping with horses in Lake Pueblo State Park at this time (see Accommodations, p. 260, for alternatives). See the Trail Savvy section (p. 12), website and posted regulations for additional information.
Special Notes	Pueblo Reservoir is primarily a warm-water fishery, supporting largemouth and smallmouth bass, walleye, perch, crappie, channel catfish, northern pike, and stocked rainbow trout. Hunting for small game, upland birds, and waterfowl is permitted in designated areas. This is a semiarid region; please remember to bring plenty of water for you and your horse. Keep your eye out for prairie rattlesnakes and take appropriate precautions. Both the Northshore and Southshore Marinas offer food and fuel. Be cautious of soft, sandy areas and prairie dog holes.

Directions to Trailhead

From Pueblo, drive approximately 4 miles west from I-25 on US 50. Turn left (south) on Pueblo Blvd. (CO 45) and continue approximately 4 miles to CO 96 (Thatcher Rd.). Turn right (west) on CO 96 and drive 6 miles to the sign on the right side of the road at the entrance to the Lake Pueblo State Park. Continue 0.6 mile to a left fork. At 0.4 mile (you will have passed the visitor center and entrance station) make a left into the Arkansas Point Campground and park to your right. Additional parking is available at the overflow parking at the boat dock and Southshore Marina.

The Lake Pueblo State Park comprises approximately 25 square miles of semiarid desert state park lands and is home to the Arkansas Point Trail System. The trailhead is approximately 0.1 mile south of the trailer parking area. The Arkansas Point Trail System kiosk is on the west side of the campground visitor center and south of the parking area, and both the Conduit Trail and the Arkansas Point Trail head out to the west from the kiosk. Trail guides are available at the visitor center.

The trails are relatively flat single tracks consisting of sandy dirt with occasional loose rock. Carsonite markers let you know where you are. The Conduit Trail goes to your right (southwest) to eventually intersect a double-track road. This road was once part of the Colorado Fuel and Iron Company (CF&I) conduit that carried water from the Arkansas River to the steel plant in Pueblo prior to the damming of the reservoir. As you continue west, you intersect the Skull Canyon Trail traveling south. Turn right (north) to head back toward the reservoir or to return to the trailhead.

The Conduit Trail can also connect to the Broken Hip Trail for an additional loop. Retrace your original path to the intersection of the Conduit Trail and turn left to ride the Arkansas Point Trail loop. Stay to the right at all trail junctions to arrive at the top of the bluff at the far eastern edge. Look for interpretive signs along the trail that explain the history of the area. Soon the trail descends again; stay to the left as you drop down the face of the bluff. This is the only potentially challenging portion of the trail, as it is steep and has some significant steps down the trail.

At this point, the route returns to the trailhead. The Greenhorn Mountains, the Sangre de Cristo Mountains, and the Spanish Peaks can be seen in the distance, framed by the blue water of the reservoir. The surrounding flora is short-grass prairie accented with cholla and prickly pear cactus, saltbush, and yucca. Piñon pine, sage, and juniper can be seen on the prairie and in and around the surrounding bluffs and cliffs. The area fauna includes ground squirrels, foxes, skunks, raccoons, badgers, coyotes, deer, and pronghorn.

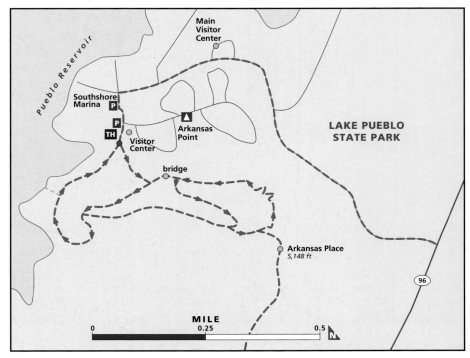

92 Dam Trail/Lake Pueblo State Park

Overall Ride Rating	○○○○○
Trail Rating	Easy
Distance	16.5 miles one way
Elevation	4,380–4,600 feet
Best Season	Year-round depending on weather. The summer months can be hot, so we advise riding early or late or avoiding hot summer days entirely.
Main Uses	Equestrian, hiking, fishing, mountain biking, hunting, boating
Trailhead Amenities	The Cottonwood day-use area accommodates 8–10 rigs, depending on size and other vehicles, and offers restrooms and potable water. Equestrians can also park at the Northshore Marina (restrooms and water available), the Arkansas Point Campground (no restrooms or water), and the Southshore Marina overflow (no restrooms or water).
Dogs	On leash at all times
Shoes	Barefoot okay. Equestrians are permitted to ride on the pavement or on the wide earthen shoulder next to the pavement.
Maps	DeLorme *Colorado Atlas & Gazetteer,* p. 73; Lake Pueblo State Park map (http://parks.state.co.us)
Contact	Lake Pueblo State Park
Fees	$5 daily entrance fee or $55 annual state parks pass required
Regulations	No overnight camping with horses (see Accommodations, p. 260, for alternatives). Horses are not allowed on swim beaches. Build fires only in the fire rings that are provided. See the Trail Savvy section (p. 12), website and posted regulations for additional information.
Special Notes	Pueblo Reservoir is primarily a warm-water fishery, supporting largemouth and smallmouth bass, walleye, perch, crappie, channel catfish, northern pike, and stocked rainbow trout. Hunting for small game, upland birds, and waterfowl is permitted, but only in designated areas. This is a semiarid region; please remember to bring plenty of water for you and your horse. Keep your eye out for prairie rattlesnakes and take appropriate precautions. Both the Northshore and Southshore Marinas offer food and fuel.

Directions to Trailhead

From Pueblo, drive approximately 4 miles west from I-25 on US 50. Turn left (south) on Pueblo Blvd. (CO 45) and continue approximately 4 miles to CO 96 (Thatcher Rd.). Turn right (west) on CO 96 and drive 6.5 miles to the second park entrance. The Cottonwood day-use area is the best trailhead for the Dam Trail. Follow the park map and signs to this lot.

Lake Pueblo State Park has traditionally been popular with sun lovers, boaters, water-skiers, sailors, swimmers, runners, anglers, and bicyclists. Today, the new breed of recreationist enjoying the 7,000-acre park is the equestrian. Exceptional, dramatic views of sandstone bluffs; 4,500 surface acres of cool, refreshing water; miles of level, rock-free, and tree-lined trails; and mild weather almost year-round make Lake Pueblo State Park an up-and-coming place to ride. The Dam Trail offers riders several routes to choose from:

Option 1: From the Cottonwood day-use area, ride north toward Anticline Lake. At the lake, the trail travels to the southeast and then to northwest. Follow the trail east and then south toward the fishing pond. Your ride could be extended by continuing in a southeast direction to connect with the 12-mile Pueblo River Trail which travels along the Arkansas River. The Greenway and Nature Center of Pueblo is just 3 miles east of the park toward the city of Pueblo and offers a nice spot along the river to stop for lunch at their café, although there is currently no place to tie horses.

Option 2: From the Cottonwood Day use area, take the trail north to Anticline Lake then west. The trail will then make a sharp turn to the north and travel around the northern boundary of the park, offering expansive views of the dam and Rock Canyon. Continue west for lingering waterfront vistas as you make your way past a sailboard launch and picnic areas on to the Northshore Marina. From the Northshore Marina, you can continue riding northwest to the end of the park, where the Division of Wildlife manages an additional 4,000 acres of public land at the Pueblo Reservoir State Wildlife Area.

Option 3: From the Cottonwood day-use area, head south, paralleling the dam. This portion of the trail leads past the fish hatchery, maintenance headquarters, and Division of Wildlife headquarters, eventually crossing the main park road; please use caution as you cross. The route continues south to the visitor center and Southshore Marina, terminating at Arkansas Point, where you can explore additional miles of trail (See Ride 91, p. 270).

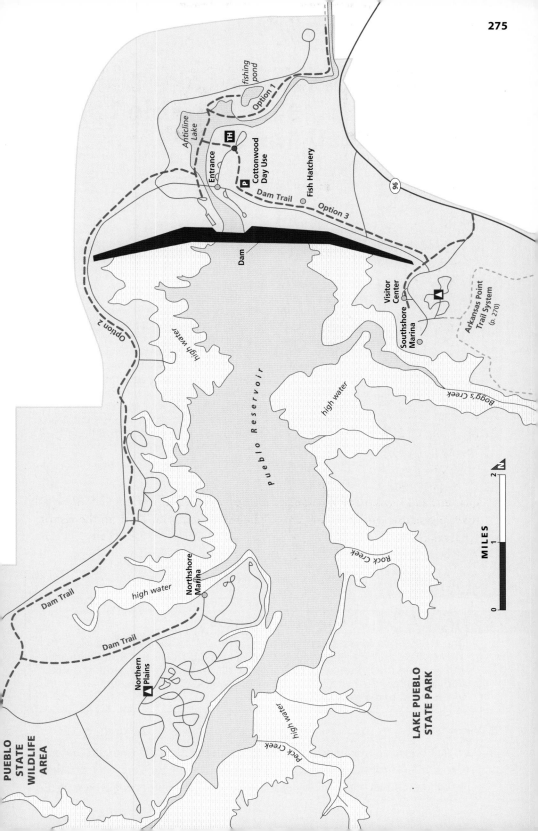

PUEBLO STATE WILDLIFE AREA

LAKE PUEBLO STATE PARK

Pueblo Reservoir

fishing pond

Option 1

Anticline Lake

Entrance

Cottonwood Day Use

Fish Hatchery

Dam Trail

Option 3

96

Dam

Visitor Center

Arkansas Point Trail System (p. 270)

Southshore Marina

Bogg's Creek

high water

Option 2

high water

Rock Creek

high water

Dam Trail

Northshore Marina

high water

Dam Trail

Northern Plains

Peck Creek

high water

N

MILES

0   1   2

93

Comanche Lake Trail (No. 1345)/Venable Lake Trail (No. 1347)

Overall Ride Rating	♘♘♘♘♘
Trail Rating	Moderate to difficult
Distance	10.5-mile loop
Elevation	9,000–12,800 feet
Best Season	Late spring to fall
Main Uses	Equestrian, hiking, backcountry and trailhead camping, hunting
Trailhead Amenities	A nice large loop serves as the parking lot for many of the trails in this area; there is room for at least six large rigs. Vault toilets and a hitching post are also located here, but no water. The Alvarado Campground has three sites that allow horse camping, but there is no fencing or method of containment. The best option is using a picket line tethered between the trees. Medium to long rigs will have difficulty negotiating the parking between trees in this fairly small loop. Future plans, however, call for potential enlargement and enhancement of the area, so check back. There are a few grassy areas nearby (not in the immediate campsite) where setting up your electric fence could be an option, but be prepared with a picket line as a backup. The sites can be reserved ahead of time with the National Recreation System at 877-444-6777, or www.recreation.gov.
Dogs	On leash in campgrounds, but not allowed on trails
Shoes	Recommended
Maps	DeLorme *Colorado Atlas & Gazetteer*, p. 71; National Geographic *Trails Illustrated Map 138, Sangre de Cristo Mountains*
Contact	San Isabel National Forest, San Carlos Ranger District
Fees	$5 day-use fee
Regulations	See the Trail Savvy section (p. 12), website and posted regulations for additional information.

Directions to Trailhead

The trailhead is located approximately 9.5 miles southwest of the town of Westcliffe. From Westcliffe, head west on Hermit Rd. 2 miles to CR 137. Turn left, travel 1 mile south, then turn right onto CR 150 and go west for another 1 mile. Turn left onto CR 141 and continue 2 miles south. At CR 140, turn right and head 2 miles west to the campground.

This 10.5-mile loop trail receives heavy use by equestrians and hikers. The trail begins approximately 0.1 mile north of the Alvarado Campground and proceeds in a southwestern direction along the Comanche Lake Trail through pine, willow, and aspen, climbing past Comanche Lake on up to the crest of the

Sangre de Cristo Mountain Range. At this point, you can choose to take the Phantom Terrace north to the Venable Lake Trail, turn back toward the trailhead, or continue west via the Comanche Trail (No. 746), along the Middle Fork of North Crestone Creek.

The Phantom Terrace connects to the Venable Lake Trail via a steep, narrow, and rocky route. This portion requires extreme caution as the trail slopes off dramatically along the edges. Horses should be in excellent condition before making Phantom Terrace's 3,800-foot climb. Should you and your partner choose to brave the Terrace, you will return along Venable Creek, pass Venable Lakes, and exit about 0.5 mile north of Alvarado Campground on the Rainbow Trail. The scenery is outstanding, offering views of Rito Alto Peak, Spread Eagle Peak, and the Wet Mountain Valley below. If you're interested in more riding in the area, the Comanche Lake and Venable Lake trails also connect to the Rainbow Trail (No. 1336), the North Crestone Creek Trail (No. 744), and the Comanche Trail (No. 746).

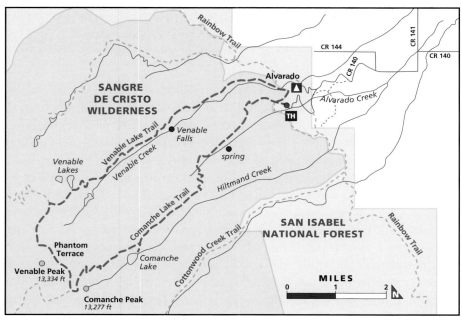

Chapter 8

The Eastern Plains

Picket Wire Canyon offers riders the chance to see dinosaur tracks and prehistoric rock art.

The Colorado plains begin at the eastern border of the state at a low elevation of 3,500 feet along the Arkansas River. Emerging gradually from the grasslands of Kansas and Nebraska, Colorado's High Plains slope gently upward for a distance of some 200 miles to the foothills of the Rocky Mountains, eventually reaching an elevation of about 6,500 feet (see DeLorme *Colorado Atlas & Gazetteer* maps 94–103). Major features of the Eastern Plains are the two shallow river valleys of the Arkansas and the South Platte Rivers and a large expanse of rolling grassland between and on either side of them. The plains are characterized by rolling short- and midgrass prairies broken by occasional bluffs and canyons, and divided by higher country and hills extending eastward from the mountains. The landscape is often decorated with wildflowers during the summer months and occasionally accented with unique rock outcroppings. Landscapes vary: Portions of the region are semiarid desert and others are wetland riparian habitats. Generally, the plains offer milder winter temperatures, providing excellent late-fall, early-spring, and even winter riding opportunities for equestrians. But be aware of the harsh winds that sometimes frequent the plains. On the whole, this rural and far less populated region is a great place for riding, providing a surprisingly ideal retreat from the rush of urban life.

Accommodations

Arrowhead Stables

42918 CR 19
Haxtun, CO 80731

970-520-1942
E-mail: ttimm@pctelcom.coop

Tom and Tammi Timm are the friendly hosts of this very nice horse hotel in northeastern Colorado. They welcome horses and their owners, and offer 12-by-12-foot stalls in a newly built barn. The stalls include feeders, fresh water, and 30-foot runs. Living-quarter trailers can park right at the barn and access water and electrical. The stable is conveniently located near the town of Haxtun, between North Sterling State Park and Bonny Lake State Park. The nearby historic Haxtun Inn has good food and lodging. Call for pricing and availability.

Bent County Fairgrounds

1499 Ambassador Thompson Blvd.
Las Animas, CO 81507

719-456-0764 (grounds)

The Bent County Fairgrounds in Las Animas offers overnight stays for horses, trailers, and campers, with some water and electrical hookups available. Contact Garrett Godfrey for reservations and arrangements at 719-456-1512. (Note that this is Mr. Godfrey's daytime business number at the First National Bank of Las Animas.) Horse owners are required to provide their own feed, buckets, and clean up. This is a great place to stay if you need a layover on your way to John Martin Reservoir State Park or the Comanche National Grassland.

JB's Horse Motel

19790 Hwy. 385
Burlington, CO 80807

719-346-8217

Joan B. Chandler is the owner and manager of this overnight equine boarding facility. She offers seven nice indoor stalls with runs in a safe and clean barn. Feed is available at an extra charge if you don't have your own. Camper hookups and overnight parking are an option at the barn. JB's is located 20 miles from Bonny Lake State Park. Call for pricing, reservations, and detailed directions.

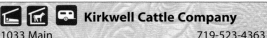

Kirkwell Cattle Company

1033 Main	719-523-4363
Stage Stop Hotel, Ste. 13	www.kirkwellcattle.com
Springfield, CO 81073	E-mails: blackjack@rural-com.com; wesm@ria.com

Kirkwell Cattle Company is a working cattle ranch offering customized group equestrian adventures the "Old West way." Their packages can be tailored for any skill level, from novice to expert. You're welcome to bring your own horse or use one of the excellent ranch horses. They can provide food, accommodations, equipment, knowledgeable guides, and even cowboy entertainment. Activities include the spring and fall Kirkwell Cattle roundups, visits to the Comanche National Grassland by horseback or wagon, cross-country riding through Colorado, Oklahoma, and New Mexico, camping at 9,000 feet, and exploring the San Juan Mountains on horseback.

West Pawnee Ranch Bed-and-Breakfast

29451 Weld CR 130	970-895-2482
Grover, CO 80729	www.westpawneeranch.com

This working ranch is situated on 7,000 acres in the heart of the remote, peaceful Pawnee National Grassland. Innkeepers Paul and Luanne Timm welcome you and your horse to ride their ranch or the surrounding region. Birding is a favorite activity of many of their guests, as there are more than 250 species known to inhabit the area. Accommodations include two bedrooms in the main house, each with its own bath. You can also stay in the Prairie House, which sleeps up to six people. A hearty prairie breakfast is included. Your horses may stay in a paddock with shelter from the elements or in a stall with advance arrangements. This is a pleasant and tidy place to stay, with wonderful company from the hosts. Reservations may be made for evening meals in advance. This is a good plan, given that the nearest restaurant is more than 30 miles away.

Rides

Idalia
94 Bonny Lake State Park.......... 281

Greeley
95 Pawnee National Grassland... 283

La Junta
96 Picket Wire Canyon/Comanche
    National Grassland 285

97 Red Shin Trail/John Martin
    Reservoir State Park 288

98 Vogel Canyon/Comanche
    National Grassland 291

Springfield
99 Homestead Trail/Picture Canyon/
    Comanche Nat'l Grassland.... 294

Sterling
100 South Shoreline Trail/North
    Sterling State Park 298

94 Bonny Lake State Park

Overall Ride Rating	♡♡♡♡♡
Trail Rating	Easy
Distance	One short designated nature trail, plus 26 miles of shoreline for cross country riding
Elevation	3,690 feet
Best Season	Year-round; highly recommended in spring and fall
Main Uses	Fishing, boating, hunting, campground camping
Trailhead Amenities	Horse trailer parking is allowed at the Foster Grove Campground (see park map for directions); Hale Ponds (from the south end of the dam go 2 miles east on CR 3.5, turn north or left on Road LL.5 for 0.5 mile, go past the volunteer fire dept. and turn right or east on CR4, go 4.5 miles to Hale Ponds); and the South Republican State Wildlife Area (from CO 385 go east or right on CR2 or CR3 and follow the signs to arrive at the SWA before reaching the reservoir). Horse camping is allowed in the Foster Grove Campground in campsites 31–42. Horses must be kept and constrained by electric fence or portable panels behind the trees west of the campsites. There are no trees for highlining in this area. The campsites all have picnic tables and fire grates. Shared amenities include restrooms, common water spigots, a shower facility, a dumpster for manure at the end of the trees, and a dump station. Sites 40–42 have electricity. Day parking is also available at the Visitor Center and Wagon Wheel Campground.
Dogs	On a leash at all times; prohibited on swim beaches
Shoes	Barefoot okay
Maps	DeLorme *Colorado Atlas & Gazetteer,* p. 102; Bonny Lake State Park map (http://parks.state.co.us)
Contact	Bonny Lake State Park
Fees	$5 daily park pass or $55 annual state parks pass required. Camping is $16 per day. Reservations can be made online at www.parks.state.co.us or by calling 800-678-CAMP (outside of Denver) or 303-470-1144 (in Denver).
Regulations	Keep horses off the swim and water-ski beaches and out of other campsites. See the Trail Savvy section (p. 12), website and posted regulations for additional information.
Special Notes	Be cautious during hunting season

Directions to Trailhead

From Burlington, travel north on CO 385 toward Idalia (following the signs). Turn right (east) on CR 3 at the signs to Bonny Lake State Park. The Foster Grove Campground and payment kiosk are just east on CR 3. The trail travels around the lake and can be accessed 0.2 mile south of the Foster Grove campsites.

This 6,900-acre state park is best known for its quality water-based recreation around beautiful 1,900-acre Lake Bonny. The facilities include four campgrounds, two beaches, boat ramps, and a marina. While the park is renown for excellent fishing (walleye, northern pike, and a variety of bass), boating, swimming, windsurfing, and water-skiing, it is also a bird-watching paradise. The park is home to many upland birds, bald eagles, white pelicans, migratory waterfowl, and a variety of shore birds. Additional wildlife viewing opportunities include turkey, whitetail deer, coyote, bobcats, rabbits, and a myriad of other small creatures.

The park lies on the eastern plains of northern Colorado along the Republican River and is often called the "oasis on the plains." Vast expanses of gently rolling prairies combine with beautiful, sandy beaches and extensive riparian habitats scattered with mature cottonwood and dense willow. The lovely setting is a pleasant and peaceful surprise. Just as pleasant and more surprising is the freedom you experience to enjoy your mount, exploring nature and the beauty of the park with very little restriction. If you have not visited here, you should definitely add it to your must-ride list. It is a wonderful place to spend time with your horse and is especially nice when the park is less crowded and cooler in the fall and spring. It would even make a wonderful weekend getaway on one of Colorado's warm, sunny winter weekends. Enjoy this delightful surprise.

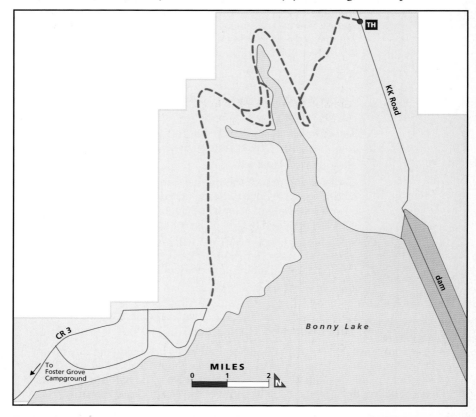

95 Pawnee National Grassland

Overall Ride Rating	◡◡◡◡◡
Trail Rating	Easy
Distance	1.5 miles one way on the Pawnee Buttes Trail (No. 840); unlimited cross-country riding on 193,060 acres of open grassland
Elevation	5,200–5,400 feet
Best Season	Year-round
Main Uses	Equestrian, hiking, dispersed camping, mountain biking, hunting, motorized vehicles (on routes marked by number posts), bird-watching
Trailhead Amenities	Park or camp anywhere within 300 feet of an open road or at the road's edge, but do not block traffic. There is no easily accessible drinking water for humans or horses. Ranch ponds and stock tanks are spread far and wide and you may not find one in the area in which you are riding or camping. Tying to trailers or portable corrals are the only options for overnight horse containment, as there are no trees for highlining. There is a Forest Service recreation area with a developed campground and picnic area 0.25 mile north of Briggsdale on CR 77; it has a parking lot, restrooms, and drinking water during warm months. But, like all other developed campgrounds, horses are not allowed. Access to the grassland from the recreation area is limited due to surrounding private land.
Dogs	Allowed under voice control
Shoes	Barefoot okay
Maps	DeLorme *Colorado Atlas & Gazetteer,* p. 94; Pawnee National Grassland Forest Service map
Contact	Pawnee National Grassland
Fees	None
Regulations	There are closures at the Pawnee Buttes from March 1 through June 30 for raptor nesting season. Riders must remain on the Pawnee Buttes Trail and stay at least 300 yards away from all nests during this time. The east butte is accessible only across private land. There is no camping or campfires within 200 feet of parking lots or windmills. See the Trail Savvy section (p. 12), website and posted regulations for additional information.
Special Notes	Start out with a full tank of gas and a spare tire, as facilities are limited. Most roads are gravel or dirt and can be dangerous when wet. Look for Forest Service and private property signs and please respect private land, which is heavily interspersed with government land. Most improvements are installed to control or benefit livestock. If a gate is open, leave it open; if you open it, close it. Don't go through a gate and leave it open until your return. Leave water tanks and windmills alone. A mill or tank is either running or shut off for a reason that may not be obvious to you. When camping, remember that high winds are possible, so be careful when setting up tents. Camping in the bottom of draws is not recommended due to summertime flash floods.

Directions to Trailhead

To get to the Pawnee Buttes Trail by following the Pawnee Pioneer Trail, a Colorado Scenic and Historic Byway, take US 85 north from Greeley to Ault and turn right on CO 14. This road will take you into the grassland. At Briggsdale, turn left (north) on CR 77, passing the Crow Valley Recreation Area and Campground. Continue north 15 miles to CR 120 and turn right, going 6 miles to Grover. Take gravel CR 390 southeast out of Grover another 6 miles to CR 112 and turn left (east). Follow this road 8 miles to GR 685 and turn left for the Pawnee Buttes trailhead. East-west county roads have even numbers and north-south have odd.

The Soil Conservation Service (SCS) transferred these lands to the Forest Service in 1954. Prior to this, the SCS acquired the prairie from failing homesteaders during the Dust Bowl days of the 1930s. The 300-foot-high tops of the buttes were once contiguous with the surface of the Chalk Bluffs to the north. They are now detached remnants of the High Plains surface. This is hardy, open land where you may ride unhindered for miles upon miles. You have an opportunity to ride here all day without encountering other people.

This is also an excellent area for birding, with over 250 species to be seen throughout the year. Short-grass prairie consisting of buffalo, grama, and wheat grasses dominates the landscape. Shade is nearly nonexistent. The only trees that you will see are occasional cottonwood and willow in drainage areas. Yucca and prickly pear cactus, with their sharp spines, abound. Prairie dogs, coyotes, foxes, pronghorn, and mule deer are among the local inhabitants. Speedy jackrabbits are prolific also. Occasional prairie cabins still stand, affording a rare glimpse into early 20th-century homesteading days and the hardships that the pioneers endured.

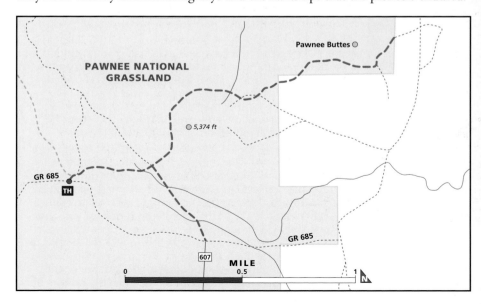

96 Picket Wire Canyon/ Comanche National Grassland

Overall Ride Rating	♡♡♡♡♡
Trail Rating	Easy to moderate
Distance	Corrals to Withers Canyon trailhead: 3.2 miles; trailhead to dinosaur tracks: 5.3 miles; trailhead to Rourke Ranch: 8.7 miles
Elevation	4,325–4,650 feet
Best Season	Year-round; recommended in fall and spring. Temperatures in the canyon can rise to more than 110 degrees in the summer months.
Main Uses	Equestrian, hiking, trailhead camping, mountain biking, Forest Service vehicle tours in April, May, September, and October
Trailhead Amenities	At the junction of GR 25/County Road 25 and GR 500A/County Road 500A are three corrals (two medium and one small), a vault toilet, a gravel parking area large enough to accommodate five to six trailers, and an informational kiosk. At the Withers Canyon trailhead are a vault toilet, juniper trees, and a gravel loop with several long spurs to accommodate many trailers. You can also park alongside the road. There is enough room to allow for large groups, depending on the amount of privacy desired and the parking configuration. Camping is allowed at the GR 25/GR 500A junction and the trailhead. Juniper trees at the second area are hard to use for highlining. If camping here, horses need to be in a portable corral or tied to trailers. There is no water available on the canyon rim. Bring your own water. A water purifier is also recommended. Horses can also be watered along the river. Pack a collapsible bucket and plan your ride accordingly. Vault toilets are at the dinosaur tracks, the Rourke Ranch, the corrals and the parking area on the rim.
Dogs	Under voice control
Shoes	Recommended
Maps	DeLorme *Colorado Atlas & Gazetteer,* p. 100; Comanche National Grassland Forest Service map (www.fs.fed.us/r2/psicc/coma)
Contact	Comanche National Grassland
Fees	None
Regulations	The canyon is open from dawn to dusk. No camping or unauthorized vehicles allowed in Picket Wire Canyon. Withers Canyon trailhead is the only public access into Picket Wire Canyonlands. Horses are not allowed at the dinosaur tracks site. See the Trail Savvy section (p. 12), website and posted regulations for additional information.
Special Notes	Riders should watch for prairie rattlesnakes, scorpions, and cacti. Horses' lower legs should be checked for spines after riding. Be careful not to drive over the cacti when parking off-road.

Directions to Trailhead

From La Junta, drive south on CO 109 for 13 miles. Turn right (west) on GR 802 (David Canyon Rd.) and continue for 8 miles. Turn left (south) on GR 25 (Rourke Road) and travel another 6 miles. Turn left at the sign for Picket Wire corrals onto GR 500A. Park here if you wish to use the corrals, or continue past the gate (if it is open) another 3 miles to park at the Withers Canyon trailhead. **Note:** The gate can be closed when the road is too wet to drive to the trailhead. If that is the case, parking will be restricted to the lot at the corrals. This area is subject to flash floods and winter snowstorms, which can make the gravel roads temporarily impassable.

Picket Wire Canyon contains historic attractions from all eras, starting with the largest documented dinosaur track site in North America. It extends across 0.25 mile and contains more than 1,300 visible tracks. Later, prehistoric American Indians left their mark in the form of rock art images. The river and canyon's original name came from stories about the Spanish explorers of the 17th century; it was "El Rio de las Perdidas en Purgatorio," or the River of Lost Souls in Purgatory, after the unfortunate treasure seekers who died without benefice of clergy. In the 18th century, French trappers dubbed it the Purgatoire, and its pronunciation later evolved to "Picket Wire" by English-speaking home-steaders. This trail takes you by the Dolores Mission and Cemetery, built by Mexican pioneers between 1871 and 1889; you then pass the dinosaur tracks and finally come to the Rourke Ranch (also known as the Wineglass Ranch), established in the 19th century to raise cattle and horses. When the ranch was sold in 1971 at well over 52,000 acres, it was known as one of the oldest and most successful enterprises in southeastern Colorado.

If you parked at the corrals, follow the road east 3.2 miles to the trailhead. Watch for a cattle guard with a gate roughly 0.5 mile down the road. From the trailhead, ride past the bathroom and pick up a rocky trail that descends Withers Canyon approximately 300 feet in 0.3 mile down to the canyon floor. Once in the canyon, the trail loops farther north and east around a ridge to reveal Picket Wire Canyon and the Purgatoire River. Sizeable cottonwood trees indicate the added moisture of the river bottom compared with the rim above. From this point on, the double-track trail travels generally in a southwest direction. While riding, watch both sides of the river for remains of dwellings that tell the story of the canyon's history. At almost 4 miles, remnants of the Dolores Mission and Cemetery will be on both sides of the trail. Please respect these sites and do not ride horses within the ruins, especially the fenced cemetery. Along the south side of the cemetery, a short trail goes up the hill to a viewing site for prehistoric American Indian rock art. Horses can be ridden up to it, but do not touch the carved areas. Follow this side trail back to the main trail. This is one of the river access points for watering horses, but the river is about 0.5 mile away. Keep this additional mileage in mind if the Rourke Ranch is your final destination.

From the mission site on, the trail becomes an old road; the mission marks the end of the Forest Service vehicle tour. The dinosaur track site is 1.5 miles farther. Horses can be ridden to a river crossing just south of the tracks by following the trail east out of the parking area to a cluster of signs describing the history of the area (these are worth a stop to read) and then taking a trail to the right and down to the river. This also makes a good lunch stop.

After "oohing" and "aahing" at the tracks, return to the parking lot, take advantage of the facilities, and continue south about 0.5 mile to the "window rock" on the right side of the trail. This makes for a really striking picture opportunity, which can include your horse. About 0.5 mile down the trail is another rock art viewing opportunity. Once again, a single-track trail leads off to the right and can be ridden up to a larger site. Backtrack to the main trail, where it is an additional 2.5 miles to the historic Rourke Ranch. If riding to the ranch, take the left Y, avoiding the private driveway.

At every stop, keep in mind the time, the mileage to return out of the canyon, and the hours of daylight remaining, as the day can quickly slip away from you. The sun and temperatures can drop rapidly, especially on spring or fall evenings. We always recommend dressing in layers and wearing a hat and sunscreen.

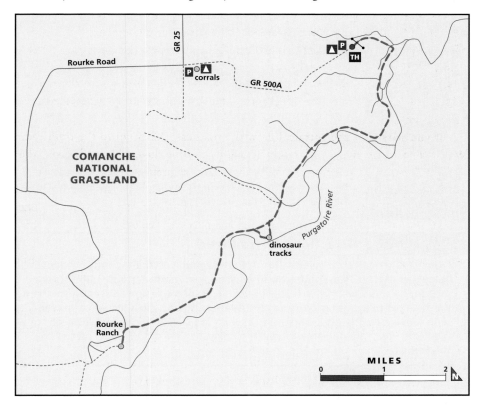

97 Red Shin Trail/ John Martin Reservoir State Park

Overall Ride Rating	♡♡♡♡♡
Trail Rating	Easy
Distance	4.5 miles one way
Elevation	3,850–4,015 feet
Best Season	Year-round
Main Uses	Equestrian, hiking, fishing, boating, water sports
Trailhead Amenities	The Lake Hasty parking area has room for numerous large rigs, with a restroom, water spigot, and picnic area with fire grills at the trailhead. An RV dump station is located across from the Lake Hasty entrance on the state park road.
Dogs	On leash
Shoes	Barefoot okay
Maps	DeLorme *Colorado Atlas & Gazetteer*, p. 99; John Martin State Park map (http://parks.state.co.us)
Contact	John Martin Reservoir State Park
Fees	$5 for daily fee or $55 for an annual state parks pass
Regulations	No camping with horses. See the Trail Savvy section (p. 12), website and posted regulations for additional information.
Special Notes	From mid-April to late August, the shores of the reservoir are home to the threatened Piper Plover and endangered Interior Least Tern. In addition, threatened bald eagles winter at John Martin Reservoir and Lake Hasty. Look for potential trail improvements and possibly equestrian camping in the next few years. Be cautious of rattlesnakes. In the miles and miles of trails we trekked during the writing of this book, this is the only place where we actually ran into a rattlesnake on the trail.

Directions to Trailhead

From La Junta, travel 20 miles east on US 50 through Las Animas and another 16 miles east to Hasty. Turn right (south) on School St. The street sign might still be missing on this small street; however, you can't miss the signs directing you to the state park. Proceed approximately 2 miles south on School St. The visitor center is located on the right (west) side as the road curves to the east. Proceed to the Lake Hasty area and park near the spillway, dam, and fishing pier at the southernmost parking lot.

The Red Shin Trail heads south from the parking area at Lake Hasty on a gravel double-track path. It quickly changes directions, turning east along the spillway and the Arkansas River. After approximately 0.5 mile, cross the paved State Park Rd.,(which receives minimal traffic), then the trail swings north through a sandy riparian area of salt cedars northwest of the Arkansas River. The trail becomes fainter as it wanders through this area, but finding the way should not present a problem for most riders. Continue traveling north, keeping the East Group Picnic Area and the Caddoa Group Camping Area on your left side. The trail curves to the west, crossing the State Park Rd. again at the visitor center, where you can visit the Santa Fe Trail Historic Site. From here, turn around and return the way you came. The John Martin Reservoir was built in 1948 as part of a flood-control management plan for the Arkansas River basin. The water acreage varies from 1,500 to 3,000 surface acres.

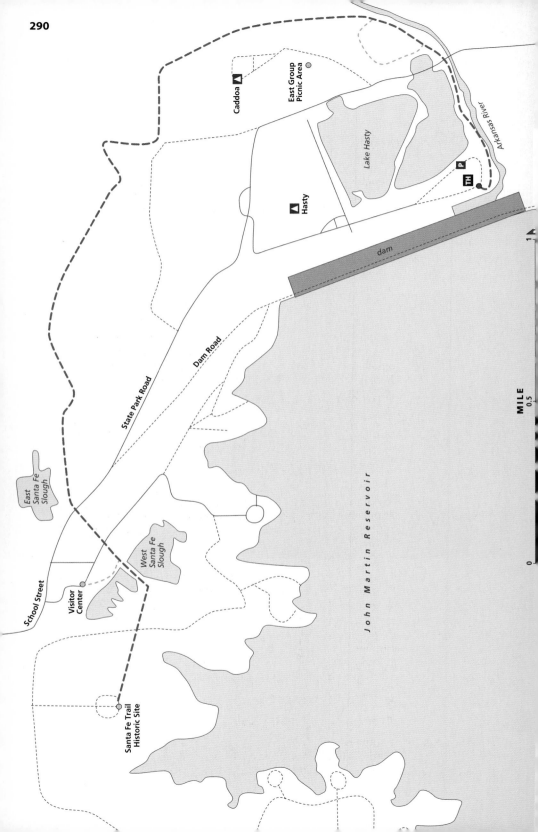

Caddoa

East Group
Picnic Area

Lake Hasty

Hasty

Arkansas River

P

TH

dam

Dam Road

State Park Road

East
Santa Fe
Slough

West
Santa Fe
Slough

School Street

Visitor
Center

John Martin Reservoir

Santa Fe Trail
Historic Site

MILE

0.5

1

0

98 Vogel Canyon/Comanche National Grassland

Overall Ride Rating	♘♘♘♘♘
Trail Rating	Easy, with moderate segments at the canyon descent and ascent
Distance	Overlook Trail: 0.5 mile one way; Canyon Trail: 1 mile one way; Mesa Trail: 0.5 mile from trailhead to fence; 0.5 mile from Prairie Trail to fence; Prairie Trail: 1.5 miles one way from Canyon Trail to Stagecoach tracks
Elevation	4,300–4,400 feet
Best Season	Year-round, but recommended in fall and spring. Temperatures in the canyon can rise to more than 100 degrees in the summer months.
Main Uses	Equestrian, hiking, trailhead camping, mountain biking
Trailhead Amenities	Vault toilet, covered picnic tables, two wood hitching rails, and loop-around parking for three to four trailers. Camping is allowed in the parking area only. Horses will need to be tied to trailers or the hitching rails or enclosed in portable corrals. There is no drinking water for people or horses.
Dogs	Under voice control
Shoes	Recommended
Maps	DeLorme *Colorado Atlas & Gazetteer*, p. 100; Comanche National Grassland map (www.fs.fed.us/r2/psicc)
Contact	Comanche National Grassland
Fees	None
Regulations	Do not touch or apply any photographic enhancing or replication materials to prehistoric rock art. See the Trail Savvy section (p. 12), website and posted regulations for additional information.
Special Notes	There is no potable water in the canyon or on the rim. Bring at least one gallon of drinking water per person per day and a water purifier into the canyon, especially if planning a summer ride. Pack a collapsible bucket to access water for horses from the permanent springs located in the canyon. Take care to avoid spring and summer afternoon storms, which can bring lightning or cause flash floods. Riders may encounter prairie rattlesnakes, tarantulas, and scorpions throughout the area—avoid tall grass and watch where you place your hands and feet.

Directions to Trailhead

From La Junta, drive south on CO 109 for 13 miles. Turn right (west) on GR 802 (David Canyon Rd.) and continue for 1 mile. Turn left (south) at road sign that reads Vogel Canyon and head 2 miles to the parking lot.

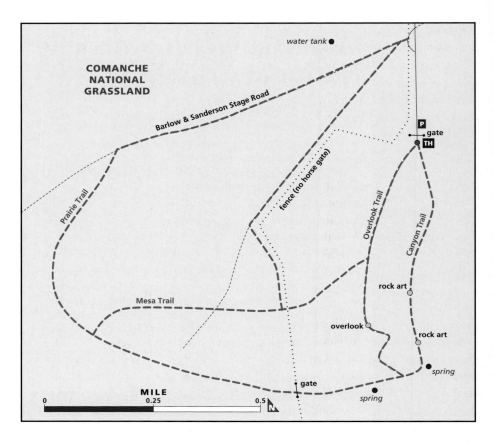

Vogel Canyon is a tributary of the Purgatoire River drainage during runoff, although it does not have active running water. Like Picket Wire Canyon (see Ride 96, p. 285), Vogel Canyon has a rich history. American Indians lived in the canyon 300–800 years ago and left rock art images that are visible from two places along the Canyon Trail. During the 1870s, the Barlow & Sanderson mail and stage line developed a spur of the Santa Fe Trail running from Las Animas to Trinidad. The Prairie Trail follows a section of the old stagecoach road. Stone ruins from Depression-era homesteads still stand, as well.

Although trail mileage within Vogel Canyon is limited, the area makes a pleasant and relaxing second-day ride when combined with the long Picket Wire Canyon ride (see p. 285) the previous day. Start at the area information sign and continue through the gate in the fence. The wide crusher-fine Overlook Trail leads for 0.5 mile to exactly to what the name implies, an overlook of the canyon and another informational sign. Prior to this point, riders can take a short but pretty jaunt on the Mesa Trail, but must turn around at 0.5 mile at a fence without a gate.

From the overlook, a short, rocky trail drops riders into the canyon and onto the intersection of the Prairie and Canyon trails. Caution should be used here, as there are narrow rock Vs as well as steps that can challenge a green or careless horse. The unnamed trail straight ahead takes riders into the main part of the canyon, but quickly ends at a private property fence line. Turning left onto the Canyon Trail eventually will return you up to the parking lot along a smaller but rocky finger of the canyon. Here is the location for two rock art observation spots. Horses will need to be held while riders climb the stairs to get a closer look and read the informational signs. On the opposite side of this smaller canyon, on a spur trail, are the remains of the Westbrook homestead. Locating the large cottonwoods will lead you to the two permanent springs, which make relaxing lunch spots.

To the right is the Prairie Trail. Watch for a fence with a wire gate for horses. Toward the end of the canyon, past a ruins site, is an intersection with the Mesa Trail. The left Y is the Prairie Trail and takes riders to the Barlow & Sanderson stage road. Follow this route toward the entrance road to the water tank (with no windmill) to get a drink for the horses. Note the wider tracks where ranchers have driven trucks to the water tank compared to the narrower original wagon tracks closer to the fence. The fence along the road has no gate, preventing horses and riders from heading south to the parking lot. Riders can either backtrack to the Mesa Trail intersection, or follow the fence line south to the midpoint of the Mesa Trail, where, to the left, there is a step structure over the fence, which is used by hikers, but impassable for horses. But a right turn on the Mesa Trail will wind you 0.5 mile through juniper and across sandstone slabs back to the Prairie Trail, where a left turn will lead you back through the gate in the fence that you passed through earlier. Return to the parking lot by either climbing back up the Overlook Trail or by taking the Canyon Trail and winding up the picturesque sandstone wash, following some rock cairns.

99 Homestead Trail/Picture Canyon/Comanche National Grassland

Overall Ride Rating	♘♘♘♘♘
Trail Rating	Easy to moderate
Distance	8-mile signed trail, plus unlimited riding on unsigned open grassland and old ranch roads
Elevation	4,200–4,450 feet
Best Season	Year-round
Main Uses	Equestrian, hiking, trailhead camping, biking, mountain hunting, motorized vehicles on developed roads only
Trailhead Amenities	A large, level, grassy area just north of the trailhead and picnic area on the west side of the road is recommended for equestrian parking/camping. If the developed picnic area is relatively empty and your rig is not too large, you should be able to park and camp here. Amenities include three covered tables and one vault toilet. The main parking lot is a large gravel parking area. There is also an open grassy area to the west of the main lot; together an unlimited number of trailers can be accommodated. No trash service is available in the area so please plan to "pack it out." Plan to bring water for horses and people.
Dogs	On leash
Shoes	Recommended
Maps	DeLorme *Colorado Atlas & Gazetteer,* p. 100; Comanche National Grassland Forest Service map
Contact	Comanche National Grassland
Fees	None
Regulations	Do not touch or apply any photographic enhancing or replication materials to prehistoric rock art. See the Trail Savvy section (p. 12), website and posted regulations for additional information.
Special Notes	There are several water sources for your horses along the way, including springs and cattle tanks, but these may not always be dependable. You should plan to bring water for your horses and tank up before leaving the trailhead. Be sure to carry water for human consumption.

Directions to Trailhead

From the intersection of US 287 and US 160 in Springfield, take US 287 south for 20 miles to the small town of Campo. Turn right (west) onto CR J, which soon changes from pavement to a well-maintained gravel road. Proceed 10 miles to GR 18 and turn left (south). Drive 4.8 miles on this dirt road to the entrance of Picture Canyon on your right side. The trailhead is 2 miles ahead.

When one thinks of the grasslands, the image that usually comes to mind is miles upon miles of sameness. The Comanche National Grassland is anything but monotonous, offering equestrians an exhilarating riding experience unlike any other in Colorado. While the area can be hot and dry during the summer months, the spring and fall are particularly good times to enjoy the lower elevations. The plains are dominated by short-grass prairie decorated by sagebrush, yucca, and a variety of cacti. When combined with the midgrass prairies, scrub oak, piñon pine, and juniper set against the multicolored layers of rock in the canyon walls, a beautiful and diverse landscape emerges. Sandy washes are marked by beautiful shady cottonwood trees. Thousands of years of wind, rain, snow, ice, and erosion have hewn incredible rock formations, which become impromptu art as they take on the shapes of eagles, turtles, cats, arches, and even wisdom teeth. Canyon walls display pictographs and petroglyphs that tell of ancient civilizations dating as far back as 3,000 years. Remnants of old homesteads remind us of the area's early settlement in the 1800s and early 1900s.

Spectacular views reach as far as Oklahoma and New Mexico. This country is home to over 275 bird species, 20 fish species, 60 mammal species, and 30 reptile species, including two poisonous snakes (the prairie rattlesnake and the massasauga). This particular section of Comanche National Grassland, referred to as the Carrizo Unit, lies south and west of Springfield and covers more than 435,000 acres. This is a "must-ride" on one's list of equestrian journeys. The

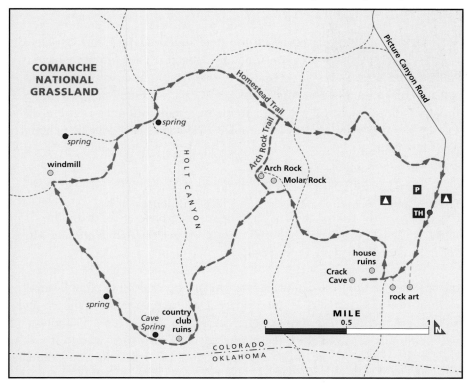

Homestead Trail provides a wonderful 8.1-mile signed trail (9.1 miles including the spurs). However, there is much more to see if you are willing to leave the signed trail and explore a little on your own.

Begin the Homestead Trail by riding south from the picnic/parking area on a trail that quickly joins a dirt road. Before the road forks at about 0.3 mile, cut across the grassy field toward the canyon wall, heading in a southeast direction. Where the fence line meets the canyon wall, you'll reach a gate that will allow you entrance to see the pictographs and petroglyphs left behind by previous

inhabitants of the land. Please do not touch the wall, as this can cause further deterioration, and please close the gate when leaving in order to protect this natural resource.

From here, return to the dirt road and take the right fork of the road to its end to see the remains of an old homestead and Crack Cave. Some experts believe that the markings on the wall within the cave may have been used to help with crop planting and harvesting. (Due to vandalism, a locked gate now prevents visitors from entering the cave.) Return to the road. The trail heads north, or right (left if you are coming east from the cave), from the intersection with the fork of the road.

In 0.2 mile, you arrive at a sign pointing to Arch Rock and the Homestead Trail; turn left here and continue until you reach a sign with a black, right-pointing arrow. Turn right onto an unmarked trail and follow the wooden posts that serve as trail markers. The trail takes you through juniper trees until you come to the next right fork onto a cattle path. Ride up and out of the canyon to the ridge until you reach a double-track trail just before the next wooden post at about 0.8 mile. Continue riding northwest across the double-track trail.

Next you arrive at a large wooden post with no signs. Turn left (west) and follow the rock cairns down a slickrock canyon. In 0.2 mile, the Homestead Trail intersects the Arch Rock Trail (the sign is incorrect—it is not another 7.5 miles). It is, well, worth the 0.25-mile side trip to see the Arch Rock and Molar Rock (also called Wisdom Tooth Rock).

After visiting the Arch Rock and Molar Rock, you can choose a short or longer riding option. For a shorter ride stay on the Arch Rock Trail heading north until it intersects the Homestead Trail, and return to the trailhead and parking area by riding east. For a longer ride return to the Homestead loop trail by riding south until you reach the intersection of the Homestead and the Arch Rock trails. At this point continue southwest until you reach the next landmark at the 3-mile point, rumored to be the ruins of an old country club. Just 0.3 mile farther is Cave Spring (water should be treated here before drinking). Look inside the cave and on the canyon walls for pictographs. Just to the left of the cave on the canyon wall, surveyors have carved a quasi-map indicating the locations of Colorado, Utah, Oklahoma, Arizona, and New Mexico. Continue down the road past Cave Spring through a lovely stand of cottonwood trees to arrive at a rock formation resembling a boot and another set of house ruins.

After emerging from this little canyon, head north toward the windmill on the horizon. Once at the windmill and cattle tank, you have ridden 4.5 miles. Here, the trail takes off to the right (east) along some cattle paths (continue to look for the wooden sign posts; some may have fallen). At 5 miles, you come across a post leading down to the edge of the canyon and over into the next canyon. Bear right when you arrive at the road at 5.1 miles. At 5.3 miles, take the left fork in the road and at 5.5 miles take the right fork. At 5.9 miles bear right onto the trail where it meets the road again. Continue another mile to the junction of the Arch Rock Trail. Stay on the Homestead Trail and do not turn

right (south), as it will take you back the way you came. Cross a road heading southeast into Picture Canyon and continue riding east until you reach Picture Canyon Rd. Turn right (south) to follow it south back to the trailhead.

100 South Shoreline Trail/ North Sterling State Park

Overall Ride Rating	○○○○○
Trail Rating	Easy
Distance	3 miles one way
Elevation	4,100 feet
Best Season	Year-round; use caution during waterfowl hunting season
Main Uses	Equestrian, hiking, mountain biking, fishing, hunting, boating
Trailhead Amenities	The trailhead for the South Shoreline Trail is south of the main entrance station for North Sterling State Park, with parking for six to eight large rigs. No other trailhead amenities. Camping with horses is currently not allowed. However, the park management is very horse-friendly and interested in expanding its equestrian amenities.
Dogs	On leash
Shoes	Barefoot okay
Maps	DeLorme *Colorado Atlas & Gazetteer*, p. 95; North Sterling State Park map (www.parks.state.co.us)
Contact	North Sterling State Park
Fees	$5 daily park pass or $55 annual state parks pass required
Regulations	See the Trail Savvy section (p. 12), website and posted regulations for additional information.

Directions to Trailhead

From W. Main Street in Sterling (CO 114), turn north on N. 7th Ave. (CR 39) and travel 12 miles. CR 39 becomes CR 37. Turn left (west) at the park signs at CR 37 and CR 46 and travel 2 miles to the south park entrance. The trailhead is left (south) on CR 33 approximately 0.2 mile on the right (west) side of the road.

The trail starts to the southwest side of the trailhead and travels west through a gate. The double-track trail is a relatively level mixture of dirt, sand, and gravel and parallels the shoreline of the reservoir. The views of the Eastern Plains and the surrounding bluffs framing the blue waters of the reservoir make this a unique and enjoyable ride. However, it can be quite warm in the middle of the summer, so we recommend riding here in the spring or fall. During the summer, aim for early-morning or late-afternoon rides, as there is little to no shade. Watering the horses is not a problem as long as they don't mind the sound of the waves lapping at the shore.

Simply follow the trail from the east trailhead to the west trailhead and then turn around and return the way you came. Along the way, the route borders the southern end of the reservoir through grassy open meadows alternating with tree-covered riparian areas.

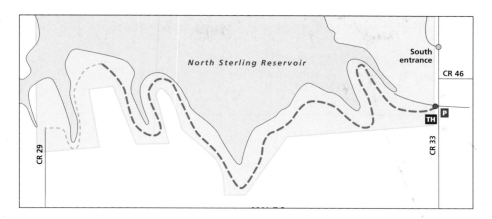

North Sterling State Park encompasses 1,500 acres of recreational land and is a great place for wildlife viewing. Be observant and you may see deer, coyotes, badgers, rabbits, waterfowl, upland birds, eagles, shorebirds, and pelicans. The reservoir is also an excellent warm-water fishery featuring largemouth bass, crappie, perch, walleye, bluegill, catfish, and wiper. A marina concession is located at the northeast corner of the reservoir.

Appendix A: Public Agency Contact Information

BUREAU OF LAND MANAGEMENT
Royal Gorge Field Office • 3170 E. Main St., Cañon City, CO 81212
719-269-8500 • www.co.blm.gov/ccdo/canon.htm

CITY PARKS AND RECREATION

**City of Boulder Open Space
and Mountain Parks**
P.O. Box 791
Boulder, CO 80306
720-913-0696
www.bouldercolorado.gov

**City of Colorado Springs
Parks, Recreation, and
Cultural Services**
1401 Recreation Way
Colorado Springs, CO 80905
719-385-6540
www.springsgov.com

Denver Mountain Parks
300 Union
Morrison, CO 80465
303-697-4545
www.denvergov.org/
   mountain_parks/

**Denver Parks and
Recreation Department**
201 W. Colfax Ave., Dept. 601
Denver, CO 80202
303-937-4654
www.denvergov.org/
   Recreation2/default.asp

**Denver Water
Recreation Office**
1600 W. 12th Ave.
Denver, CO 80204
303-628-6000
www.denverwater.org

**City of Fort Collins
Natural Areas**
200 W. Mountain
Fort Collins, CO 80521
970-221-6600
www.ci.fort-collins.co.us/
   naturalareas/

**Garden of the Gods
Visitor and Nature Center**
1805 N. 30th St.
Colorado Springs, CO 80904
719-634-6666
www.gardenofgods.com

**City of Lakewood/
Bear Creek Lake Park**
Community Resources Dept.
15600 W. Morrison Rd.
Morrison, CO 80465
303-697-6159
www.lakewood.org

Town of Parker
20120 E. Mainstreet
Parker, CO 80138
303-841-4500
www.parkeronline.org

**City of Pueblo Parks
and Recreation**
800 Goodnight Ave.
Pueblo, CO 81005
719-553-2790
www.pueblo.us

Pueblo Mountain Park
9161 Mountain Park Rd.
Beulah, CO 81023
719-485-4444
www.hikeandlearn.org

COUNTY PARKS AND RECREATION

**Arapahoe County Public
Works and Development**
10730 E. Briarwood Ave.
Centennial, CO 80112
720-874-6500
www.co.arapahoe.co.us/
   Departments/PW

**Douglas County Parks
and Trails**
100 3rd St.
Castle Rock, CO 80104
303-660-7495
www.douglas.co.us/
   publicworks/parksandtrails/
   index.html

**El Paso County Parks
and Recreation**
2002 Creek Crossing
Colorado Springs, CO 80906
719-520-6375
http://adm2.elpasoco.com/
   Parks/prktrail.asp

**Jefferson County
Open Space**
700 Jefferson County Pkwy.
Golden, CO 80419
303-271-5925
www.co.jefferson.co.us/
   openspace/

**Larimer County Parks
and Open Lands**
1800 S. CR 31
Loveland, CO 80537
970-679-4570
www.larimer.org/parks

STATE PARKS AND RECREATION
Colorado Division of Wildlife Offices

BERGEN PEAK STATE
WILDLIFE AREA
6060 Broadway
Denver, CO 80216
303-297-1192

FORT COLLINS
SERVICE CENTER
317 W. Prospect
Fort Collins, CO 80526
970-472-4300

SOUTHEAST REGION
SERVICE CENTER
4255 Sinton Rd.
Colorado Springs, CO 80907
719-227-5200

For more information visit http://wildlife.state.co.us/LandWater/StateWildlifeAreas/

Colorado State Parks

BARR LAKE STATE PARK
13401 Picadilly Rd.
Brighton, CO 80603
303-659-6005

DENVER ADMINISTRATIVE
OFFICE
1313 Sherman St., No. 618
Denver, CO 80203
303-866-3437

LORY STATE PARK
708 Lodgepole Dr.
Bellvue, CO 80512
970-493-1623

BONNY LAKE STATE PARK
30010 CR 3
Idalia, CO 80735
970-354-7306

GOLDEN GATE CANYON
STATE PARK
92 Crawford Gulch Rd.
Golden, CO 80403
303-582-3707

MUELLER STATE PARK
P.O. Box 49
Divide, CO 80814
719-687-2366

CHATFIELD STATE PARK
ADMINISTRATIVE OFFICES
11500 N. Roxborough Park Rd.
Littleton, CO 80125
303-791-7275

JOHN MARTIN RESERVOIR
STATE PARK
30703 CR 24
Hasty, CO 81044
719-829-1801

NORTH STERLING
STATE PARK
24005 CR 330
Sterling, CO 80751
970-522-3657

CHERRY CREEK STATE PARK
4201 S. Parker Rd.
Aurora, CO 80014
303-699-3860

LAKE PUEBLO STATE PARK
640 Pueblo Reservoir Rd.
Pueblo, CO 81005
719-561-9320

ROXBOROUGH STATE PARK
4751 Roxborough Dr.
Littleton, CO 80125
303-973-3959

For more information visit http://parks.state.co.us/

NATIONAL FORESTS AND GRASSLANDS

Arapaho and Roosevelt National Forests

CANYON LAKES
RANGER DISTRICT
2150 Centre Ave., Bldg. E
Fort Collins, CO 80526
970-295-6700
www.fs.fed.us/r2/arnf/

Comanche National Grassland

CARRIZO UNIT
P.O. Box 127
27204 I-287
Springfield, CO 81073
719-523-6591
http://www.fs.fed.us/r2/
  psicc/coma/

TIMPAS UNIT
1420 E. 3rd St.
La Junta, CO 81050
719-384-2181
http://www.fs.fed.us/r2/
  psicc/coma/

Gunnison National Forest

GUNNISON
RANGER DISTRICT
216 N. Colorado
Gunnison, CO 81230
970-874-6600 or 970-641-0471
(8:30 am to 4:30 pm)
www.fs.fed.us/r2/gmug/

PAONIA RANGER DISTRICT
N. Rio Grande Ave.
P.O. Box 1030
Paonia, CO 81428
970-527-4131
www.fs.fed.us/r2/gmug/

Pawnee National Grassland
660 O Street
Greeley, CO 80631
970-353-5004
www.fs.fed.us/r2/arnf/about/
organization/png/index.shtml

Pike National Forest
PIKES PEAK RANGER
DISTRICT
601 S. Weber
Colorado Springs, CO 80903
719-636-1602
http://www.fs.fed.us/r2/psicc/pp/

SOUTH PARK RANGER
DISTRICT
320 Hwy. 285
P.O. Box 219
Fairplay, CO 80440
719-836-2031
http://www.fs.fed.us/r2/
 psicc/sopa/

SOUTH PLATTE RANGER
DISTRICT
19316 Goddard Ranch Ct.
Morrison, CO 80465
303-275-5610
http://www.fs.fed.us/r2/psicc/spl/

Rio Grande National Forest
DIVIDE RANGER DISTRICT
13308 W. Hwy. 160
P.O. Box 40
Del Norte, CO 81132
719-657-3321
www.fs.fed.us/r2/riogrande/
 contact/districts

San Isabel National Forest
SALIDA RANGER DISTRICT
325 W. Rainbow Blvd.
Salida, CO 81201
719-539-3591
www.fs.fed.us/r2/psicc/sal/

SAN CARLOS RANGER
DISTRICT
3170 E. Main St.
Cañon City, CO 81212
719-269-8500
www.fs.fed.us/r2/psicc/sanc/

San Juan National Forest
COLUMBINE RANGER
DISTRICT
367 S. Pearl St.
P.O. Box 439
Bayfield, CO 81122
970-884-2512
www.fs.fed.us/r2/sanjuan/

DOLORES RANGER DISTRICT
100 N. 6th Street
Dolores, CO 81323
970-882-7296
www.fs.fed.us/r2/sanjuan/

PAGOSA RANGER DISTRICT
180 2nd St.
P.O. Box 310
Pagosa Springs, CO 81147
970-264-2268
www.fs.fed.us/r2/sanjuan/

White River National Forest
ASPEN RANGER DISTRICT
806 W. Hallam
Aspen, CO 81611
970-925-3445
www.fs.fed.us/r2/whiteriver/

BLANCO RANGER DISTRICT
317 E. Market St.
Meeker, CO 81641
970-878-4039
www.fs.fed.us/r2/whiteriver/

DILLON RANGER DISTRICT
680 Blue River Pkwy.
P.O. Box 620
Silverthorne, CO 80498
970-468-5400
www.fs.fed.us/r2/whiteriver/

SOPRIS RANGER DISTRICT
620 Main St.
Carbondale, CO 81623
970-963-2266
www.fs.fed.us/r2/whiteriver/

NATIONAL PARKS AND MONUMENTS

National Park Service
Department of the Interior
1849 C St. NW
Washington, D.C. 20240
www.nps.gov/

**Great Sand Dunes National
Park and Preserve**
11999 CO 150
Mosca, CO 81146
719-378-6300
visitor center: 719-378-6399
www.nps.gov/grsa

**Rocky Mountain
National Park**
1000 Hwy. 36
Estes Park, CO 80517
970-586-1206
www.nps.gov/romo

Appendix B: Trail Accommodations

• Indicates that there may be nearby overnight stabling and/or lodging available, but information is not included in this book.

Ride	Trail Name	TH or Campground Camping	Dispersed Camping	Backcountry Camping	Nearby overnight stabling &/or lodging
32	Abyss Lake Trail	Yes	Yes	Yes	•
11	Alderfer / Three Sisters Park	No	No	No	Yes
14	Apex Park	No	No	No	Yes
91	Arkansas Point Trail System / Lake Pueblo State Park	No	No	No	Yes
24	Barr Lake State Park	No	No	No	•
25	Bear Creek Lake Park	No	No	No	Yes
4	Bear Creek Regional Park	Yes	No	Yes	Yes
59	Beaver Meadows Resort and Trails	Yes	No	Nearby	Yes, on site
30	Ben Tyler Trail	Yes	Yes	Yes	•
70	Big Ridge Trail	Yes	Yes	Yes	Yes
5	Black Forest Regional Park	No	No	No	Yes
50	Bobcat Ridge Natural Area	No	No	No	Yes
94	Bonny Lake State Park	Yes	No	No	Yes
34	Brookside McCurdy Trail	Yes	Yes	Yes	•
37	Browns Creek Trail	Yes	Yes	Yes	Yes
46	Bulwark Trail	Yes	No	Yes	•
33	Burning Bear Trail	Yes	Yes	Yes	•
81	Burnt Timber Trail	No	No	Yes	Yes
73	Capitol Creek Trail	No	Yes	Yes	Yes
61	Carhart Trail	Yes	No	Yes	Yes
17	Chatfield State Park	Yes	No	No	Yes
26	Cherry Creek Regional Trail (Parker)	No	No	No	Yes
27	Cherry Creek State Park (Aurora)	Yes	No	No	Yes
76	Cliff Creek / Beckwith / Three Lakes Trail	Yes	No	Yes	•
39	Colorado Trail from Avalanche TH	Yes	Yes	Yes	Yes
38	Colorado Trail from Browns Creek TH	Yes	Yes	Yes	Yes
93	Comanche Lake / Venable Lake Trail Loop	Yes	No	Yes	•
35	Craig Park Trail	Yes	Yes	Yes	•
92	Dam Trail / Lake Pueblo State Park	No	No	No	Yes
77	Dark Canyon Trail	Yes	No	Yes	Yes
19	Deer Creek Canyon Park	No	No	No	Yes
9	Dome Rock State Wildlife Area	No	No	No	Yes
1	Doudy Draw and Community Ditch Trails	No	No	No	•
78	Dyke / Lake Irwin Trails	Yes	No	No	Yes
51	Eagle's Nest Open Space Trails	No	No	No	Yes
66	East Marvine Creek Trail	Yes	Yes	Yes	Yes
12	Elk Meadow Park	No	No	No	Yes
56	Fish Creek Trail	Yes	Yes	Yes	•
57	Flowers Trail	Yes	Yes	Yes	•
6	Fountain Creek Regional Trail	No	No	No	Yes
7	Fox Run Regional Park	No	No	No	Yes
8	Garden of the Gods	No	No	No	Yes
15	Golden Gate Canyon State Park	Yes	No	No	Yes
44	Goose Creek Trail	Yes	Yes	Yes	•
90	Great Sand Dunes Nat'l Park / Preserve	No	No	Yes	Yes
2	Greenbelt Plateau / Marshall Mesa Tr.	No	No	No	•
28	Greenland Trail	No	No	No	Yes
74	Hay Park Trail	Yes	Yes	No	Yes
18	Highline Canal Trail	No	No	No	Yes
62	Himes Peak Trail	Yes	No	Yes	Yes

Ride	Trail Name	TH or Campground Camping	Dispersed Camping	Backcountry Camping	Nearby overnight stabling &/or lodging
29	Homestead Ranch Park	No	No	No	Yes
52	Horsetooth Mountain Park	No	No	Yes	Yes
20	Indian Creek Trail	Yes	No	Yes	•
58	Jacks Gulch	Yes	Yes	Yes	•
97	John Martin Reservoir State Park	No	No	No	Yes
13	Lair O' the Bear Park	No	No	No	Yes
48	Lawn Lake Trail	No	Yes	Yes	•
42	Lily Pad Lake	No	No	Yes	Yes
40	Little Browns Creek Trail	Yes	Yes	Yes	Yes
68	Long Park Trail	No	No	Yes	
53	Lory State Park	No	No	No	Yes
69	Lost Creek Trail / Lost Park Trail	No	No	Yes	
75	Maroon, East Maroon, & West Maroon Creek	No	No	Yes	Yes
67	Marvine Creek Trail	Yes	Yes	Yes	Yes
41	Meadow Creek Trail	No	No	Yes	Yes
3	Mesa Trail	No	No	No	•
88	Middle Frisco Trail	Yes	Yes	Yes	Yes
79	Mill Castle Trail	No	No	Yes	Yes
71	Mirror Lake Trail	Yes	Yes	Yes	Yes
22	Monument Preserve	No	No	No	Yes
10	Mueller State Park	No	No	No	Yes
23	New Sante Fe Regional Trail	No	No	No	Yes
47	North Fork Trail	Yes	No	Yes	•
60	North Lone Pine Trail	No	Yes	Yes	•
100	North Sterling State Park	No	No	No	Yes
95	Pawnee National Grassland	Yes	Yes	Yes	Yes
36	Payne Creek Trail	Yes	Yes	Yes	•
96	Picket Wire Canyon / Comanche National Grassland	Yes	No	No	Yes
99	Picture Canyon / Comanche National Grassland	Yes	No	No	Yes
84	Piedra River Trail	No	No	Yes	Yes
82	Pine River Trail	Minimal	No	Yes	Yes
54	Pineridge Natural Area	No	No	No	Yes
45	Platte River Trail	No	No	Yes	•
87	Pueblo Mountain Park	No	No	No	Yes
21	Sharptail Ridge Trail System	No	No	No	Yes
43	Shelf Road Recreation Area	Yes	Yes	Yes	•
72	Snell Creek Trail	No	No	Yes	Yes
34	South Park Trail	Yes	Yes	Yes	•
63	Stillwater Trail	Yes	No	Yes	Yes
80	Transfer Corral and Area Trails	Yes	No	Yes	Yes
64	Trappers Lake Trail	Yes	No	Yes	Yes
83	Vallecito Trail	No	No	Yes	Yes
55	Vespers Trail	Yes	No	No	Yes, on site
98	Vogel Canyon / Comanche National Grassland	Yes	No	No	Yes
65	Wall Lake Trail	Yes	No	Yes	Yes
85	Weminuche Trail	No	No	Yes	Yes
89	West Frisco Trail	Yes	Yes	Yes	Yes
16	White Ranch Park	No	No	Yes	Yes
86	Williams Creek Trail	No	No	Yes	Yes
49	Ypsilon Lake Trail	No	No	Yes	•

*Indicates that there may be nearby overnight stabling and/or lodging available, however there is no information included in this book.

Appendix C

Appendix D

Back Country Horsemen of America

"Join us on our journey to the other side of the mountain where the packer and his stock are living symbols that connect America's past to its future."

The BCHA is a national grassroots non-profit organization made up of recreational trail riders just like you who are concerned about continued pack and saddle stock access to our favorite trails. BCHA was formed in 1973 specifically to unite equestrians as one large, recognizable voice rather than unheard, individual voices. States across the nation have BCHA chapters made up of local equestrians working in their own backyards assisting their land managers with the tremendous backlog of trail maintenance projects. The state of Colorado currently has eight active BCHA chapters. The Back Country Horsemen of America is a service organization working in and educating users of the back country. These two elements, along with a determination to protect and preserve the historical use of recreational stock in the back country are primary factors for our existence.

Our mission is to:
- Perpetuate the common sense use and enjoyment of horses in America's back country
- Work to insure that public lands remain open to recreational stock use
- Assist various government and private agencies with trail maintenance and management
- Educate, encourage and solicit active participation in the wise use of back country resources
- Develop and grow new chapters of BCHA

Please visit our state or national websites for locations and membership information. If you do not find a chapter close to you, please consider forming your own chapter. Startup help is provided by state officers and nearby chapters as well as the national office. If leadership or membership is not for you, tax deductible donations are always welcome.

If you care about having trails to ride in the future...get involved today!

BACK COUNTRY HORSEMEN
OF AMERICA

BCHA National
P.O. Box 1367
Graham, WA 98339-1367
1-888-893-5161
www.backcountryhorse.com

BCHA Colorado
970-884-8021
www.bchcolorado.org

Index

Note: Citations followed by the letter "m" denote maps; those followed by the letter "p" denote photos.

A

Abyss Lake Trail ride, 112–114, 114m
Alderfer/Three Sisters Park ride, 51–52, 52m
altitude sickness, 14
Apex Park and Lookout Mountain Park ride, 57–58, 58m
Arkansas Point Trail System/Lake Pueblo State Park ride, 270–272, 272m
Arrowhead Stables, 279
Aspen Loop Trail ride, 239, 240m
Aspen/Snowmass, 215–222
Aurora, 93–96
Avalanche Trailhead ride, Colorado Trail from, 128–130, 131m

B

Bailey, 105–122
Barr Lake State Park ride, 83–84, 84m
Bayfield/Durango, 242–249
Bear Creek Lake Park ride, 85–86, 87m
Bear Creek Regional Park and Palmer/Red Rock Loop Trail ride, 32–34, 34m
Beaver Meadows Resort, 149

Beaver Meadows Resort Ranch ride, 182–183, 183m
Beckwith Pass Trail/Three Lakes Trail/Cliff Creek Trail ride, 223–225, 225m
Beddin' Down Bed, Breakfast and Horse Hotel, 103
bees, 14
Bent County Fairgrounds, 279
Ben Tyler Trail ride, 105–106, 107m
Beulah, 261–262
Big Ridge Trail ride, 207, 208m
Black Forest Regional Park ride, 35–36, 37m
Bobcat Ridge Natural Area ride, 158–159, 159m
Bonny Lake State Park ride, 281–282, 282m
Boulder, 26–31
Box Canyon Trail ride, 239, 240m
Breckenridge Equestrian Center, 103
Breckenridge/Frisco, 134–137
Brighton, 83–84
Brookside McCurdy Trail ride, 108–109, 110m
Browns Creek Trailhead ride, Colorado Trail from, 125m, 126–127
Browns Creek Trail ride, 123–124, 125m
Bruno (or Buno) Gulch Area, 111–119
Buena Vista/Salida, 123–133

The corrals at Transfer Trail are a good starting point for many scenic rides in Mancos.

Buford Lodge and Store, 187–188
Bulwark Ridge Trail ride, 151–152, 152m
Bureau of Land Management office, 300
Burning Bear Trail ride, 115–116, 119m
Burnt Timber Trail ride, 242–243, 243m

C

campfires, 19
camping, types of, 11
camping gear checklist, 21
Cañon City, 138–142
Capitol Creek Trail ride, 215–216, 217m
Carhart Trail ride, 190–191, 191m
Chatfield State Park ride, 64–66, 66m
checklists, 20–21
Cherry Creek Regional Trail ride, 88–90,
    91m, 92
Cherry Creek State Park ride, 93–96, 96m
Chicken Creek Trail ride, 239, 240m
city and county parks and recreation
    departments, 300
Cliff Creek Trail/Beckwith Pass Trail/
    Three Lakes Trail ride, 223–225, 225m
Colorado Springs, 32–45
Colorado Trail from Avalanche Trailhead
    ride, 128–130, 131m
Colorado Trail from Browns Creek
    Trailhead ride, 125m, 126–127
Comanche Lake Trail/Venable Lake Trail
    ride, 276–277, 277m
Comanche National Grassland/
    Homestead Trail/Picture Canyon ride,
    294–297, 295m
Comanche National Grassland/Picket
    Wire Canyon ride, 285–287, 287m
Comanche National Grassland/Vogel
    Canyon ride, 291–293, 292m
Community Ditch and Doudy Draw
    Trails ride, 26–27, 28m
Copper Top Acres, 149
Cortez/Mancos, 238–241
Cozy Point Ranch, 214
Craig Park Trail ride, 110m, 120
Crested Butte, 223–233
Cross Creek Ranch, 149
Cutoff Trail/Jacks Gulch Trail ride,
    176m–177m, 180–181

D

Dam Trail/Lake Pueblo State Park ride,
    273–274, 275m
Dark Canyon Trail ride, 226–227, 228m
Deer Creek Canyon Park ride, 69–71, 71m
dehydration, 14
Del Norte, 263–266
Divide, 46–50
Dome Rock State Wildlife Area ride,
    46–47, 48m
Double Spur Lodge & Ranch, The, 258
Doudy Draw and Community Ditch
    Trails ride, 26–27, 28m
Durango/Bayfield, 242–249
Dyke Trail/Lake Irwin Trail ride,
    229–230, 230m

E

Eagle's Nest Open Space ride, 160–161,
    162m
East Maroon Creek Trail/West Maroon
    Creek Trail/Maroon Creek Trail ride,
    220–221, 222m
East Marvine Creek Trail ride, 199–200,
    200m
Elbert, 100–101
Elk Meadow Park ride, 53–54, 54m
Estes Park and Rocky Mountain National
    Park, 151–157
etiquette, trail, 15–16
Evergreen/Morrison, 51–56

F

Fireside Inn Cabins, 235
Fish Creek Trail ride, 174–175,
    176m–177m
Flowers Trail ride, 176m–177m, 178–179
Fort Collins/Loveland, 158–172
Fountain Creek Regional Trail ride,
    38–39, 39m
Fox Run Regional Park ride, 40–41, 41m
Frisco/Breckenridge, 134–137

G

Garden of the Gods ride, 42–45, 44m
gear checklists, 20–21
Golden, 57–63

Golden Gate Canyon State Park ride, 59–60, 61m

Gold Run Trail ride, 239, 240m

Goose Creek Trail ride, 143–144, 145m

Granite Peaks Ranch, 236

Great Sand Dunes National Park & Preserve, 267–269

Greeley, 283–284

Greenbelt Plateau and Marshall Mesa Trails ride, 28m, 29

Greenland Trail ride, 97–99, 98m

Gunnison County Fairgrounds, 214

H

Hay Park Trail ride, 218–219, 219m

Highline Canal Trail ride, 66m, 67–68

Himes Peak Trail ride, 191m, 192

Historic Pines Ranch, The, 259

Homestead Ranch Park ride, 100–101, 101m

Homestead Trail/Picture Canyon/Comanche National Grassland ride, 294–297, 295m

Horsethief Campground and Trappers Lake Trails, 189–197

Horsetooth Mountain Park ride, 163–164, 165m

H2 Ranch Bed & Breakfast and Horse Motel, 23

hypothermia, 14

I

Idalia, 281–282

Indian Creek Trail ride, 72–73, 74m

J

Jacks Gulch Campground and Trails at Pingree Park, 173–181

Jacks Gulch Trail/Cutoff Trail ride, 176m–177m, 180–181

JB's Horse Motel, 279

Jefferson County Fairgrounds, 23

John Martin Reservoir State Park/Red Shin Trail ride, 288–289, 290m

Jolly Rancher, The, 236

K

Kirkwell Cattle Company, 280

L

Lair O' the Bear Park ride, 55–56, 55m

La Junta, 285–293

Lake George/Florissant, 143–147

Lake Irwin Trail/Dyke Trail ride, 229–230, 230m

Lake Pueblo State Park/Arkansas Point Trail System ride, 270–272, 272m

Lake Pueblo State Park/Dam Trail ride, 273–274, 275m

Lakewood, 85–87

Larkspur, 97–99

Lawn Lake Trail ride, 154–155, 156m

Leave No Trace principles
  being considerate of others, 19
  campfires, 19
  leaving what you find, 19
  planning ahead, 17
  respecting wildlife, 19
  traveling and camping surfaces, 18
  waste disposal, 18

lightning, 14

Lily Pad Lake Trail ride, 135m, 136–137

Little Browns Creek Trail ride, 125m, 132–133

Little Medano Creek Trail/Sand Ramp Trail ride, 268, 269m

Littleton, 64–76

Lodge Motel, 259

Long Lost Trailhead, 202–205

Long Park Trail ride, 203, 204m

Lookout Mountain Park and Apex Park ride, 57–58, 58m

Lory State Park ride, 166–167, 168m

Lost Creek Trail ride, 204m, 205

Lost Park Trail ride, 204m, 205

Loveland/Fort Collins, 158–172

M

Mancos/Cortez, 238–241

map, statewide rides, 8m–9m

Maroon Creek Trail/East Maroon Creek Trail/West Maroon Creek Trail ride, 220–221, 222m

Marshall Mesa and Greenbelt Plateau Trails ride, 28m, 29

Marvine Campground and Trailhead, 198–201

Marvine Creek Trail ride, 200m, 201
Meadow Creek Trail ride, 134–135, 135m
Medano Pass Trail ride, 268, 269m
Mesa Trail ride, 28m, 30–31
Middle Frisco Trail ride, 263–264, 266m
Mill Castle Trail ride, 231–232, 233m
Mirror Lake Trailhead, 206–209
Mirror Lake Trail ride, 208m, 209
M Lazy C Ranch, 103–104
Monument, 77–82
Monument Preserve ride, 77–79, 79m
Morrison/Evergreen, 51–56
Morrison Trail ride, 239–240, 240m
Mosca, 267–269
Mosca Pass Trail ride, 268, 269m
Mount Princeton Riding Stables &
    Equestrian Center, 104
Mueller State Park ride, 48m, 49–50

N

national forests and grasslands offices,
    301–302
national parks and monuments offices,
    302
New Santa Fe Regional Trail ride, 80–81,
    82m
Norris-Penrose Event Center, 24
North Fork Trail ride, 152m, 153
North Lone Pine Trail ride, 184–185,
    185m
North Sterling State Park/South Shoreline
    Trail ride, 298–299, 299m

P

Pagosa Springs, 250–257
Palmer/Red Rock Loop Trail and Bear
    Creek Regional Park ride, 32–34, 34m
Parker, 88–92
parks and recreation departments, city
    and county, 300
parks and recreation offices, state, 301
Pawnee National Grassland ride,
    283–284, 284m
Payne Creek Trail ride, 110m, 121–122
Picket Wire Canyon/Comanche National
    Grassland ride, 285–287, 287m

Picture Canyon/Comanche National
    Grassland/Homestead Trail ride,
    294–297, 295m
Piedra River Trail ride, 250–252, 251m
Pineridge Natural Area ride, 169–170,
    171m
Pine River Trail ride, 244–245, 246m
Pingree Park, Jacks Gulch Campground
    and Trails at, 173–181
Platte River Trail ride, 146–147, 147m
Pueblo, 270–275
Pueblo Mountain Park ride, 261–262,
    262m
Pueblo West Campground, Cabins &
    Arena, 260

R

ratings, ride and trail, 10
rattlesnakes, 13
Red Feather Lakes Area, 182–185
Red Rock/Palmer Loop Trail and Bear
    Creek Regional Park ride, 32–34, 34m
Red Shin Trail/John Martin Reservoir
    State Park ride, 288–289, 290m
regulations, trail, 16
Rim Trail ride, 240m, 241
River Camp RV Park, Campground, and
    Horse Hotel, 188
Rocky Mountain National Park and
    Estes Park, 151–157

S

safety
    altitude sickness, 14
    bees, 14
    dehydration, 14
    general guidelines, 12–13
    hypothermia, 14
    lightning, 14
    rattlesnakes, 13
    weather changes, 14
Salida/Buena Vista, 123–133
Sand Ramp Trail/Little Medano Creek
    Trail ride, 268, 269m
Sand Ramp Trail ride, 268–269, 269m

Sauls Creek Stables, 237
711 Ranch and Fossil Guide Service, 213
Sharkstooth Trail ride, 240m, 241
Sharptail Ridge Trail System ride, 75–76,
     76m
Shelf Road Recreation Area ride,
     138–142, 140m
Snell Creek Trailhead, 210–211
Snell Creek Trail ride, 210–211, 211m
Snowmass/Aspen, 215–222
South Park Trail ride, 117–119, 119m
South Shoreline Trail/North Sterling State
     Park ride, 298–299, 299m
Springfield, 294–297
SS2 Bed, Barn & Breakfast, 24
state parks and recreation offices, 301
Sterling, 298–299
Stillwater Trail ride, 193, 194m

T

tack checklist, 20
Three Lakes Trail/Cliff Creek
     Trail/Beckwith Pass Trail ride,
     223–225, 225m
Three Sisters/Alderfer Park ride, 51–52,
     52m
Tip Top Guest Ranch, 150
trail etiquette, 15–16
trail regulations, 16
Transfer Corral and Area Trails, 238–241
Transfer Trail ride, 240m, 241
Trappers Lake and Horsethief
     Campground Trails, 189–197
Trappers Lake Trail ride, 195, 196m
trip planning checklist, 20

V

Vallecito Creek Trail ride, 247–248,
     249m
vehicle checklist, 21
Venable Lake Trail/Comanche Lake Trail
     ride, 276–277, 277m
Vespers Trail ride, 172
veterinary supplies checklist, 21
Vogel Canyon/Comanche National
     Grassland ride, 291–293, 292m

W

Wall Lake Trail ride, 196m, 197
waste disposal, 18
weather changes, 14
Weminuche Trail ride, 253–254, 254m
Westcliffe, 276–277
West Frisco Trail ride, 265, 266m
West Mancos Trail ride, 240m, 241
West Maroon Creek Trail/Maroon Creek
     Trail/East Maroon Creek Trail ride,
     220–221, 222m
West Pawnee Ranch Bed-and-Breakfast,
     280
White Bears Ranch, 25
White Ranch Park ride, 62–63, 63m
wildlife, respecting, 19
Williams Creek Trail ride, 255–256,
     257m

Y

Ypsilon Lake Trail ride, 156m, 157

About the Authors/Photographers

Sherry Snead, the primary author, photographer, and team leader for *Saddle Up, Colorado!*, has had a love affair with horses since the ripe old age of five. She was born and raised in the "Horse Capital of the World," Lexington, Kentucky. After graduating from college at the University of Kentucky, she moved to Arizona, where she and her husband Scott were married on horseback/stagecoach and acquired their first horses and horse property. Sherry is a member of the Colorado Horse Council, the Front Range Back Country Horsemen of America, the Parker Trail Riders, the American Quarter Horse Association, and the American Paint Horse Association. Seventeen years, eight horses, hundreds upon hundreds of miles of trails, and one *Statewide Equestrian Trail & Travel Guide* later, Sherry enjoys exploring Colorado from the back of one of her four-legged friends and documents everything she can to share with fellow equestrians.

Scott Snead grew up in Arizona, with a love of the outdoors and a passion for fishing, hiking, camping, hunting, and wildlife viewing. This led to his pursuit of a formal education from Arizona State University in zoology, chemistry, and biology. His love of animals developed into a specialty as a sociobiologist (studying the social behavior of animals) and an early career as a research biologist. Scott now works in business management, running a division of a Denver-based organization. Scott lives in Colorado, where he spends as much time as possible exploring the wilderness by horseback with Sherry, his loving wife of 17 years. Scott is a member of the American Quarter Horse Association, the Parker Trail Riders, the Front Range Back Country Horsemen of America, and the Colorado Horse Council.

Contributing Authors

Julie Chaney is a director and past president of the Front Range Back Country Horsemen, treasurer of the Back Country Horsemen of Colorado, and a director of the Colorado Horse Council. Julie is certified as a Leave No Trace trail ethics trainer and is a trail crew leader and a crosscut/chainsaw sawyer. Julie is a member of and has held various board positions for the Parker Trail Riders and Buffalo Bill Saddle Club. She also has experience in the show ring, including Western, English, reining, speed events and cross-country jumping.

Jim Chaney, a veteran horseman, has been involved in raising, training, showing, packing, and back country riding for over 25 years. He is also a past president of the Front Range Back Country Horsemen. Jim manages many trail maintainence projects and teaches the lost art of packing. He is the former president and current arena chairman of the Parker Trail Riders and a repeat guest speaker at the Rocky Mountain Horse Expo's Trail Rider Conference.